MOLLIE KATZEN'S
STILL LIFE WITH MENU
COOKBOOK

Ten Speed Press

MOLLIE KATZEN'S
STILL LIFE
WITH MENU
COOKBOOK

Over 200 Delicious Vegetarian
Recipes With Original Art

FOR CARL

Special acknowledgments for *Mollie Katzen's Cooking Show:*

Funding provided by AkPharma Inc., the makers of **beano**
Accommodations provided by Parc Oakland
Furnishings provided by Noriega Furniture, San Francisco and Kohler Sinks and Faucets
Appliances provided by Dacor; GE Appliances; Oscartielle Equipment, California;
  and Russell Range
Food provided by Berkeley Bowl; Whole Foods; and Straus Family Creamery
Publicity by The Thacker Group

Special thanks to All-Clad Metalcrafters, Inc.; Chantal Cookware Corp.; Chicago Metallic
Bakeware; Corning Consumer Products Company; Draeger's; J. A. Henckels; Le
Creuset; Noah's Bagels; Odwalla Juice, Inc.; Pottery Barn; Rival; San Francisco League
of Urban Gardeners (SLUG); Taylor & Ng; Ten Speed Press; Williams-Sonoma; Yan
Can Cook, Inc.; Z Gallerie; Zyliss USA Corp.

Much gratitude to the generous and gifted producers, specialists, support staff, and crew
who all had a hand in creating *Mollie Katzen's Cooking Show:* Carl Shames, Molly Roth
Hamaker, Peggy Lee Scott, Brian Murphy, Tina Salter, Kate Zilavy, Gerd Mairandres,
Heidi Gintner, Lorraine Battle, Ron Louie, Carl Abbott, Joyce Quan, Robert Erdiakoff,
Ron Haake, Heidi Jane Rahlmann, Mike Morgan, Brad Cochrane, Steele Douglas, Greg
Overton, Mike Ratusz, Jack Butterfield, Rich Bucher, Martie Bruce, Dave Sotelo, Jean
Tuckerman, Marty Glickman, Bernice Chuck Fong, Christine Swett, Helen Soehalim,
Jack Ervin, Joseph Strebler, Robindranuth Basdeo, Chris Greenwald, Richard Sloss, Ed
Rudolph, Sam Lehmer, Jade Alburo, Robert Brown, Cathyn Fan, Harriet Garfinkle,
Wendy Lane, Keri Menacho, Max Savishinsky, Lauren Williams, Ed Cosci, Richard
Hartwig, Michael Anderson, Norman Bonney, Richard Jett, Conrad Slater, Richard
Favaro, and Alan Steinheimer. Personal thanks to AkPharma and Patricia Smith.

TEN SPEED PRESS
P.O. Box 7123
Berkeley, California 94707

All illustrations on the cover and throughout this book were done in soft pastel
  on paper by Mollie Katzen.
Book and Cover Design by Nancy Austin, Mollie Katzen,
  and Hal Hershey.
Artwork Photography by Jerry Kapler.
Printed by R. R. Donnelley & Sons Company, Inc., Willard, Ohio

Library of Congress Cataloging-in-Publication Data
    Katzen, Mollie, 1950-
    Still life with menu cookbook / Mollie Katzen.
    256 p. cm.
    Includes index.
    ISBN 0-89815-669-6
    1. Cookery. 2. Menus. I. Title
    TX714.K37 1988 641.5—dc 19 88-20075

First Printing, 1994

Printed in the United States of America

    4   5   6 — 99   98   97

ACKNOWLEDGMENTS

I am greatly indebted to the following people whose skills and generous efforts assisted me greatly with the revision of this book: Nancy Austin, Jackie Wan, Hal Hershey, Carl Shames, Jo-Lynne Worley, Toni Tajima, Catherine Jacobes, Lara Cartwright, Frances Bowles, George Young, Leili Eghbal, Mariah Bear, Joanie Shoemaker, and Molly Roth Hamaker. Thank you to Joel Singer, who helped me test recipes for the first edition, and to Dawn Van Hee who worked on the second round.

Thank you to my mother, Betty Katzen, for her encouragement for everything always (and for her sponge cake recipe in particular); to my lovely friend, Julie Goodman, who gave me the idea for Middle Eastern Spinach Soup; to Jody Hirsh, who generously shared his original recipe for Tunisian Eggplant Appetizer; to Rachel and David Biale, who conveyed the Challah recipe from Joan Shore, of Putney, Vermont; to Isabel Buerschaper, for her excellent Molasses Crinkle recipe; to Peggy Stein, for sharing her knowledge about Latin American cuisines, to Terry McCarthy, for his patience in photographing me; to Jerry Kapler, for the artwork photography; to Daniel Katzen, Carol Stewart, and Naomi Schalit, who retested recipes for the first edition when I needed some objectivity; and to Ina Cooper and Brent Beck, for encouraging my artistic expansion.

Certain friendships, lasting over years and miles, have been major sources of nourishment for me: Sarah Gowin, Patricia Cronin, Sarah Sutro, Susan Ostertag, Susan Savishinsky, Joel Savishinsky, Tara Blau, Ruth Scovill, and Barbara Felsinger all have been such friends. I also want to express my appreciation for the love, support, and shared purpose I've had the privilege to exchange with Frances Moore Lappé, Donna Korones, Ronnie Gilbert, Deborah Kaufman, Janis Plotkin, and Virginia King.

Without the extraordinary daycare providers and teachers at the Child Education Center and Berkwood Hedge School, who have taken such loving care of my children Sam and Eve, I couldn't have gotten this revised edition together. And thanks to Sam and Eve for being so wonderful.

I acknowledge the illustrator Clement Hurd, whose death in February 1988 saddened many of us who loved his work. The illustration for Chocolate Eclipse is an homage to him. Thanks to his son and daughter-in-law, Thacher and Olivia Hurd.

Thank you, finally, to all the people who have read and used my cookbooks, and who have written to me to express all sorts of comments, suggestions, and appreciation. I take it all to heart!

PREFACE

I AM HONORED to present you with this new series of menus and pastel drawings. It represents almost six years of recipe testing, writing, and long intensive hours in my painting studio—all of which has been a wonderful privilege for me. The privilege is enhanced now, as the book comes out into the world and into your hands.

Once again, as in my other two books, the cuisine is vegetarian, reflecting a growing preference for lighter, simpler, and more healthful eating. Many people would like to have the option of eating less meat, and that option is exactly what these recipes and menus attempt to provide.

My love for art and for cooking spring from the same source. Both interests are lifelong, and at times they have readily intertwined. As a toddler I was seriously involved in Mud as an art form, replete with food metaphors. As an art student in college I studied painting by day and cooked in restaurants at night. The following decade was spent writing and illustrating the *Moosewood Cookbook* and *The Enchanted Broccoli Forest*, and trying to find as much studio time as possible on the side. For me, the boundary between these two creative channels is a soft one, sometimes disappearing altogether. This book is an embodiment of that relationship.

I hope that these pictures and recipes will bring pleasure into your lives, and that you and your loved ones will continue to be well fed in all ways.

Mollie Katzen

CONTENTS

LIST OF RECIPES

INTRODUCTION

THE PURPOSE OF THIS BOOK

IN 1972, WHEN I BEGAN WORKING on my first cookbook, I didn't know anyone who worked a 9-to-5 full-time job. Most of my contemporaries were either in graduate school (indefinitely) or following creative, self-motivated, very flexible styles of living. Accordingly, it didn't occur to me to consider convenience needs when plotting out recipes. I just assumed that people would cook whatever they felt like eating and adjust their schedules to what they were cooking. If that meant being in a kitchen all day long, stirring and kneading and grinding by hand, other endeavors would just get postponed. I eventually posted "preparation time" notices on each recipe, but that was mainly to give an overview of what was involved in preparing a dish, not because I thought that anyone might be in a hurry.

But those days have evolved into these days, and now everyone I know has made serious commitments to life and work, and is very, very busy. Many of us who once paid careful attention to everything we ate—and could afford the time to be conscientious about healthy "natural" eating—frequently find ourselves grabbing food on the run. In our hearts, perhaps, we've continued to admire and appreciate the idealistic approach to cooking we once had time for, but we come home tired and hungry, and in many cases we have more than just ourselves to feed. We need convenience, and often that means we end up eating things that would have made us cringe fifteen years ago. Or we splurge and buy attractive, more-or-less healthful take-out foods from fancy delis—but who can afford to do this on a regular basis?

The purpose of this book is to help reintroduce good eating into our increasingly complex schedules; to provide encouragement and ideas as well as recipes and menus; and to make interesting, genuine, and inexpensive food as accessible and convenient as possible. It takes some thought and planning to get our kitchens and ourselves into gear when so much of our time and energy is spent elsewhere. But the effort will be well rewarded. We will all be the richer for it, and our lives might even be that much longer.

ABOUT THE CUISINE AND THE MENUS

The cuisine in this book has been influenced by many ethnic traditions, largely from the Mediterranean, Asia, Southeast Asia, Eastern Europe, Central and South America, France, Northern

Italy, and the Southwest United States. The primary ingredients are fresh vegetables and fruits, grains, tofu, legumes, pastas, nuts, and dairy products. Accessibility, aesthetics, and an awareness of nutrition have been my primary concerns in creating these recipes.

The menus are put together with careful attention to contrast, balance, nutrition, and convenience (including the availability and expense of ingredients). Many people have been cooking vegetarian for quite a few years now, but still get nervous about what goes with what. It's difficult in our meat-oriented culture to be comfortable without a clearly designated "main dish" in the meal, and there is wide-spread insecurity about whether or not a meal contains enough protein. By composing these menus for you, I hope to take some of the anxiety out of meatless cooking. Rest assured that the meals are nutritious, and that you will get enough protein and whatever else you need.

As my own cooking abilities have developed, and as I've become aware of a general concern over diet, I've been striving to cook with fewer milk products in general, and to reduce the butterfat content considerably (without detracting too much from the creamy flavor) when using dairy products. A decade and a half ago, in the pioneer days of creative vegetarian cookery, a lot of us young chefs felt like part of a large experiment. We were a little shaky, sometimes, about the appeal of our cooking. Those of us running restaurants, especially, felt compelled to win people over to meatless cuisine, which was still considered a fringe activity at that time. So we would dump in extra butter, cream, or sour cream at the last minute, which was the best way we knew to assure that the food would be really delicious. The cuisine has matured over time, and so have many of our skills. We are now learning how to cook with a lighter touch, to make high-fat ingredients go farther in a given dish, and to use seasonings in sophisticated ways that make it unnecessary to rely on a rich dairy content. These recipes, with the butterfat pared down, reflect this shift in my own cooking. Feel free to alter the recipes even further in this direction.

You will notice that the menus generally are not designated as breakfast, lunch, or dinner. This is to encourage flexibility in your meal planning. Very often you will find that a good soup, salad, and homemade bread make a perfect supper, and sometimes a hearty, filling lunch is in order. Consider how you define different types of meals for different times of the day or evening. Menu planning is a very personal endeavor, and should reflect one's own individual rhythms. Experiment with ideas that defy traditional assumptions. Whole new worlds (or at least a few new avenues) may open up for you.

I have tried to keep the menus as seasonably flexible as possible. I live in California, where the produce markets overflow with ripe perfection twelve months a year. But I spent many years in an area of upstate New York where the winters go on for at least six months, spring lasts about fifteen minutes, and the summer growing season is often clipped short by September frosts. So I know what it's like to have a precious growing season followed by many cold months when fresh produce is limited. You won't have to spend long February evenings wistfully reading recipes that you have to wait until summer to enjoy. You should be able to find many of the ingredients—no matter what the local climate—much of the year.

HOW TO USE THIS BOOK

All the menus with more than two dishes—and any degree of complexity—are preceded by an introduction that breaks down the meal preparation into tasks that can be done one, two, and three days ahead. Spreading out the work in this way can make cooking more enjoyable—and increases the chances of the meal getting made at all! Read through all advance preparation information, as well as the individual recipes, before embarking on any of these menus. I've broken them down according to my own habits and judgment, but you can revise anything in this book to suit *your* style. Most of the schedules attempt to minimize same-day presentations, assuming you are working and will not have a lot of time (or desire) to put in much labor right after getting home. I've also tried to coordinate things for you, so you can mince garlic for two different dishes at the same time or bake a casserole and a dessert together (and perhaps streamline your utility bill just a touch).

Even if you choose not to follow the do-ahead suggestions as they are written, I hope they will help demystify the work involved, so it can seem less intimidating than it otherwise might. At first glance, freshly baked bread on a Thursday night seems like a fantasy. But read on, and discover that you can put up the bread dough and form the loaves several days earlier, and that the loaves can be stored in the refrigerator and proceed directly into a hot oven from there. Similarly, starting a salad or a vegetable dish from scratch at 6:15 P.M. on a Tuesday night may seem like an overwhelming task. But if the salad greens are all cleaned and dried in advance, the dressing made, the vegetables chopped, the cheese grated, and the rice cooked and ready to reheat, the entire dinner can be an unimposing endeavor.

In order for this to work, you have to be willing to put in a modest amount of time at least several evenings a week. Take thirty or forty minutes to put up the bread dough, chop the vegetables for the next night, etc. Many of the advance preparations include activities like soaking or cooking beans, which require little or no supervision. While tomorrow's soup gently simmers, you can be fixing lunches, opening your mail, or making a phone call or two. Advance preparations require only a small effort during an evening when you are going to be puttering around at home anyway.

If you don't feel like making the entire menus as they are written, you can certainly change things around, and mix and match individual recipes in any number of combinations. String several menus together if you want to make a large feast, or just make one recipe at a time. This book is designed to be used either way. Each recipe contains all the information necessary, so that it can be made independently.

Desserts are entirely optional. I would actually be surprised if you had time to make them regularly. But they are there if you want them—either for special occasions, or for ordinary nights when you feel you could use a little special something.

HELPFUL TOOLS

Certain gadgets, appliances, and even simple small objects can make an enormous difference in the amount of time you end up spending in your kitchen. If you want to have quality food with a minimum of labor, here is a short list of highly recommended items.

FOOD PROCESSOR

For me, this appliance has become indispensable. There are all sorts of things I prepare frequently with a food processor, but would probably not bother with very often if I had to do them by hand. Grating, mixing pie and biscuit dough, puréeing soups, dips, and pâtés, certain kinds of vegetable chopping—all of these get done in a matter of seconds in a food processor. Also try using a mini-processor. It has about a one-cup capacity, and is perfect for mincing garlic or small amounts of fresh herbs.

BLENDER

This has not been totally replaced by the food processor; there are still a few things it does better. It can sometimes make a smoother puréed soup than a processor, and is very useful for chopping or blending medium-sized amounts of things that might get lost in a larger machine. I also find that nothing works better than a blender for grinding small amounts of nuts and seeds either to a coarse meal or a fine powder. Just a few quick pulses and it's done.

MICROWAVE OVEN

Microwaves are extremely helpful to people who need to do a lot of their cooking in advance, as most busy lives require. With a microwave, you can heat leftovers without overcooking them and without having to wash any caked-on pots and pans. Vegetables cooked in a microwave actually retain more thiamine and ascorbic acid than those prepared by any other method, as nutrients deteriorate through extended exposure to elevated temperatures. In a microwave, the duration of the heat is so brief and so little water is needed that the cooking action occurs within the vegetable itself. Very little breakdown of color or fiber occurs.

TIMER WITH A BELL

Keep a timer with a bell by your side when you are doing advance preparations on a busy weekday evening. The bell will remind you that you are boiling beans or sautéing onions while you are helping your children with their homework or preparing your own work for the next day. Things on the stove are very easy to forget.

PAPER AND PENCIL,
PLASTIC CONTAINERS OF
ALL SIZES, LABELS,
PLUS A SYSTEM
FOR ALL OF THIS

Keep menus and shopping lists, plus a list of the current freezer inventory. Label and date containers of leftovers, and make a list of whatever you have done ahead for a given meal (remind yourself what meal it is—and for which night!). Keep these things in a special place where they won't fall in with miscellaneous other items. You can create a custom-made system for your household, and it will really help!

FREEZER

If you get serious about using the freezer, your repertoire can be greatly expanded and meal preparation can be simplified. Many foods freeze beautifully. Read on for details.

THINGS YOU CAN
PREPARE AHEAD
AND FREEZE

↬ MINCED GARLIC AND GINGER: Prepare several tablespoons at a time and wrap tightly in plastic wrap in a little log shape. Whenever you need some, just take out the log and slice off what you need. (An average-sized clove of garlic equals about 1/2 teaspoon minced.)

↬ CHOPPED ONIONS, FRESH BERRIES, PITTED CHERRIES, SLICED PEACHES OR APRICOTS, GRATED CHEESES (EXCEPT PARMESAN), AND PARBOILED VEGETABLES: Spread them out on a tray and freeze until solid. Then transfer to a plastic bag, seal it, and return to the freezer. This way the pieces will stay separate, so you can use as much or as little as you want at a time without having to defrost a whole clump.

- ✧ PARMESAN CHEESE: Freeze in any amount for long periods of time. Use as needed, direct from the freezer.
- ✧ FRESH HERBS: Wrap airtight in a plastic bag. They will lose their color, but will remain quite fragrant.
- ✧ PIE CRUST: All rolled out and in the pan, or still in a ball. Either way, wrap airtight in a plastic bag.
- ✧ BISCUIT DOUGH: Make a log shape, wrap tightly in foil. Then you can "slice 'n' bake."
- ✧ PIZZA DOUGH: See page 226.
- ✧ BREAD DOUGH: Freeze unbaked loaves for up to several weeks. Be sure to wrap airtight in a plastic bag.
- ✧ TOMATO PURÉE: Freeze in 1-cup batches (perfect amount for a 12-inch pizza) in small containers.
- ✧ TOMATO PASTE: Store in units of 1 to 2 tablespoons in plastic-wrap-lined ice cube trays. Seal the trays in plastic bags.

SOME FREEZING TIPS

Label and date everything you freeze, so you won't have to peer into containers of unrecognizable frozen matter, wondering what it could be and who could have put it there.

- ✧ Every now and then, chop extra of something (onions, garlic) that you are chopping anyway, and freeze for a later time. This will save on labor.
- ✧ Any time you open a can of tomato paste or purée, automatically freeze what you don't use. (Don't forget to label.)
- ✧ Group things together that might get used for the same dish. For example, put pizza dough, tomato purée, garlic, and grated provolone and/or mozzarella together in the same corner (or even in a little basket). Then you can avoid having to spend two hours looking for that one missing ingredient.
- ✧ Try to keep a current list on the outside of the freezer reminding you of what's in there and when you put it in. Cross things off as you use them.

INGREDIENTS

Here is a rundown of the basic ingredients used in this book. I've tried to steer clear of exotic items as much as possible. For one thing, they are usually expensive. Second of all, they can be hard to find outside of major metropolitan areas (especially if they are imported). It has been my personal challenge to figure out ways to make ethnic dishes as authentic as possible using only American supermarket ingredients. I want to make this kind of food accessible to as many people as I can. As far as fancy foods are concerned (fruit-flavored vinegars, nut oils, etc.), I do use them in modest quantities, as they can be exquisitely delicious. Wherever these high-class grocery items occur, I have given suggestions for where to find them, plus ideas for substitutions, so you won't feel pressured to use them. I want to stress flexibility in these recipes and not provoke anxiety over ingredients. The purpose of this book, after all, is to make your life easier!

I can't emphasize enough how important good shopping habits are to the overall functioning of your kitchen. Having the ingredients in the house is half the battle. Try to make a long, thorough list, and do a major marketing trip once a week. Then you will probably only have to supplement it once or twice with a quick run for fresh produce or tofu.

You can make just about every recipe in this book from the following inventory.

- ❧ BAKING SUPPLIES: Baking soda, baking powder, salt, pure vanilla extract, unsweetened chocolate, unsweetened cocoa, semisweet chocolate chips.

- ❧ BEANS AND LEGUMES (DRIED AND/OR CANNED): Kidney beans, black beans, pinto beans, chick-peas, white beans, green and yellow split peas, lentils, black-eyed peas.

- ❧ BUTTER: Unsalted or lightly salted.

- ❧ CANNED FOODS: Artichoke bottoms or hearts, beans (for quick tortilla entrées, see page 230), green chilies, olives, pineapple (packed in juice), tomato products (paste, purée, whole tomatoes), water chestnuts.

- ❧ CORNMEAL: Finer grained for corn bread and muffins, coarser for polenta. (Both types store well in the freezer.)

- ❧ DAIRY: Cheddar, Swiss, mild white cheese (Monterey jack or something similar), feta, Parmesan, buttermilk, lowfat milk, yogurt and/or sour cream, cream cheese (or Neufchâtel), cottage cheese; also keep nonfat dry milk in your cupboard for back up.

- ❧ EGGS: These recipes were tested with Grade A large eggs.

- ❧ FLOURS: Unbleached white, whole wheat, rye. Also try oat or barley flour. High-gluten bread flour can be used in place of unbleached white flour in any yeasted bread recipe.

- ❧ FRUIT: Lemons, limes, and oranges at all times, plus whatever else is in season. (It's nice to keep a bowlful within easy reach for healthful snacking.) Dried apricots, currants, dates, raisins.

❧ GARLIC: Always keep several fresh bulbs on hand; buy frequently enough so it stays fresh. (There is a big difference between fresh and old garlic.)

❧ GINGER: Fresh ginger root keeps well, either by itself, in a jar of wine in the refrigerator, or minced and frozen.

❧ GRAINS: Brown rice, basmati rice, white rice, bulgur, millet, rolled oats, wheat berries, pearl barley.

❧ HERBS AND SPICES: *Dried:* Keep a current list of what you're out of (or running out of) posted somewhere, such as inside a cupboard or on the refrigerator. About once a month go to the spice shelves in the supermarket with your list and pick out all the things you need.

Fresh: Parsley is always in season; buy other fresh herbs as available. They freeze fairly well. Also consider planting an herb garden, indoors or out.

❧ MISO: This is a fermented paste made from soybeans and grains, and is used as a base for soups and sauces. It is sold in most Japanese grocery stores and natural food stores, and it comes in many different varieties. Miso keeps indefinitely in the refrigerator.

❧ NUTS, NUT BUTTERS, SEEDS: Almonds, cashews, hazelnuts (also called filberts), peanuts, pecans, walnuts; peanut butter, almond butter, sesame butter or tahini; sesame, sunflower, and poppy seeds.

❧ OILS: Extra virgin olive oil (from the first pressing of the olives) is best for salads. For cooking you can use virgin or pure olive oil. Canola or multi-purpose vegetable oil can be used in recipes that don't mention a specific type of oil. Refined peanut oil works very well for stir-fries. Walnut and other nut oils have a strong, deep flavor. Use them in salads in small amounts or to season other oils. Buy nut oils in the gourmet section of the grocery store, or in specialty shops. If you store them in the refrigerator they will last a long time and you will get your money's worth. Chinese sesame oil has a deep, dark, inimitable flavor. It is used primarily as a seasoning and occasionally for sautéing. Look for it in Asian grocery stores.

❧ PASTA: All the pasta recipes in this book can be made with fresh *or* dried pasta. Keep a variety of shapes and sizes of dried pasta in your cupboard at all times. Also, soba noodles, udon noodles, and ramen instant soup mix (see page 231) should be part of your basic stock items.

↝ SOY MILK: It comes in boxes, refrigerated or not, in natural food stores and in some grocery stores. Use it to replace cow's milk in any recipe.

↝ SOY SAUCE: Japanese soy sauces (tamari or shoyu) are stronger and slightly sweeter than Chinese soy sauces, which tend to be saltier. Kikkoman is one of the better brands of Japanese soy sauce. Use whichever type you like best.

↝ SUGARS: Granulated sugar, light or dark brown sugar, honey, molasses, corn syrup (for occasional baking needs), real maple syrup.

↝ TOFU: Generally comes packed in water or vacuum packed. There are many different varieties, from very soft to very firm, silken, savory-baked, five-spiced, etc. Tofu has a short refrigerator life—one week at most if you store it in water in the refrigerator and conscientiously change the water every day.

↝ TORTILLAS: Corn and flour tortillas, plus tortilla chips are all good to have around as staples (see page 230). Tortillas freeze well.

↝ VEGETABLES: Onions, carrots, celery, potatoes, and cleaned, dried salad greens should be on hand at all times. Add to this list whatever is in season.

↝ VINEGARS: Red wine, cider, rice (from Asian grocery stores), fruit-flavored or special wine-flavored (champagne), and balsamic. These latter three types are expensive, but you use only a small amount at a time. Use them to flavor other vinegars or to lightly dress salads. They are a luxury, but really very exciting and delicious. Look for exotic vinegars in the gourmet department of your grocery store, or in specialty shops.

↝ WINES AND LIQUORS: Mirin (Japanese cooking sake, available in Asian grocery stores), dry sherry, dry white and red wines, moderately fruity white wine, brandy, rum.

↝ YEAST: Active dry yeast comes in three-part packages and keeps for a long time in the refrigerator. Keep it on hand so you can bake bread whenever the spirit moves you.

CONVERSION TABLE

DRY INGREDIENTS

Cornmeal, coarse (polenta), 1 cup = 170 grams

Cornmeal, fine, 1 cup = 150 grams

Herbs, dried = $1/3$ to $1/4$ amount of fresh herbs

Flour, rye, 1 cup = 170 grams

Flour, white, unbleached, 1 cup = 140 grams

Flour, whole wheat, 1 cup = 170 grams

Grains, dried (rice, bulgur, millet, wheat berries), 1 cup = 200 grams

Oats, rolled, 1 cup = 90 grams

Sugar, brown, 1 cup (packed) = 200 grams

Sugar, confectioners', 1 cup = 130 grams

Sugar, granulated, 1 cup = 200 grams

BULK INGREDIENTS

Beans (black beans, lentils, chick-peas, pinto beans, white beans), $1/2$ cup = 100 grams

Cheese, 1 lb. = 4 to 5 cups (packed) grated

Nut butter (peanut, almond, cashew, etc.), 1 cup (8 oz.) = 250 grams

Nuts, chopped, $1/3$ to $1/2$ cup (2 oz.) = 50 grams

Onion, 1 small to medium-sized = 1 cup, chopped

Raisins, $1/3$ cup (2 oz.) = 50 grams

Sesame seeds, $3/4$ cup = 100 grams

LIQUIDS

1 cup (8 oz.) = 250 ml

1 tablespoon ($1/2$ fluid oz.) = 16 ml

16 tablespoons = 1 cup

The season for this menu ranges from late spring to midsummer, when the tail end of an early vegetable harvest and the beginning of plum season overlap. If that doesn't happen in your neck of the woods (I know it's easier in California than in other places!), make this meal with whatever is available whenever you can.

CREAM OF RED PEPPER SOUP
SPRING VEGETABLE SALAD
FRUITED GRAIN SALAD
PRALINE-BUTTERSCOTCH BARS

3 DAYS AHEAD: cook grains for Fruited Grain Salad / roast and peel peppers for soup (optional)

2 DAYS AHEAD: cut onions and peppers for soup / prepare vegetables for Spring Vegetable Salad (prepare garlic for soup and salad at the same time) / for spring salad, steam and marinate potatoes

1 DAY AHEAD: prepare soup, steps 1 through 4 / for spring salad, steam vegetables and mix with potatoes (don't add herbs yet) / assemble grain salad, except fresh fruit

SAME DAY: assemble and bake praline bars / finish soup / add herbs and lemon juice to spring salad / add fruit to grain salad

CREAM OF RED PEPPER SOUP

PREPARATION TIME: 50 MINUTES.

YIELD: 4 TO 6 SERVINGS.

1 to 2 tablespoons butter or
   olive oil

2 cups minced onion

2 large cloves garlic, minced

1 teaspoon salt

freshly ground black pepper

1/2 teaspoon ground cumin

5 medium-sized red bell
   peppers, sliced

1 tablespoon unbleached white
   flour

1/2 cup stock or water

2 1/2 cups milk (lowfat or
   soy okay), room temperature or warmer

OPTIONAL TOPPINGS:

thinned sour cream (thinned
   by whisking lightly)

minced fresh cilantro

minced fresh basil

An indescribable shade of creamy red-orange, this is a beautiful-looking, rich-tasting soup that is actually quite easy to make. Steps 1 through 4 can be done as much as two days ahead. Heat the soup to room temperature, or a little warmer, before purée-ing it with the milk. (Be sure, also, that the milk is at least room temperature.)

As an extra-special alternative way of preparing the peppers, you may roast them first. Place them on an oiled tray in a 350° oven for 20 to 30 minutes, or until the skin puckers. (Turn the peppers every 5 to 8 minutes during roasting, so the skin will blister evenly.) Place the hot peppers in a plastic or paper bag for 3 to 5 minutes. When they are cool enough to handle, remove the peppers and discard the core, seeds, and skin. (Use a sharp paring knife. The skin should come right off.) Proceed with the recipe exactly as it's written.

1. Melt the butter or heat the oil in a soup pot or Dutch oven. Add onions and garlic and cook slowly with salt, pepper, and cumin.

2. After about 5 to 8 minutes (when the onions are clear and soft), add bell peppers. Stir and cover. Cook over low heat 10 to 15 minutes, stirring intermittently.

3. Gradually sprinkle in flour. Cook, stirring, another 5 minutes.

4. Add stock or water, stir, cover, and cook 2 to 3 minutes. Remove from heat.

5. Purée, bit by bit, with milk. Put the puréed soup in a soup pot or double boiler. (OPTIONAL: You may strain the soup to get a smoother texture.) Heat very gently.

6. Serve topped with sour cream and minced herbs, if desired.

SPRING VEGETABLE SALAD

PREPARATION TIME: ABOUT
45 MINUTES, PLUS TIME
TO CHILL.

YIELD: 5 TO 6 SERVINGS.

¹/₄ pound baby carrots

*¹/₂ pound fresh green beans,
as slender as possible*

¹/₂ pound snow peas

8 to 10 very small red potatoes

1 small head cauliflower

*1 or 2 small yellow summer
squash*

*¹/₂ pound asparagus, pencil
thin, if possible*

*2 to 3 medium cloves garlic,
minced*

¹/₄ cup extra virgin olive oil

1 teaspoon salt

lots of black pepper

*4 to 5 tablespoons mayonnaise
(see page 68) (optional)*

*a small handful each of finely
minced fresh basil, fresh
tarragon, fresh marjoram,
fresh dill, and fresh chives*

¹/₂ cup fresh lemon juice

The ideal vegetables for this salad are the thinnest, youngest, most angelic: miniature squash, baby carrots, slender green beans, flat snow peas, pencil-thin asparagus, etc. But if you can't find such perfection in your produce store, buy what you can and make the salad anyway. It will still be good.

Also, feel free to substitute other vegetables according to their availability and your own taste.

The salad can be assembled a day in advance. Just hold off on adding the lemon juice until shortly before serving. (If the vegetables sit too long in an acidic substance, their colors will fade.)

NOTE: The weights of the vegetables are approximate.

If you can't get all the different types of fresh herbs, use whatever you can find, or substitute dried.

1. Prepare the vegetables: Trim both ends of the carrots, green beans, and snow peas. If desired, cut them in half. Or leave them whole. Halve the potatoes, separate the cauliflower into 1-inch pieces, and slice the squash. Snap off and discard the coarse lower ends of the asparagus. Cut off the tips, and slice the middle parts into 1¹/₂-inch pieces. Group the vegetables as follows:

   ∾ potatoes
   ∾ carrots, cauliflower, asparagus middles, green beans
   ∾ snow peas, asparagus tips, squash slices

2. Steam the potatoes until just tender, about 10 to 15 minutes. While potatoes are cooking, place the garlic and olive oil in a large bowl. When the potatoes are done, transfer them—still hot—to the bowlful of garlic and oil.

3. Steam the next group of vegetables until just tender, for about 8 to 10 minutes. Refresh under cold water immediately upon removing from heat. Drain well and transfer to the bowl. Repeat with the last group of vegetables, which will take about 5 minutes to cook. Mix gently but thoroughly.

4. Add remaining ingredients, except for the lemon juice, and stir again. Cover tightly and chill until very cold.

5. Stir in the lemon juice within about 15 minutes of serving time.

FRUITED GRAIN SALAD

PREPARATION TIME: ABOUT
1 HOUR FOR THE GRAINS TO
COOK, ONLY A FEW MINUTES
THEREAFTER.

YIELD: LOTS! AT LEAST 8 TO
10 SERVINGS.

1 cup uncooked wheat berries

1 cup uncooked pearl barley

1 cup uncooked short-grain
    brown rice

3 tablespoons cider vinegar

1 tablespoon lemon juice

3 tablespoons canola or
    vegetable oil (optional)

1/2 teaspoon salt

1 1/2 cups (packed) golden
    raisins

3/4 cup (packed) minced fresh
    chives (scallions may be
    substituted—be sure to
    mince them very fine)

6 to 7 large fresh mint leaves,
    minced—or more, to taste
    (or 1 to 2 teaspoons dried
    mint)

4 to 5 ripe firm red plums,
    sliced

1 or 2 tart green apples, sliced
    (in addition to, or instead
    of, the plums) (optional)

This is a simple, yet unusual-tasting salad. Each grain—barley, whole wheat berries, brown rice—has its own distinct personality, especially if you take the slight trouble to cook each of them correctly. The addition of golden raisins, chives, mint, and plums (and/or apples) makes it taste both exotic and yet homey and familiar. Do try to find fresh mint for this salad. It's an important component, and dried mint is not quite the same thing.

The grains need to cook separately. You can cook them in advance and store them in tightly covered containers until you are ready to make the salad. You can also prepare the salad a night or two before you plan to serve it. (Add everything except the fresh fruit, which should go in shortly before serving.) It takes very little work. Most of the preparation time allotted is for cooking the grains, so you can easily make it during an evening when you are home doing other things.

This salad keeps very well, and is great to have on hand for lunches and snacks.

NOTE: This can be made with no oil.

1. Soak the wheat berries for about 30 minutes. Meanwhile, wash the barley several times, until the water in which it is rinsed looks clear. Put the barley and 2 1/2 cups water in a saucepan. Bring to a boil, partially cover, and simmer until tender (about 30 minutes).

2. Place the rice and 1 3/4 cup water in a small saucepan. Bring to a boil, partially cover, and simmer very quietly for about 35 minutes, or until tender.

3. Drain the wheat berries and place in a saucepan with 2 1/2 cups water. Bring to a boil, cover and simmer until tender. This will take about 1 to 1 1/4 hours. Check the water level. You may have to add just a little extra if it seems dry.

4. When all the grains are cooked, combine them in a large bowl. Stir to let excess steam escape. Add remaining ingredients except the plums and/or apples. Cover and chill well before serving. This will keep up to three days. Add plum and/or apple slices, and mix them in gently just before serving.

PRALINE-BUTTERSCOTCH BARS

PREPARATION TIME: 30 TO
35 MINUTES TO PREPARE,
15 TO 20 TO BAKE.

YIELD: 20 MEDIUM-SIZED BARS.

1 cup (2 sticks) butter
³/₄ cup (packed) brown sugar
1 cup coarsely chopped
    pecans
2 eggs
1¹/₂ teaspoons vanilla extract
1¹/₂ cups flour
2 teaspoons baking powder
a pinch of salt (optional)

This is a light butterscotch brownie baked in a pan coated with butter, brown sugar, and pecans. Turn each bar upside down and the coating becomes a crunchy topping.

1. Preheat oven to 350°.

2. Place ¹/₄ cup of the butter (¹/₂ stick) in a 9 x 13-inch pan, and place it in the oven for a few minutes until it melts. Remove from the oven, and tilt the pan until the butter is evenly distributed. Sprinkle with ¹/₄ cup brown sugar and the pecans. Set aside.

3. Cream together the remaining ³/₄ cup butter and ¹/₂ cup brown sugar at high speed with an electric mixer. Add the eggs one at a time, beating well after each addition. Stir in the vanilla extract.

4. Sift together the dry ingredients, then add this to the butter mixture. Stir until well mixed.

5. Spoon the batter onto the pecans in the prepared pan, placing dollops here and there. Then very gently spread it, using a rubber spatula or a plain dinner knife. Try not to dislodge the pecan mixture too much. The batter will seem sparse, and it may not reach all the way to the edges of the pan, but just do the best job possible. It will expand properly and even itself out during baking.

6. Bake 15 to 20 minutes, until a knife or toothpick inserted into the center comes out clean. Cool at least to room temperature before cutting into bars.

7. Invert each bar before serving so the crunchy praline coating will be on top.

~

Middle Eastern Spinach Soup is thick with potatoes or rice. Mediterranean Lentil Salad is delicately seasoned, yet full-bodied. Together they make a fortifying meal. Serve them with a good brand of sesame crackers (ak-mak or lavosch), and follow them up with light, light Lemon Snaps.

MIDDLE EASTERN SPINACH SOUP
MEDITERRANEAN LENTIL SALAD
SESAME CRACKERS
LEMON SNAPS

3 DAYS AHEAD: cook lentils (step 1 of salad)

2 DAYS AHEAD: cook potatoes or rice for soup / clean spinach / assemble salad, short of adding bell peppers or herbs (this can also be done 1 day ahead)

1 DAY AHEAD: assemble soup through step 3 / make cookie dough and refrigerate

SAME DAY: bake cookies / heat soup and add yogurt / add peppers and herbs to salad

MIDDLE EASTERN SPINACH SOUP

PREPARATION TIME: 45 MINUTES.

YIELD: 6 TO 8 SERVINGS.

1 medium-sized potato, or
   3 cups cooked white rice
   (1 cup uncooked; see
   instructions below)

2 to 4 cups water

1 to 2 tablespoons butter or
   olive oil

2 large cloves garlic, minced

4 cups chopped onion

2 teaspoons salt (or to taste)

1 teaspoon ground cumin

1/2 teaspoon turmeric

a dash of cinnamon (or more,
   to taste)

2 pounds fresh spinach,
   cleaned, stemmed, and
   chopped

1 1/2 cups firm yogurt, room
   temperature

black pepper and cayenne,
   to taste

Yogurt binds everything together in this hearty, soothing, and beautifully green soup, and gives a lemony accent to the already unusual seasonings.

You can make this soup with either potatoes or rice. The potatoes may be cooked up to several days in advance. Store them in their cooking water in a closed container in the refrigerator. The rice may also be cooked a day or two in advance.

OPTIONAL SHORTCUT: If you are just too tired to face that big pile of raw spinach, substitute two 10-ounce packages frozen, chopped spinach. (Defrost before using.)

WITH POTATOES:

1. Peel and dice the potatoes, and cook potatoes in 2 to 4 cups water, covered, until tender. (This should take about 10 to 15 minutes.) Set aside, water included.

2. Melt the butter or heat the oil in a Dutch oven or soup pot, and sauté garlic and onion over medium heat along with the salt and spices until tender (8 to 10 minutes).

3. Add cooked potatoes with their water, and spinach. Cover and simmer another 10 to 15 minutes. At this point the soup can be left as is, or partially or completely puréed. Use a blender or steel blade attachment of a food processor. It's fun to experiment with various textures. A complete purée can be quite elegant.

4. Stir in yogurt. Add pepper and cayenne to taste. This soup is equally good served hot or cold.

WITH RICE:

1. Put 2 cups water in a saucepan and bring to a boil. Sprinkle in 1 cup uncooked white rice. Lower heat to the gentlest possible simmer, cover, and cook about 20 minutes, or until all the water is absorbed and the rice is tender. Set aside.

2. Sauté onions and garlic with spices exactly as in step 2 above.

3. Add spinach and 2 cups additional water. Cover and simmer for 10 to 15 minutes.

4. As in the instructions above, all or some of the soup can be puréed. Stir in the rice and yogurt after puréeing.

5. Heat very gently before serving. This variation actually tastes best neither hot nor cold, but somewhere in between.

MEDITERRANEAN LENTIL SALAD

PREPARATION TIME: 40 MINUTES
TO PREPARE, PLUS SEVERAL
HOURS TO CHILL.

YIELD: SERVES 6, EASILY.

2 cups dried lentils

1/4 cup extra virgin olive oil

3/4 teaspoon salt

1 to 2 oranges, peeled and
    sectioned

1 large clove garlic, minced

3 tablespoons fresh lime juice

3 tablespoons balsamic vinegar
    (cider vinegar will also
    work)

1/4 cup very finely minced
    red onion

1/4 to 1/2 teaspoon each grated
    orange and lime rind

1/2 cup (packed) dried currants

1 small carrot, finely minced

1/2 each red and yellow bell
    pepper, minced

a handful each of finely
    minced fresh parsley, fresh
    chives, and fresh mint

Sweet and savory combine harmoniously in this fruity marinated salad. Streamline the preparation time by getting everything else ready while the lentils are cooking. The whole salad can be made up to two days ahead of time, but postpone adding the bell pepper and fresh herbs until shortly before serving.

1. Rinse the lentils in a colander. Meanwhile, set a large potful of water to boil—at least 6 cups of water. After the water has reached the boiling point, lower the heat to a simmer. Add the lentils, and cook very gently in the simmering water, partially covered, until they are tender. (Try to prevent the water from getting agitated while the lentils are cooking, as that will cause them to burst and lose their shape. The goal is to have perfectly cooked lentils—light and distinct.) Cooking time should be around 20 to 30 minutes. Check the water level and add more if necessary. Drain the lentils when they are done, and gently rinse in cold water. Drain again and place in a large bowl.

2. Add remaining ingredients except bell pepper and fresh herbs, cover tightly, and chill at least 4 hours.

3. Add the bell pepper and herbs within an hour of serving.

LEMON SNAPS

PREPARATION TIME: 30 MINUTES.

YIELD: 2 DOZEN COOKIES.

$^1/_2$ cup butter, softened

$^1/_2$ cup (packed) brown sugar

2 tablespoons granulated sugar

1 egg

2 tablespoons lemon juice

$^1/_2$ teaspoon grated lemon rind

1 cup unbleached white flour

$^1/_4$ teaspoon salt

$^1/_8$ teaspoon nutmeg

The flavor of butter is essential to the success of these cookies. The lemon is present, but subtle. If you like more of a kick in there, you can increase the amount of lemon rind to $^3/_4$ teaspoon.

Lemon snaps are hard to stop eating, especially when they're about one hour old. So if there are going to be a lot of people coming through your kitchen right after you bake these cookies, you might consider doubling the recipe.

1. Preheat oven to 375°. Lightly grease a cookie sheet.

2. Cream together the butter and sugars at high speed with an electric mixer for 3 to 5 minutes.

3. Add the egg, and beat well for another 2 to 3 minutes.

4. Stir in remaining ingredients. Mix until well combined.

5. Drop by rounded teaspoons at least 2 inches apart on the greased cookie sheet.

6. Bake 12 to 15 minutes or until brown around the edges. Remove from the tray right away, and cool on a rack.

∾

No one will wonder where the main dish or dessert is, especially if this menu is served as a late summer lunch. The presence of grapes and pecans in the rice salad and the cakelike quality of the scones give a feeling of completeness.

LIGHT TOMATO SOUP
JEWELED RICE SALAD
YOGURT SCONES

2 DAYS AHEAD: make soup (this can also be done 1 day ahead) / cook rice for salad

1 DAY AHEAD: assemble salad / get scone ingredients ready: measure flour and combine dry ingredients

SAME DAY: assemble and bake scones (baking can be done while you put together salad and heat soup) / reheat soup / garnish salad

LIGHT TOMATO SOUP

PREPARATION TIME: 40 TO
45 MINUTES.

YIELD: 4 TO 5 SERVINGS.

*3 pounds fresh and perfectly
ripe tomatoes, cut into
chunks*

*4 medium-sized cloves garlic,
chopped*

*6 to 8 fresh basil leaves
(or 1 full stalk fresh basil)*

*1 to 2 tablespoons brown
sugar or honey*

1 teaspoon salt

*freshly ground black pepper,
to taste*

*optional garnishes: minced
fresh parsley and/or
fresh dill*

This tomato soup is mostly tomatoes. It also features several of the tomato's best friends and closest associates, i.e., garlic, basil, parsley, and dill. A touch of sugar cuts the acidity, so there is no need for any oil or dairy products. This soup can be made several days in advance, and reheats nicely.

1. Place tomatoes, garlic, and basil in a soup pot, large saucepan, or Dutch oven. Cover and cook over medium heat for 10 to 15 minutes, or until tomatoes are quite liquefied.

2. Remove from heat, and cool to the point at which you feel confident about puréeing it. (Dodging hot splatters is not a lot of fun.) Fish out the basil, and purée the tomatoes and garlic in a food processor or blender until quite smooth.

3. Strain through a medium-fine strainer back into the soup pot, and season with brown sugar or honey, salt, and freshly ground black pepper.

4. Heat just before serving. If desired, sprinkle each bowlful with a light touch of minced fresh parsley and/or dill.

JEWELED RICE SALAD

PREPARATION TIME: 45 MINUTES
TO PREPARE, PLUS TIME TO
CHILL.

YIELD: AT LEAST 6 SERVINGS.
(MORE, DEPENDING ON WHAT
ELSE IS SERVED.)

2 cups uncooked short-grain
  brown rice

3 cups water

¹/₃ cup extra virgin olive oil

6 to 8 tablespoons fresh lemon
  juice (to taste)

1 teaspoon salt

1 large clove garlic, finely
  minced

1 tablespoon honey

4 to 6 scallions, very finely
  minced (include both
  whites and greens)

¹/₂ cup (packed) very finely
  minced fresh parsley

1 cup chopped toasted pecans

freshly ground black pepper,
  to taste

2 cups red or green seedless
  grapes (or a combination of
  red and green)

1 cup cooked chick-peas
  (freshly cooked or from a
  can, rinsed and drained)
  (optional)

a handful of toasted pecan
  halves

This is a lemony, garlicky rice salad, greenish in hue, crunchy with toasted pecans, and adorned with grapes. The green color comes from mincing the parsley to a very, very fine state in a food processor fitted with the steel blade.

The rice can be cooked a day or two ahead of time. All other ingredients can be prepared while the rice is simmering. The salad keeps very well (for at least four or five days) if covered tightly and refrigerated.

1. Place the rice and water in a saucepan. Cover and bring to a boil. Lower heat to the slowest possible simmer and cook undisturbed for 35 minutes or until all water is absorbed and the rice is tender. Immediately transfer the cooked rice to a large platter or a long, shallow, rectangular pan and distribute it with a wooden spoon, allowing the maximum amount of steam to escape. This prevents the rice from overcooking in its own heat, and helps keep the grains separate as they cool.

2. In a large bowl combine olive oil, lemon juice, salt, garlic, and honey. When the rice has cooled to room temperature add it to this dressing and stir until well combined.

3. Add scallions, parsley, chopped pecans, and black pepper to taste. Mix well.

4. Set aside a handful or so of grapes to be left whole, for garnish. Slice the rest in half. Stir the sliced grapes into the salad, if you want the optional chick-peas, add them at this time, too.

5. Cover tightly and chill well before serving. Garnish with whole grapes and toasted pecan halves.

YOGURT SCONES

PREPARATION TIME: 30 MINUTES.

YIELD: 1 TO 1½ DOZEN.

1½ cups unbleached white
   flour

1½ cups whole wheat flour

2 teaspoons baking powder

2 teaspoons baking soda

½ teaspoon salt

6 tablespoons cold butter

2 tablespoons (packed) brown
   sugar

1¼ cups firm yogurt

2 eggs

½ cup (packed) raisins,
   sultanas, or currants

These scones are unusually light and fluffy.

Unlike most recipes for scones, this one doesn't require any rolling or cutting of the dough. In fact, the "dough" is more of a batter, and can be dropped—like cookies—directly onto the baking sheet. Because of this great shortcut, the recipe can be completely assembled in just 15 minutes or less, and the scones only bake for another 15 minutes. So pull this one out if you have guests coming for tea on short notice.

1. Preheat oven to 400°. Lightly grease a baking sheet.

2. Sift together the first 5 ingredients. Then cut together with butter and brown sugar, using a food processor (steel blade attachment), pastry cutter, or electric mixer—until uniformly blended. It should resemble coarse meal. If using a food processor, transfer everything to a bowl.

3. Beat the yogurt together with 1 egg. Make a well in the center of the dry ingredients, and add the yogurt mixture along with the dried fruit. Mix as minimally as possible, with swift, decisive strokes, until well blended.

4. Drop by rounded quarter-cup measures onto the lightly greased sheet. Beat the remaining egg. Brush the tops with beaten egg (the softness of the batter might require you to pat, rather than brush, it on).

5. Bake 12 to 15 minutes. Serve hot or warm, with butter and good preserves.

PURÉE OF YELLOW SQUASH SOUP
CORN-RYE BREAD
AVOCADO AND GRAPEFRUIT ON GREENS WITH GRAPEFRUIT VINAIGRETTE
OATMEAL COOKIE VARIATIONS

If you use frozen squash (directions are included with the recipe), this cheerful menu can be made any time of the year. The soup and bread are perfect partners. Serve them together, and let the salad be a course unto itself. Make a pot of the finest tea to accompany the cookies.

3 DAYS AHEAD: assemble bread dough; refrigerate the unbaked loaves (this can also be done 1 or 2 days ahead)

2 DAYS AHEAD: prepare soup, steps 1 through 4

1 DAY AHEAD: for the salad: make grapefruit sections, Grapefruit Vinaigrette, and clean and dry the greens / make cookie dough; bake immediately, or wait until tomorrow / bake bread

SAME DAY: purée soup with milk, and heat gently; prepare optional topping, if desired / bake cookies, if you didn't yesterday / assemble salad

PURÉE OF
YELLOW SQUASH SOUP

PREPARATION TIME: 45 MINUTES.

YIELD: 4 TO 6 SERVINGS.

*1 pound yellow squash
(approximately
6 small ones)*

2 cups chopped onion

*2 medium cloves garlic,
minced*

*1 to 2 tablespoons butter or
olive oil*

*1/2 teaspoon dried thyme
(or 2 teaspoons minced
fresh thyme)*

1/2 teaspoon dried sage

*1/2 teaspoon dried basil
(or 1 to 2 tablespoons
minced fresh basil)*

1 teaspoon salt

*1 tablespoon unbleached white
flour*

*1/2 cup dry white wine
(optional)*

*2 cups milk (lowfat or
soy okay)*

freshly ground black pepper

OPTIONAL TOPPING:

*1 small red bell pepper, cut in
thin strips*

1 clove garlic, minced

2 teaspoons olive oil or butter

minced chives

This recipe is designed primarily for yellow crookneck squash, which is available from early summer through early fall. But the soup can be made year round either from frozen yellow squash or from winter squash (acorn or butternut).

To freeze yellow squash, cut the squash into 1/4-inch slices, and drop into a saucepan of boiling water for 3 minutes. Drain and cool. Then wrap airtight in a plastic bag or container and freeze.

To use acorn or butternut squash in this recipe, peel and seed a 1-pound squash. Chop it into small pieces, and steam or boil until tender. Drain well. Then simply follow the recipe, beginning with step 2, substituting this cooked winter squash for the yellow crookneck.

1. Cut the end off the squash, and peel if the skin looks suspicious in any way. Then cut the squash into 1/4-inch slices and set aside.

2. In a large saucepan or a Dutch oven, begin sautéing onions and garlic in butter or oil over medium-low heat. After about 5 minutes, add squash, herbs, and salt. Stir, cover, and continue to cook about 10 more minutes.

3. Gradually sprinkle in the flour, stirring constantly. Continue to cook and stir over low heat about 5 minutes.

4. Pour in the optional white wine, stir briefly, cover, and let simmer 10 to 15 minutes. (NOTE: The alcoholic content of the wine dissipates with cooking, and the taste of the wine diminishes gradually. So if you let it cook a little longer at this step, you will get a more subtle result. Just be sure to stir everything up from the bottom from time to time, so it won't stick or scorch.) Remove from heat, and allow the soup to cool until it's cool enough to purée.

5. Purée the soup with the milk in a food processor or blender, and return it to a soup pot. (At this point, you may choose to strain the soup through a fine strainer or a sieve to get a smoother texture.) Adjust the seasonings. Add black pepper to taste.

6. Heat gently just before serving.

7. While the soup is heating, prepare (or don't) the optional topping. Sauté the bell pepper and garlic in olive oil or butter until *just* tender. Spoon a little bit of this into each steaming bowl of soup, and sprinkle with minced chives.

CORN-RYE BREAD

PREPARATION TIME: 4 TO 5 HOURS, MUCH OF WHICH IS RISING OR BAKING TIME.

YIELD: 2 MEDIUM-SIZED ROUND LOAVES.

1¹/₂ cups lukewarm water

1 package active dry yeast

3 tablespoons molasses

2 tablespoons soft butter or canola oil

2 teaspoons salt

1¹/₂ cups cornmeal

1¹/₂ cups rye flour

2¹/₂ to 3 cups unbleached white flour

oil for the bowl

extra cornmeal, for the baking sheet

This is a dense bread with a touch of molasses. It ages well if you keep it sealed in a plastic bag, and it tastes great (and can be sliced thin) by its third or fourth day. Cornmeal and rye flour are beautifully compatible partners: each is strong, but neither dominates. You can vary the amounts of cornmeal and rye flour, using as little as 1 cup of each and as much as 2 cups. Always add them first, and then compensate for the variations by increasing or decreasing the amount of unbleached white flour.

As with many of the yeasted breads in this book, you can choose to give the unbaked loaves their final rise in the refrigerator. The rise will be so slow that they can actually stay there for up to three days before being baked, provided the tray they are on is wrapped in a sealed plastic bag. Put them directly into a preheated oven from the refrigerator. This will enable you to have practically instant fresh-baked bread to soothe you at the end of a busy day.

1. Place the water in a large mixing bowl. Sprinkle in the yeast, and let it stand for 5 minutes until it becomes foamy.

2. Stir in molasses, butter or oil, and salt.

3. Whisk in cornmeal and rye flour, beating well after each addition.

4. Begin adding white flour ¹/₂ cup at a time, mixing after each addition with a wooden spoon. When the dough becomes too thick to mix with a spoon, begin kneading with your hand. Add just enough white flour to make a firm, unsticky dough.

5. Turn the dough out onto a floured surface and knead for about 10 minutes. Add small amounts of flour as necessary, if the dough becomes sticky.

6. Clean or wipe out the bowl, and oil it lightly. Add the kneaded dough, and oil the top surface of the dough. Cover with a clean, dry tea towel, and set in a warm (or at least draft-free)

place to rise. Leave it there for 2 hours or until it has risen to about 1$\frac{1}{2}$ times its original bulk.

7. Punch down the risen dough, and return it to the floured work surface. Knead for 5 to 10 more minutes, then divide the dough in half and form 2 round loaves. Slash the top of each loaf with an "X" (use a serrated bread knife). Then sprinkle a handful or two of cornmeal onto a large baking sheet, and place the loaves on the sheet about 4 to 5 inches apart. Cover with the towel again, and return to the rising place. Let rise 45 minutes to 1 hour more. (Alternatively, you can refrigerate the loaves at this point. Place the baking sheet in a large sealed plastic bag with room enough for the dough to rise, and leave them up to three days before baking. They can go directly from the refrigerator into a preheated oven.)

8. Preheat oven to 375°. Bake the loaves for 45 minutes, or until they give off a hollow sound when thumped emphatically on the bottom. Cool on a rack for at least 30 minutes before slicing.

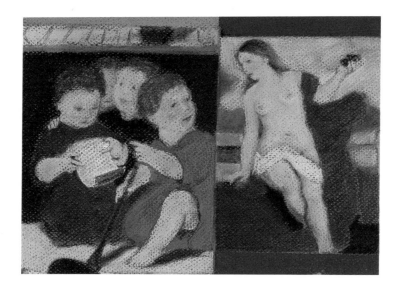

AVOCADO AND GRAPEFRUIT ON GREENS WITH GRAPEFRUIT VINAIGRETTE

PREPARATION TIME: 30 MINUTES

YIELD: 6 SERVINGS.

3 grapefruits, preferably red, but white is also fine

1 heaping teaspoon grated fresh ginger or minced sushi ginger (preserved in vinegar)

2 tablespoons walnut oil

3 to 4 tablespoons extra virgin olive oil

³/₄ to 1 teaspoon salt

1 tablespoon fresh lemon juice

3 tablespoons red wine vinegar

1 tablespoon sweetening (real maple syrup or sugar)

mixed greens (watercress, Boston lettuce, and/or other soft lettuces), well cleaned and well dried—enough for 6 servings

1 ripe avocado

The grapefruit sections, vinaigrette, and greens can all be prepared up to several days in advance. (If you prepare the greens in advance, store them wrapped in paper towels and sealed in a plastic bag. They will stay fresh if kept very dry.) The salad must be assembled at the last possible minute in order for the greens to stay crisp and the avocado to stay green.

The vinaigrette calls for a combination of walnut and olive oils. If you can't find walnut oil, just use all olive.

1. Grate enough rind from one of the grapefruits to make ¹/₂ teaspoon. Put both the grapefruit and the rind aside. Use a sharp serrated knife to prepare the other 2 grapefruits. Cut off the ends and carve off all the skin, right down to the fruit itself. Hold the peeled grapefruit over a bowl, and slice along each membrane, releasing the sections of fruit one by one. Squeeze in all the remaining juice from the membrane.

2. Strain the grapefruit sections over a second bowl to collect the juice. Put the sections aside, and measure the juice. You will need ¹/₂ cup for the vinaigrette. If there isn't enough, squeeze some more from the extra grapefruit.

3. Combine the grapefruit juice, ginger, walnut oil, olive oil, salt, lemon juice, vinegar, and sweetening, and mix well. Cover and chill until serving.

4. Just before serving the salad, arrange the mixed greens on individual serving plates.

5. Peel the avocado and cut it into about 12 slender slices. Place a couple of these on each plate. Add a few grapefruit sections (from Step 1) and drizzle on some vinaigrette. Use a moderate amount, and pass a small pitcher for people to add extra, to taste.

OATMEAL COOKIE VARIATIONS

PREPARATION TIME: 25 MINUTES TO PREPARE, 12 TO 15 TO BAKE.

YIELD: 4 DOZEN COOKIES.

¾ cup (1½ sticks) soft butter

¾ cup (packed) brown sugar

1 egg

1 teaspoon vanilla extract

1¼ cups flour

1 teaspoon baking soda

½ teaspoon salt

3½ cups rolled oats

5 to 6 tablespoons water or orange juice

1 teaspoon cinnamon

1 cup (packed) raisins

¾ cup chopped walnuts

Oatmeal cookies are a perennial favorite. The basic recipe is open to many suggestions and variations, so feel free to be creative. Meanwhile, here are two of my own favorite versions.

I. CINNAMON-RAISIN-WALNUT OATMEAL COOKIES

1. Preheat oven to 350°. Lightly grease a cookie sheet.

2. Cream together butter and brown sugar with an electric mixer at high speed.

3. Beat in the egg; stir in the vanilla.

4. Sift together flour, baking soda, and salt.

5. If you are using thick-cut rolled oats (the kind that is sold in bulk at natural food stores), grind the oats slightly in a blender or food processor, using a few quick spurts. If you are using a more refined product, like Quaker Oats, this step is unnecessary.

6. Stir flour mixture into the butter mixture, and add all remaining ingredients. Mix until everything is well combined.

7. Drop by rounded teaspoons onto a lightly greased cookie sheet, and flatten each cookie slightly with the back of the spoon.

8. Bake 12 to 15 minutes. Remove from the sheet while still hot, and cool on a rack.

II. CHOCOLATE-CHOCOLATE CHIP OATMEAL COOKIES

Follow the above recipe with these changes:

1. Substitute 5 to 6 tablespoons black coffee for the water or orange juice.

2. Omit cinnamon, raisins, walnuts.

3. Add 1 cup ground chocolate chips (ground to a coarse meal in a blender, using quick spurts) and 1 cup whole chocolate chips. Stir these in at the end.

"Composing" a platter of contrasting salads is like setting up an edible still life.

The soup and rolls alone make a satisfying lunch. Add all or some of the salads and the pie, and you have an elegant dinner.

PURÉE OF WATERCRESS, MUSHROOM, AND POTATO SOUP

RAISIN PUMPERNICKEL ROLLS

COMPOSED SALAD:
CAULIFLOWER WITH CUMIN AND CHEESE; ROASTED RED PEPPERS WITH GARLIC AND LIME; MARINATED BEETS WITH MINT

PEAR PIE WITH WALNUT CRUST

3 DAYS AHEAD: assemble rolls, short of baking, and refrigerate / make Roasted Red Peppers with Garlic and Lime / cook and peel beets

2 DAYS AHEAD: make the soup to the point at which it is puréed / make Marinated Beets, leaving out optional feta and mint garnish

1 DAY AHEAD: make Cauliflower with Cumin and Cheese / make pie crust

SAME DAY: finish soup and reheat; prepare garnishes / assemble and bake pie; bake rolls at the same time

PURÉE OF WATERCRESS, MUSHROOM, AND POTATO SOUP

PREPARATION TIME: 1 HOUR, MAXIMUM.

YIELD: 4 TO 6 SERVINGS WITH-OUT MILK, 6 TO 8 SERVINGS WITH MILK.

3 to 4 fist-sized potatoes (peeling is optional), cut into small chunks

1/2 pound mushrooms, coarsely chopped

3 cups chopped onions or leeks

4 cups water

1 to 1 1/2 teaspoons salt

4 cups chopped fresh water-cress or other leafy greens

OPTIONAL:

1 to 2 medium-sized cloves garlic (cooked with the other vegetables, either in water or sautéed)

1 to 2 tablespoons butter or canola or vegetable oil, if you wish to sauté the onions and mushrooms

1 cup milk, room temperature (lowfat or soy okay)

freshly ground black pepper, to taste

thinned sour cream (thinned by whisking slightly), for garnish

strips of fresh basil leaves, for garnish

This is a very simple purée of vegetables, which tastes delicious with or without milk added. It can be prepared either by cooking all the vegetables together in water or by sautéing some of them in butter beforehand. So one has the option of a rich-tasting, very filling purée made with little or no butter or dairy products. If you choose to add the milk, you can use lowfat or soy and still get a luxurious result.

The purée can be made several days ahead. Add everything except the milk and garnishes. To serve, heat very gently, and make sure the milk is at room temperature before stirring it in.

METHOD I:

1. In a soup pot or Dutch oven, cook potatoes, mushrooms, onions or leeks, and optional garlic in water with salt, covered, over medium heat, for about 15 minutes, or until the potatoes are very tender. Remove from heat, transfer to another container, and cool in cooking water until lukewarm.

2. Purée the vegetables with their cooking water in a food processor or blender, in batches. Gradually add all the chopped watercress or greens as you purée. Return to the soup pot or Dutch oven, and heat gently.

3. If you choose to add the milk, stir it in just before serving. (Make sure the milk is at room temperature first.) Taste to adjust seasonings. The watercress adds quite a bite, but if you prefer additional nippiness, freshly ground black pepper goes very well in here.

4. Serve hot, with or without optional garnishes of sour cream and basil.

METHOD II:

1. Put the potatoes up to boil in a medium-sized saucepan. Use all 4 cups of water.

2. Meanwhile, cook the mushrooms, onions or leeks, and optional garlic (or not) in butter or oil with salt in a large skillet over medium heat. Stir intermittently and cover between stirrings.

Continue to cook for about 10 minutes, or until everything is tender and well mingled.

3. When the potatoes are cooked, purée them together with the sautéed mushrooms et al. and the freshly chopped watercress.

4. Proceed as in Method I.

RAISIN PUMPERNICKEL ROLLS

PREPARATION TIME: 4 TO 5 HOURS, MOST OF WHICH IS RISING TIME.

YIELD: 16 ROLLS.

⅓ cup semisweet chocolate chips

3 tablespoons butter

1 cup lukewarm water

2 packages active dry yeast

½ cup molasses

1½ tablespoons Postum

1½ teaspoons salt

1 cup raisins

2 cups rye flour

2½ cups unbleached white flour

2 to 3 cups whole wheat flour, as needed

oil for the bowl and the dough

cornmeal for the baking sheet

Don't be startled by the presence of chocolate chips in this recipe. They serve to darken, moisten, and slightly sweeten the rolls but their presence will be extremely subtle.

If you don't have Postum, you can use instant coffee. You can even use strong black coffee, and just slightly adjust the amount of flour to accommodate the change. Remember that, apart from sensitivity to heat, dough is quite flexible.

Also, don't be discouraged by what seems like a major preparation time commitment. During most of those 4 to 5 hours the dough is rising, and you are free to do other things. There is only a modest amount of actual labor required. The result is really worthwhile, and the rolls keep for up to two weeks if kept in a sealed plastic bag in the refrigerator. They are delicious sliced and toasted.

NOTE: The rolls can be assembled up to three days in advance of baking. Store them in an airtight plastic bag in the refrigerator.

1. Melt the chocolate chips and butter together over very low heat, then remove from heat and cool to room temperature.

2. Place wrist-temperature water in a large bowl. Sprinkle in the yeast and let it stand 5 minutes. It will be foamy.

3. Stir in molasses with a wooden spoon. Add Postum, salt, and raisins.

4. Making sure it is no warmer than room temperature, drizzle in the chocolate mixture, mixing constantly.

5. Add rye flour and 1 cup each of the white and whole wheat. Stir as vigorously as possible with a wooden spoon.

6. Gradually knead in all the white flour plus enough additional whole wheat flour to make a smooth, nonsticky dough. Turn the dough out onto a floured surface and knead about 10 min-

utes. The dough will be dense. Let it rest while you clean the mixing bowl.

7. Lightly oil the bowl and the top surface of the dough. Put the dough in the bowl, cover with a clean towel, and let rise in a warm place for at least 3 hours. It will rise by about half of its original volume.

8. Punch down the dough and knead it on a floured surface another 5 minutes or so. Cut the dough in half, then cut each half into 8 equal parts. Knead each little piece for a minute or two, and form into a ball (it should be the approximate size of a slightly overweight golf ball).

9. Dust a baking sheet (or two, depending on the size) with cornmeal, and arrange the balls of dough at least 3 inches apart. Let the dough rise again for 45 minutes to 1 hour. (You may also let it rise in the refrigerator. Wrap the baking sheet loosely but airtight in a plastic bag and refrigerate. The rolls can remain stored this way up to three days before baking. They can go into a preheated oven directly from the refrigerator.)

10. Preheat oven to 375°. Bake for 30 minutes, or until the rolls sound hollow when thumped. Remove from the sheet and cool at least 10 minutes before serving.

COMPOSED SALAD

Individual salads can be combined to make an elegant appetizer or light main course when grouped together on a platter. Try serving the following recipes this way, as a "Composed Salad," artfully arranged and garnished. Then experiment with other combinations of salads, aiming for contrasts in color and subtle variations in seasoning and texture. Composed salads can become a creative and exciting part of your ever-expanding repertoire.

CAULIFLOWER WITH CUMIN AND CHEESE

This tasty salad has a range of applications. It can accompany the most elegant of meals, and it also makes a great snack. It's all right to make it a day or two ahead of time, if that's more convenient for you. It will keep well.

PREPARATION TIME: 30 MINUTES.

YIELD: 4 PORTIONS DEPENDING ON WHAT ELSE IS SERVED.

4 cups small cauliflorets (approximately 2 small heads cauliflower)

1 cup thinly sliced onion

3/4 teaspoon whole cumin seeds

1 to 2 tablespoons extra virgin olive oil

1/4 to 1/2 teaspoon salt

1 tablespoon cider vinegar

1 small clove garlic, finely minced

1 cup mild white cheese cubes (Monterey jack or something similar), the size of dice

3 to 4 tablespoons sour cream or yogurt, or a combination

freshly ground black pepper, to taste

1. Steam the cauliflower until tender (this should take about 5 to 8 minutes, depending on the size of the pieces), and refresh under cold running water. Transfer to a medium-sized bowl.

2. In a small skillet, sauté the onions and cumin seeds in oil with salt over medium heat until the onions are very soft (5 to 8 minutes).

3. Combine all ingredients, mix well, and taste to adjust seasonings. Serve chilled or at room temperature.

ROASTED RED PEPPERS WITH GARLIC AND LIME

PREPARATION TIME: 30 MINUTES TO ROAST THE PEPPERS; JUST A FEW MINUTES OF PREPARATION THEREAFTER.

YIELD: ABOUT 4 PORTIONS, DEPENDING ON WHAT ELSE IS SERVED.

4 to 5 large red bell peppers, in their prime

3 tablespoons fresh lime juice

3 to 4 tablespoons extra virgin olive oil

$^{1}/_{2}$ teaspoon salt

1 large clove garlic, well minced

freshly ground black pepper

Since discovering roasted peppers—and realizing how easy it is to prepare them—I've gotten addicted. Sometimes I just roast a few for fun in my spare time. It is amazing how a humble bell pepper can get transformed through this process. Strips of roasted, peeled pepper are so tender you almost don't need to chew them.

This salad can also be prepared with raw red peppers if you just can't take the time to do the roasting and peeling. It's not exactly the same thing, but it can be done, and it will taste fine. Just be sure to give the peppers at least a few hours (preferably overnight) to marinate.

This dish keeps beautifully for up to a week, so make it as many days ahead of time as you need to. Preparation time can be streamlined by getting the marinade ready while the peppers roast.

1. Preheat oven to 400°. Place the peppers on a baking sheet and bake them for 20 to 30 minutes, turning them every 5 to 8 minutes, so they will blister fairly evenly. When they are quite soft and the skins have pulled away from the peppers, remove them and place immediately in a paper bag for about 3 to 5 minutes. Remove from the bag, cut out and discard stems and seeds, and peel the peppers with a sharp paring knife. The skins should come off very easily.

2. Cut the peppers into small cubes or strips, and place them in a medium-sized bowl.

3. Add all other ingredients and mix gently.

4. Cover tightly and refrigerate at least 12 (and preferably 24) hours before serving.

MARINATED BEETS WITH MINT

PREPARATION TIME: 45 TO 50 MINUTES TO BAKE THE BEETS, OR 15 TO 20 MINUTES TO BOIL THEM; JUST A FEW MINUTES TO FINISH AFTER THAT, PLUS TIME TO CHILL.

YIELD: ABOUT 4 PORTIONS, DEPENDING ON WHAT ELSE IS SERVED.

8 medium-sized beets (about 2 inches in diameter)

2 tablespoons walnut oil

3 small cloves garlic, well minced

1 tablespoon plus 1 teaspoon fruit vinegar (recommended: raspberry, pear, or cassis)

1/2 teaspoon salt

1/4 cup (packed) coarsely minced fresh mint leaves

1/2 cup crumbled feta cheese (optional)

extra sprigs of mint, for garnish

This salad is a dark, regal shade of magenta, punctuated by bright green sprigs of mint. The walnut oil (available in the gourmet section of many grocery stores and in specialty shops) gives a distinct and pungent flavor, which enhances the staid sweetness of the beets. If you can't get walnut oil, substitute extra virgin olive oil, and consider garnishing the salad with a few toasted walnut halves. And if you don't have access to fancy vinegars, go ahead and use cider vinegar.

I prefer baking the beets to boiling them. If you follow the baking method described below, the flavor will consolidate and be much more intense and beetlike than if you boil them.

This salad keeps very well up to a week if stored in a tightly lidded container in the refrigerator. (Leave out the optional feta cheese and the mint-sprig garnish until just before serving.)

1. Cook the beets by baking them or boiling them. To bake, preheat oven to 400°. Wrap the beets in aluminum foil, leaving the stem ends slightly exposed. Bake 45 to 50 minutes, or until the beets are very tender. Rinse under cold running water, and rub off the skins. Trim the stem end with a paring knife. To boil, remove the tips, stems, and greens. Place the beets in a saucepan, and cover them with water. Bring to a boil, turn down the heat, and simmer 15 to 20 minutes, or until tender. Drain, and rub off the skins under cold running water.

2. Dry the beets on paper towels. Slice them in half lengthwise, and then into very thin half-moons. Place them in a medium-sized bowl.

3. Add all remaining ingredients (except the feta and the extra sprigs of mint) and mix well. Cover tightly and refrigerate at least 12 hours (preferably 24 hours or more). If you think of it, stir the marinating beets intermittently during this time.

4. Serve cold, topped with crumbled feta, if desired, and garnished generously with small sprigs of fresh mint.

PEAR PIE WITH WALNUT CRUST

PREPARATION TIME: 35 MINUTES,
PLUS 35 MINUTES TO BAKE.

YIELD: 1 9-INCH PIE.

CRUST:

1 tablespoon soft butter

2 cups walnuts

1/2 cup unbleached white flour

3 tablespoons (packed) brown
    sugar

1/4 teaspoon salt

1/4 teaspoon cinnamon

about 3 tablespoons water
    (as needed)

FILLING:

5 to 6 average-sized firm,
    ripe pears

2 tablespoons unbleached
    white flour

3/4 teaspoon cinnamon

2 tablespoons (packed) brown
    sugar (or more, to taste)

grated rind of 1 lemon

1 tablespoon fresh lemon juice

a dash of salt

1/2 pint heavy cream (optional)

confectioners' sugar, to taste
    (optional)

1/2 teaspoon vanilla extract
    (optional)

A cross between a pie and a tart, this dessert is especially wonderful if served slightly warm, accompanied by lightly sweetened whipped cream or vanilla ice cream.

D'Anjou, Comice, or Bartlett pears work best in here. You can use Bosc, but they cook down less, and will remain quite firm even after being baked. If you like a combination of textures, try mixing 1 or 2 Bosc pears with one of the softer kinds.

The crust can be made several days in advance. Wrap it in a sealed plastic bag and store in the refrigerator.

CRUST:

1. Generously grease a 9-inch pie pan with the butter.

2. Grind the walnuts *almost* to a paste in a food processor with the steel blade attachment or in a blender, using quick spurts. (If using a blender, grind the nuts in 3 or 4 batches rather than all at once.)

3. Combine the walnuts with flour, sugar, salt, and cinnamon in a medium-sized bowl. Mix with a fork until uniformly blended.

4. Add water 1 tablespoon at a time, mixing after each addition. Add just enough to enable the dough to adhere to itself, but not so much that it becomes sticky.

5. Use your hands to press the dough evenly into the bottom and sides of the buttered pie pan. Set aside while you make the filling.

FILLING:

1. Preheat oven to 375°.

2. Peel and slice the pears, and place them in a medium-sized bowl. Gradually sprinkle in the flour as you toss the slices gently.

3. Add cinnamon, sugar, lemon rind and juice, and salt. Stir lightly.

4. Spread the filling into the unbaked crust. Bake for 35 minutes.

5. Meanwhile, if desired, whip the heavy cream, adding confectioners' sugar to taste and 1/2 teaspoon vanilla extract. Refrigerate until serving time.

6. Serve the pie warm, topped with the whipped cream. Or, if you'd rather not bother making the whipped cream, you can serve it with vanilla ice cream.

Save this meal for the most elegant occasion. The pâté is lavishly decorated; the soup is straight from heaven. The bread makes you feel like you're in rural France, and the green beans lead to delusions that the whole meal is in fact a picnic in Monet's gardens.

Serve with a light white wine and a simple dessert of plain fresh berries, if they are in season.

GOLDEN PEAR SOUP
CHEESE-NUT PÂTÉ
COUNTRY BREAD
ROASTED AND MARINATED GREEN BEANS
WITH ONIONS AND GARLIC CLOVES
FRESH BERRIES
WHITE WINE

3 DAYS AHEAD: assemble and bake the pâté / assemble the bread; refrigerate the unbaked loaves (this can also be done 1 or 2 days ahead)

2 DAYS AHEAD: prepare soup, steps 1 through 4

1 DAY AHEAD: make Roasted and Marinated Green Beans et al. / prepare garnishes for pâté

SAME DAY: bake the bread / frost and decorate the pâté / finish the soup and heat gently

GOLDEN PEAR SOUP

PREPARATION TIME: 50 MINUTES.

YIELD: 6 SERVINGS.

1½ pounds yams or sweet potatoes (acorn or butternut squash may be substituted)

4 cups water

1 3-inch stick cinnamon

1½ teaspoons salt

3 large (average-person's-fist-sized) ripe pears (any kind but Bosc)

1 to 2 tablespoons butter

¼ cup plus 1 tablespoon dry white wine

⅓ cup half-and-half, light cream, or milk (lowfat or soy okay)

a few dashes of ground white pepper

Fresh pears and yams are puréed together and finished off with touches of cinnamon, white wine, and cream. This unusual soup is slightly sweet, slightly tart, and deeply soothing. It is easy to make, and it's hard to believe something that tastes this good can be born of such a low-keyed effort.

Steps 1 through 4 can be done ahead of time, and the purée can be refrigerated for a day or two before the finishing touches are added and the soup is heated and served.

1. Peel yams (or sweet potatoes or squash), and cut into small pieces. Place in a large saucepan with water, cinnamon stick, and salt. Bring to a boil, cover, and simmer until tender (about 15 minutes). Remove the cover and let it simmer an additional 5 minutes over medium heat. Remove and discard the cinnamon stick. Set aside.

2. Peel and core the pears, and cut them into thin slices.

3. In a heavy skillet, sauté pears in butter for about 5 minutes over medium heat, stirring frequently. Add ¼ cup wine, cover, and simmer 10 to 12 minutes more over medium heat.

4. Using a food processor with the steel blade or a blender, purée the yams and their water together with the pears au jus until smooth. (You may have to do this in several batches.) Transfer to a heavy soup pot or Dutch oven.

5. Add the cream or milk and the remaining tablespoon of wine. Sprinkle in the white pepper. Heat very gently just before serving. (Don't cook it or let it boil.)

CHEESE-NUT PÂTÉ

PREPARATION TIME: 20 MINUTES TO ASSEMBLE, I HOUR TO BAKE. AFTER SEVERAL HOURS OF CHILLING, ABOUT 20 MINUTES TO PREPARE FOR SERVING.

YIELD: SERVES 8 TO 10 AS AN APPETIZER.

2 tablespoons melted butter (to grease the pan)

I cup finely minced onion

I tablespoon butter

8 ounces cream cheese (lowfat okay)

I pound cottage cheese (lowfat okay)

I cup ground almonds and walnuts, combined (use a food processor with steel blade or a blender, in quick spurts)

½ teaspoon salt (or to taste)

lots of black pepper

I tablespoon minced fresh dill (or I teaspoon dried)

2 teaspoons prepared mustard

2 to 3 teaspoons fresh lime or lemon juice

2 cups (packed) grated cheddar

TOPPINGS:

I cup ricotta

a few walnut halves, whole almonds, and whole or chopped olives

radishes, cucumber slices, and parsley

I think I've made this pâté more than any other recipe in this book. It is especially easy if you use a food processor, first to grate the cheddar, and then to purée everything together.

You can get truly artful with the decorations. The pâté gets frosted all over with ricotta cheese, and then embellished ad infinitum with vegetable slices, minced herbs, nuts, olives, etc. The dish creates a festive event in and of itself, and your guests will feel flattered.

The pâté can be assembled and baked up to four days ahead. Wrap it airtight and store in the refrigerator. Frost and garnish within hours of serving.

1. Preheat oven to 325°. Melt and distribute 2 tablespoons butter in a standard loaf pan.

2. In a small pan, sauté onions in 1 tablespoon butter until soft.

3. Combine and whip together all ingredients (except those for topping). Use the steel blade attachment on a food processor, or high speed on an electric mixer.

4. When mixture is uniform, spread evenly into greased loaf pan.

5. Bake 1 hour. (When you take it out of the oven it will look suspiciously loose, but don't worry. It firms up as it chills.) Allow to cool completely in the pan, then chill for at least several hours before turning out onto a serving platter.

6. To get the pâté out of the pan, loosen it with a spatula. Invert it onto a larger plate, holding the pan in place against the plate. Shake firmly several times (or give it a whack). Remove the loaf pan. The pâté should emerge in one piece. If it breaks, you can easily mold it back together. (Don't be discouraged by how ugly it looks in its predecorated state. It will be transformed by the ricotta and the garnishes.)

7. To decorate, spread a layer of ricotta cheese all over, as if frosting a cake. Place whole or half nuts, olives, radishes, cucumber slices, and parsley in the design of your choice. Serve with dark bread or good crackers.

COUNTRY BREAD

PREPARATION TIME: 3 TO
4 HOURS, MOST OF WHICH
IS RISING TIME.

YIELD: 1 LARGE OR 2 SMALL
LOAVES.

1 1/2 cups lukewarm water

1 package active dry yeast

3 to 4 tablespoons (packed)
brown sugar

4 tablespoons soft butter

1 1/2 teaspoons salt

2 cups oat flour

1 cup rye or whole wheat
flour

3 cups unbleached white flour
(more or less)

oil for the bowl and the dough

cornmeal for dusting the
baking sheet

Oat flour gives these tender loaves a slightly sweet flavor. You can find oat flour at most natural food stores, packaged in 2-pound bags. Or you can easily make it yourself by grinding rolled oats to the consistency of fine meal in a blender.

The unbaked loaves can be stored for several days in the refrigerator. Just be sure you wrap them airtight in a plastic bag. They can go directly from the refrigerator into a preheated oven.

1. Place the water in a large bowl. Sprinkle in the yeast and the sugar, and let it stand 5 minutes, until foamy.

2. Add butter and salt, and mix well.

3. Add flour, 1 cup at a time, beginning with all the oat and rye or whole wheat. Then add as much white flour as needed to make a firm dough. Mix between additions with a wooden spoon at first, and then graduate to your hands as the mixture thickens.

4. Turn the dough out onto a floured surface, and knead for 5 to 10 minutes, until it is smooth and elastic. Add small amounts of additional flour if it gets sticky.

5. Oil the bowl (it isn't necessary to clean it first), put the kneaded dough in the bowl, and oil the top surface of the dough. Cover with a clean tea towel, and set it in a warm place to rise until doubled in bulk. (This can take anywhere from 1 1/2 to 2 hours, depending on the temperature of your kitchen.)

6. Punch down the dough, and turn it out again on a floured surface. Knead 5 minutes more and then form 1 large or 2 small loaves, either round or baguette shaped. Make a few small slashes on top of each loaf with a sharp knife.

7. Sprinkle a baking tray generously with cornmeal. Place the loaf or loaves on top, and let them rise for about 45 minutes. NOTE: At this point, the loaves may be wrapped loosely in a very large sealed plastic bag and refrigerated for up to 48 hours before baking. The loaves can go directly from the refrigerator into the oven.

8. Preheat oven to 375°. Bake for about 50 minutes (large loaf) or 40 to 45 minutes (small ones) or until the bread gives out a hollow sound when thumped resolutely on the bottom. NOTE: For a crustier surface, lightly spray the baking loaves every 10 minutes with water from a plant mister.

ROASTED AND MARINATED GREEN BEANS WITH ONIONS AND GARLIC CLOVES

PREPARATION TIME: 10 MINUTES
TO PREPARE, 20 TO 30
TO BAKE.

YIELD: ABOUT 4 SERVINGS.

3 to 4 tablespoons olive oil

1 pound fresh green beans, cleaned, trimmed, and patted dry

1 medium-sized yellow or red onion, cut in thin slices or rings

6 to 8 medium-sized cloves garlic, peeled and halved lengthwise

a scant 1/2 teaspoon salt

1 to 2 tablespoons balsamic vinegar

freshly ground black pepper

Here is a fine alternative to steaming or sautéing green beans. Just roast them in the oven on a lightly oiled tray. The flavor and texture will be so enhanced that only minimal additional seasoning will be necessary to make this a special and delicious preparation.

You can experiment with roasting other vegetables as well: carrots cut into matchstick pieces, broccoli stalks, cauliflowerets, whole asparagus, mushrooms...try a combination. Snow peas also taste wonderful cooked this way. They take considerably less time to roast, so add them during the last 5 minutes if you're cooking them in combination with other vegetables.

NOTE: The recipe calls for medium-sized cloves of garlic sliced in half lengthwise. You can also use small ones and leave them whole. If you can't get balsamic vinegar, use champagne vinegar or some fruity variety. If none of these is available, cider vinegar or red wine vinegar will also work.

1. Preheat oven to 400°. Brush a large baking tray with 2 tablespoons olive oil.

2. Spread green beans, onions, and garlic on the tray. Salt lightly, and drizzle with another tablespoon or two of olive oil.

3. Bake the vegetables for 20 to 30 minutes, interrupting several times to shake the tray or stir briefly. After 20 minutes, tastetest a green bean to see if it's done to your liking. The baking time is somewhat flexible.

4. When all the vegetables are tender, remove from the oven and transfer to a bowl. Drizzle immediately with vinegar. Apply freshly ground black pepper to taste.

5. Serve hot, at room temperature, or cold.

Try this menu for brunch or lunch. If you want to make it a little more substantial, add a platter of assorted cheeses and olives.

TUSCAN BEAN SOUP
MARINATED EGGPLANT
RICH BAGUETTE
BALSAMIC STRAWBERRIES

3 DAYS AHEAD: soak beans for soup / prepare the baguettes; refrigerate the unbaked loaves (this can also be done 1 or 2 days ahead)

2 DAYS AHEAD: cook beans; cut vegetables for soup

1 DAY AHEAD: assemble soup (leave out lemon juice and garnishes) / prepare Marinated Eggplant

SAME DAY: (early in the day) clean, hull, and slice strawberries; sprinkle with sugar and refrigerate / bake baguettes / heat and finish soup / allow strawberries to come to room temperature; 30 minutes before serving, sprinkle with vinegar

TUSCAN BEAN SOUP

PREPARATION TIME: THE SOAKED BEANS NEED ABOUT 1½ HOURS TO COOK. AFTER THIS, THE SOUP TAKES 1 HOUR.

YIELD: 4 TO 6 SERVINGS (EASILY MULTIPLIED).

1½ cups dried white beans

2 medium-sized cloves garlic, crushed

2 stalks celery, chopped

2 medium-sized carrots, sliced

½ pound fresh green beans, cut in 1-inch lengths

6 to 8 scallions, minced (whites only)

2 tablespoons butter or olive oil (or a combination)

2 teaspoons salt

lots of freshly ground black pepper

2 to 3 teaspoons dried basil

2½ cups stock or water (bean-cooking water, if possible)

3 tablespoons fresh lemon juice

parmesan cheese and minced fresh parsley for the top

This is a vegetable soup featuring white beans and green beans in a lightly seasoned broth.

There are several different varieties of white beans available. Great Northern beans work really well in this soup, but you can also use white pea beans. Unlike thicker bean soups, this one calls for cooking the beans until just tender, so they remain distinct and can float in the broth, rather than merge with it.

The beans can be cooked up to several days in advance. The entire soup can also be made a day ahead as it reheats well. Just be sure to add the parmesan and parsley to each serving just before bringing it to the table.

1. Soak the dried beans for several hours or overnight. Cook in plenty of gently boiling water until just tender (about 1 to 1½ hours). Save any extra cooking water for the soup.

2. In a large, heavy soup pot, sauté the garlic and all the vegetables in butter and/or olive oil, with the salt, pepper, and basil, over medium heat for about 5 minutes. Cover, turn the heat way down, and cook gently 10 to 15 minutes.

3. Add the beans and 2½ cups liquid (bean-cooking water or plain water). Cover and simmer for 30 minutes. Add lemon juice and simmer 10 minutes more.

4. Serve hot, topped with parmesan and parsley.

MARINATED EGGPLANT

PREPARATION TIME: 30 TO
40 MINUTES TO PREPARE,
AT LEAST 2 TO 3 HOURS
TO MARINATE.

YIELD: 4 TO 5 SERVINGS,
DEPENDING ON WHAT ELSE IS
SERVED. VERY EASILY MULTI-
PLIED.

1 medium-sized eggplant,
    unblemished and firm

salt

1 to 2 tablespoons extra virgin
    olive oil

2 tablespoons fresh lemon
    juice

1 to 2 medium-sized cloves
    garlic, minced

freshly ground black pepper

fresh marjoram, fresh dill, and
    fresh parsley, very finely
    minced

Round eggplant slices are baked until tender, lightly moistened with olive oil and lemon, redolent of garlic, and accented gently with snippets of fresh herbs. If prepared at least 24 hours in advance of serving, the eggplant gets an opportunity to really soak up all the flavors, and the ingredients will be in peak harmony.

1. Preheat oven to 375°. Lightly oil a baking sheet.

2. Slice eggplant into circles, a scant ½ inch thick. Arrange the slices on the baking sheet and salt very lightly.

3. Let stand for about 15 to 20 minutes, then pat the eggplant dry with paper towels. Bake until the eggplant is very tender (20 to 25 minutes).

4. Remove the slices from the baking sheet and place them on a large serving platter—ideally, one with a rim. The slices can be arranged in a slightly overlapping pattern.

5. While the eggplant is still hot, drizzle with 1 to 2 tablespoons olive oil and the lemon juice. Spread—or in some way distribute—the crushed garlic over the eggplant. Sprinkle liberally with black pepper and minced fresh herbs.

6. Cool to room temperature. Cover the plate very tightly with plastic wrap and chill for at least several hours, preferably overnight. Serve cold or at room temperature.

RICH BAGUETTE

PREPARATION TIME: 3½ HOURS,
START TO FINISH (MOST OF
WHICH IS RISING OR BAKING
TIME).

YIELD: 2 SUBSTANTIAL LOAVES.

1 cup lukewarm water

1 package active dry yeast

6 tablespoons sugar

1 egg

6 tablespoons butter

1 cup dry milk

1 teaspoon salt

3½ to 4 cups unbleached
  white flour

oil or soft butter for bowl,
  dough, and baking sheet

½ cup milk for the crust
  (optional)

This is one of my all-time favorite bread recipes. The presence of dry milk gives it an indescribable tenderness. Try it for sandwiches or toast, or just by itself. It will make you feel very, very good.

The unbaked loaves may be stored in the refrigerator for several days before baking. From there they can go directly into a preheated oven.

1. Pour the water into a large bowl. (Be sure it is no warmer than your wrist!)

2. Sprinkle in the yeast, and let it sit several minutes until foamy.

3. Beat in sugar, egg, butter, dry milk, and salt.

4. Add the flour 1 cup at a time, beating with a wooden spoon after each addition. Gradually begin mixing with your hand as the dough thickens. Eventually you will find yourself kneading rather than mixing. Stop adding flour when the dough becomes smooth and unsticky.

5. Turn the dough out onto a floured surface, and knead 5 to 10 minutes.

6. Oil or butter the bowl, add the dough, and grease the top surface of the dough. Cover with a clean tea towel, and set in a warm place to rise for 1 to 2 hours, or until doubled in bulk.

7. Punch down the dough, return it to the floured surface, and knead another 5 minutes. Divide the dough in half, and form 2 long slender loaves about 2 inches in diameter. Place them 4 to 5 inches apart on a lightly greased baking sheet.

8. Place the loaves in a warm place to rise again for 1 hour. Or seal the entire baking sheet in a large plastic bag, leaving room in the bag for the bread to expand, and place it in the refrigerator. The dough can stay in there for up to three days before baking.

9. Preheat oven to 375°. OPTIONAL: Brush the risen bread with milk for a soft, brown crust. Bake 25 to 35 minutes, or until the loaves give a distinct hollow sound when thumped on the bottom. Remove from the sheet immediately, and cool on a rack.

BALSAMIC STRAWBERRIES

PREPARATION TIME: 10 TO
15 MINUTES, PLUS SEVERAL
HOURS TO SIT.

YIELD: 4 TO 6 SERVINGS.

2 pints (1 quart) strawberries

4 to 6 teaspoons sugar

1 tablespoon balsamic vinegar

A traditional Italian way to serve fresh berries is simply to let them sit and macerate for a few hours with a small amount of sugar, then to drizzle in a little vinegar just before serving. Perfectly ripe berries taste exquisite prepared this way. It is also a magical way to salvage imperfect berries, especially those that may have been picked too soon and would otherwise suffer the fate of being considered boring and disappointing.

Balsamic vinegar is a special aged variety made in Modena, Italy. It is deep reddish brown, and has a full-bodied, slightly sweet flavor that sets it apart from other vinegars. In recent years it has become widely poplar and increasingly available in the United States. It can be found in specialty or gourmet shops, as well as in some grocery stores, either with the other vinegars or in the gourmet department. If you can't get balsamic vinegar, you could substitute another variety. If not exactly transcendent, the result will still be good.

The strawberries can be sliced and sugared up to a day in advance. The vinegar should be applied within 30 minutes of serving.

1. Clean the strawberries by wiping them with a damp paper towel. (If they are washed directly in water, they will absorb it and their flavor will become diluted.)

2. Hull the strawberries, and halve or slice them, depending on their size. Place them in a shallow pan (a 10-inch glass pie pan works well) and sprinkle with sugar.

3. Cover tightly with plastic wrap, and let sit for at least several hours, stirring them or shaking the pan every now and then. (If they are going to sit for much longer than 3 or 4 hours, cover and refrigerate them, but allow them to return to room temperature before serving.)

4. Sprinkle on the vinegar within a half hour of serving, and serve in small individual bowls.

The ingredients for this menu should be readily available from midfall throughout the winter. The soup vegetables can be varied according to whatever is available. Irish Soda Bread is a perennial favorite, and you can make it over and over again with a different combination of flours each time. (It's good for the soul to keep freshly baked breads coming out of the oven regularly during the cold season.)

AUTUMN VEGETABLE SOUP
GREEN SALAD WITH PEARS, WALNUTS, AND FETA
IRISH SODA BREAD

2 DAYS AHEAD: cut soup vegetables, except chard or greens, tomato, and pepper

1 DAY AHEAD: assemble soup through step 2 / clean and dry greens; toast nuts for salad / combine all dry ingredients for the bread

SAME DAY: assemble and bake the bread / cut chard or greens, tomato, and pepper for soup; heat and complete / prepare pears and assemble salad

AUTUMN VEGETABLE SOUP

PREPARATION TIME: 45 TO 50 MINUTES, MUCH OF WHICH IS SIMMERING TIME.

YIELD: 5 TO 6 SERVINGS.

1 to 2 tablespoons butter or oil (olive or canola)

1¹/₂ cups chopped leeks

1¹/₂ cups quartered Brussels sprouts

1 large carrot, chopped

1 stalk celery, chopped

1 large potato, chopped

1 cup peeled chopped acorn or butternut squash (and/or pumpkin and/or sweet potato)

³/₄ teaspoon salt (adjust to taste)

freshly ground black pepper, to taste

cayenne, to taste

2 large cloves garlic, minced

3 cups stock or water

1 cup (packed) chopped Swiss chard or collard greens

1 large firm tomato, chopped

1 bell pepper, chopped—green, red, or yellow

1¹/₂ teaspoons dried dill

¹/₂ teaspoon each dried marjoram and basil

2 teaspoons soy sauce (or to taste)

1 tablespoon fresh lemon juice

¹/₂ cup sour cream or yogurt, room temperature (optional)

sunflower seeds, for garnish

minced fresh parsley, for garnish

The vegetables in this soup are subject to many variations, additions, substitutions, etc. This is a good opportunity to experiment with some of those fringe vegetables you may have been reluctant to try. Consider using slices or chunks of turnip, rutabaga, kohlrabi, parsnip (surprisingly sweet and benign!) or sunchoke (also called Jerusalem artichoke).

A food processor fitted with the slicing attachment will reduce the vegetable preparation time. Also, many of the vegetables can be chopped or sliced a day or two ahead. Store them in plastic bags or airtight containers in the refrigerator. (Store cut potatoes in a container of water so they won't discolor.)

1. In a soup pot or Dutch oven, cook the first 11 ingredients (everything through the garlic) over moderate heat, covered, for 10 to 15 minutes. Stir intermittently.

2. Add stock or water. Bring to a boil, lower to a simmer. Cover and let it cook slowly until everything is tender (another 15 to 20 minutes).

3. Add Swiss chard or greens, tomato chunks, and chopped bell pepper. Simmer about 5 more minutes.

4. Add herbs, soy sauce, and lemon juice, and continue to simmer another 3 to 5 minutes.

5. If you choose to add the sour cream or yogurt, stir it in just before serving. Garnish each bowlful with sunflower seeds and parsley.

GREEN SALAD WITH PEARS, WALNUTS, AND FETA

PREPARATION TIME: 20 MINUTES.

YIELD: 4 TO 5 SERVINGS.

1 medium-sized ripe D'Anjou,
Comice, or Bartlett pear
(Bosc is not recommended;
it's a little too crunchy)

2 tablespoons fresh lemon
juice

1 small head soft lettuce
(butter, red, or green leaf)
or about 12 leaves romaine,
or a combination, cleaned
and well dried

1 to 2 tablespoons walnut oil
or extra virgin olive oil

1/2 cup coarsely chopped
walnuts, toasted (use a
toaster oven)

1/2 to 1 cup crumbled feta

1 to 2 teaspoons vinegar
(red wine, sherry, or
champagne)

freshly ground black pepper

Crisp and soft greens are combined with sweet, juicy slices of fruit and accented with toasted walnuts and soft, salty feta cheese. This is a lunch dish that leaves you so satisfied, all dessert cravings just fade away.

Please note that the proportions of ingredients are flexible, and the amounts suggested below can be adjusted to your taste. I recommend the salad be dressed very lightly, as the flavors are quite complex to begin with.

1. Cut the pear into thin slices (peeling is optional). Place in a small bowl and cover with lemon juice. Set aside.

2. Place the clean, dried lettuce in a medium-sized bowl. Pat one more time with paper towels just to be sure it is *really* dry. Break the lettuce into bite-sized pieces, drizzle lightly with oil, and toss.

3. Gently mix in walnuts and feta. Sprinkle in the vinegar and grate in some black pepper. Toss to distribute.

4. Lift the pear slices out of the bowl of lemon juice with a fork or a slotted spoon. Arrange them on top of the salad, and serve.

IRISH SODA BREAD

PREPARATION TIME: 15 MINUTES
TO PREPARE, 40 TO
50 MINUTES TO BAKE.

YIELD: 1 10-INCH ROUND PANFUL.

2 cups whole wheat flour

2 cups unbleached white flour

3 teaspoons baking powder

2 teaspoons baking soda

2 tablespoons brown sugar

1 teaspoon salt

$1/4$ cup melted butter

2 eggs

$1^1/_3$ cups yogurt

golden raisins or currants
(optional)

1 teaspoon caraway seeds
(optional)

$1/4$ cup poppy seeds
(optional)

For a superb variation on this quick and easy bread, try substituting oat and barley flours for the whole wheat and white. Buy them in a natural food store, or grind rolled oats and pearl barley in a blender or food processor.

Bring this one to the table fresh from the oven.

1. Preheat oven to 375° (350° for a glass pan). Butter a 10-inch round pan.

2. In a large bowl, sift together flours, baking powder, baking soda, sugar, and salt.

3. Beat together melted butter, eggs, and yogurt.

4. Make a well in the center of the dry ingredients, and stir in the wet ingredients. Mix briefly until reasonably well blended. (The batter does not need to be elegant.)

5. Add optional touches (raisins or currants and/or seeds)—or not.

6. Spoon dough into the prepared pan, then spread as evenly as possible. Shape it into a smooth mound, higher in the middle, tapered on the sides.

7. Bake 40 to 50 minutes—until a knife inserted all the way into the center comes out clean. The top will be quite brown.

8. Cool for 10 minutes, then remove from the pan. It may be served hot, cut into wedges, and wrapped in a clean tea towel in a big bowl. This bread is delicious warm, and is also very good at room temperature or cold.

This meal contains a wide spectrum of textures. The soup is creamy, slightly dense and smooth; the salads have many different kinds of crunch, plus soft, absorbent black mushrooms. I took the liberty of adding Strawberry Meringue Pie to this otherwise ethnically correct menu. With its ethereal texture and bright, positive flavor, it is the perfect counterpoint to the deeply, darkly seasoned dishes.

VELVET CORN SOUP

COLD CHINESE MUSHROOMS WITH BEAN THREAD NOODLES

CHINESE BROCCOLI SALAD WITH WALNUTS

STRAWBERRY MERINGUE PIE

3 DAYS AHEAD: make pie crust

2 DAYS AHEAD: soak black mushrooms (step 1 of soup) / cook bean thread noodles; store in water in refrigerator / for broccoli salad: do step 1, cover tightly and refrigerate; clean and cut broccoli; toast walnuts

1 DAY AHEAD: assemble and purée soup / assemble Cold Chinese Mushrooms with Bean Thread Noodles / steam broccoli; prepare and marinate mushrooms / for the pie: separate eggs; clean and cook strawberries (step 2); get other ingredients measured and ready

SAME DAY: make pie filling and complete the pie / reheat soup and prepare garnishes / assemble broccoli salad (at the very last minute!)

VELVET CORN SOUP

PREPARATION TIME: 20 MINUTES
AFTER THE MUSHROOMS ARE
SOAKED.

YIELD: 4 CUPS STRAINED,
5 CUPS UNSTRAINED.

*¹/₄ pound dried Chinese black
  mushrooms*

5 cups boiling water

6 cups uncooked corn

1 teaspoon salt (or to taste)

1 teaspoon soy sauce

*freshly ground black pepper,
  to taste*

*¹/₂ teaspoon Chinese sesame oil
  (or more, to taste)*

2 tablespoons dry sherry

OPTIONAL GARNISHES:

*finely minced parsely,
  scallion greens, and/or
  cilantro*

finely minced red bell pepper

This is an unusual soup with an exquisite texture and the deep flavor of Chinese black mushrooms. The mushrooms can be soaked a day or two in advance, and the preparations thereafter are quick and simple.

1. Briefly rinse the dried mushrooms under running water to clean, and place them in a large bowl. Add boiling water, cover with a plate, and let stand at least 1 hour. Drain well, reserving both the mushrooms and the water, and squeezing all excess liquid from the mushrooms. Transfer the soaking water to a soup pot; store the mushrooms in a tightly covered container in the refrigerator. The mushrooms will be used in the Cold Chinese Mushrooms with Bean Thread Noodles (following recipe).

2. Add the remaining ingredients, except garnishes, to the soup pot. Heat just to boiling; simmer 10 minutes. Purée until smooth in a blender or food processor. Return to the soup pot, and adjust the seasonings. If you want a smoother texture, strain the purée through a fine sieve.

3. Reheat just before serving. For a touch of contrast, garnish each bowlful with a very light sprinkling of finely minced garnishes.

COLD CHINESE MUSHROOMS WITH BEAN THREAD NOODLES

PREPARATION TIME: ¹/₂ HOUR AFTER THE MUSHROOMS HAVE SOAKED, PLUS TIME TO CHILL.

YIELD: 6 TO 8 SERVINGS.

¹/₄ pound dried Chinese black mushrooms, soaked (see Velvet Corn Soup)

9 ounces uncooked bean thread noodles (or enough noodles to make 3 to 4 cups cooked)

3 tablespoons Chinese sesame oil, plus a little extra for drizzling on the noodles

2 tablespoons fresh lemon juice

6 tablespoons rice vinegar

4 to 6 tablespoons apple juice concentrate (to taste)

2 tablespoons soy sauce

1 teaspoon salt (to taste)

greens, for serving

1 scallion, finely minced (whites and greens)

sesame seeds

This salad has some wonderful yet subtle textural contrasts. The Chinese mushrooms are soft and highly absorbent, soaking up the flavors of the sesame oil, lemon juice, and soy sauce. The bean thread noodles (also known as cellophane noodles) are tiny and thin, yet they have quite a bit of body to them. A light sprinkling of sesame seeds on top gives just a touch of crunch.

Bean thread noodles are available in most Asian grocery stores. If you can't find them, use thin rice noodles or plain vermicelli. You will need a total of 3 to 4 cups cooked noodles, and they can be made a day or two ahead if stored in a container of water in the refrigerator.

The black mushrooms can be soaked ahead of time and stored in the refrigerator for one or two days. If you make this recipe in conjunction with Velvet Corn Soup (which precedes) there will be just the right amount of mushrooms left for this salad after making the stock.

1. Soak the mushrooms in boiling water (follow step 1 from Velvet Corn Soup). If you are making the salad independent of the soup, you can use less water than the soup calls for. Use just enough to cover.

2. Cook the noodles in boiling water until just tender. Drain well, rinse in cold running water, and drain again. Drizzle with a little sesame oil to keep the noodles from sticking together.

3. After squeezing out all excess water from the soaked mushrooms, pull off the tough stems and discard. Slice the mushrooms into very thin strips and set aside.

4. In a medium-sized bowl, combine 2 tablespoons Chinese sesame oil, lemon juice, vinegar, apple juice concentrate, soy sauce, and salt. Mix well.

5. Stir in the mushrooms. Grind in the black pepper. Add the cooked noodles, and toss gently until everything is well combined. Cover tightly and chill until serving.

6. Serve on a bed of greens, with minced scallion and sesame seeds sprinkled lightly over the top.

CHINESE BROCCOLI SALAD WITH WALNUTS

PREPARATION TIME: APPROXI-
MATELY 40 MINUTES, PLUS
TIME TO CHILL.

YIELD: 6 SERVINGS.

1 tablespoon minced garlic

1/3 cup walnut oil

1 tablespoon Chinese sesame
 oil

1 tablespoon soy sauce

1 teaspoon salt

2 tablespoons fresh lime juice

1/3 cup rice vinegar

1 tablespoon minced fresh
 ginger

2 bunches broccoli, about
 1 pound each

6 ounces mushrooms

1 1/2 cups toasted walnut
 halves

A deeply flavored marinade, full of garlic and ginger, coats tender broccoli spears, whole mushroom caps, and toasted walnut halves. This easy salad stands strongly on its own, and it is also compatible with a wide range of other dishes.

This recipe calls for walnut oil (available in the gourmet department of many supermarkets as well as in specialty shops) and Chinese sesame oil (available in Asian grocery stores). If you can't find walnut oil, increase the Chinese sesame oil to 1/4 cup and add 1/4 cup canola or peanut oil.

All components can be prepared a day in advance. Store marinated mushrooms, steamed broccoli, and toasted walnuts in separate containers, and assemble everything soon before serving. This will help keep the broccoli green and the walnuts crisp.

1. Combine the first 8 ingredients in a large bowl.

2. Cut the broccoli into spears approximately 2 inches long, and steam until just tender and bright green. Rinse immediately under cold running water, and drain well. Refrigerate in an airtight container.

3. Clean the mushrooms and remove the stems. Add the caps, whole and uncooked, to the marinade. Mix well, cover, and chill.

4. Stir the broccoli into the marinade within 15 minutes of serving. Sprinkle the walnuts on top at the very last minute.

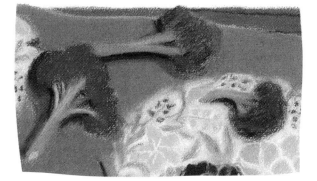

STRAWBERRY MERINGUE PIE

PREPARATION TIME: 1 HOUR.

YIELD: 1 9-INCH PIE.

This pie is cheerful, refreshing, and very pink. It tastes best if eaten the day it's made.

NOTE 1: The crust can be made several days ahead and refrigerated, unbaked, in an airtight plastic bag. It can also be frozen.

NOTE 2: Frozen unsweetened strawberries may be used for the filling. Defrost thoroughly and drain before slicing.

PIE CRUST:

1¼ cups unbleached white flour

¼ cup (½ stick) cold butter, cut into pieces

3 or 4 tablespoons cold water

extra flour

about 1½ cups dried beans

1. Use a food processor fitted with the steel blade (or a pastry cutter, or 2 forks, or 2 knives, or a fork and a knife). Cut the flour and butter together until you have a uniform mixture resembling corn meal.

2. Keep the mixture in motion as you add the water, 1 tablespoon at a time. Add *just* enough to enable the dough to adhere to itself. Then remove to a floured work surface.

3. Roll out the dough until it forms a circle that exceeds a 9-inch pie pan by about 2 inches. Transfer the dough to the pan, and form a gorgeous crust with artful edges.

4. To bake, preheat oven to 375°. Place a piece of foil on the inside of the crust and spread evenly with beans (this will help the crust to keep its shape). Bake 15 minutes, then remove the beans and foil. (Save the beans. They can be used repeatedly for this same purpose.) Bake the crust another 5 to 10 minutes, or until lightly browned. Cool thoroughly before filling.

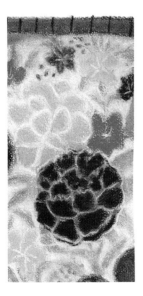

3 eggs

4 cups sliced strawberries

6 tablespoons cornstarch

1¼ cups sugar

¼ teaspoon salt

½ cup fresh lemon juice

1 teaspoon grated lemon rind

FILLING:

1. Separate the eggs, placing the yolks in a small bowl and the whites in a larger one. Cover both bowls and set aside.

2. Place strawberries in a saucepan. Cover and cook 5 to 8 minutes over medium heat (until souplike). Set aside.

3. Meanwhile, in another saucepan, combine cornstarch, sugar, and salt. Stir in the lemon juice and whisk until uniform.

4. Beat in the yolks.

5. Whisking constantly, add the hot strawberries au jus. Cook over medium heat until thick, stirring constantly. This should take about 5 more minutes.

6. Lower heat and simmer 1 minute, whisking. Add lemon rind during this time.

7. Pour into prebaked pie shell and set aside.

8. Preheat oven to 325°.

9. Beat the egg whites until stiff. Spread this meringue over the top and to the edges of the crust.

10. Bake in the preheated 325° oven for about 10 minutes, or until the meringue is delicately browned. Cool thoroughly (but do not chill) before serving.

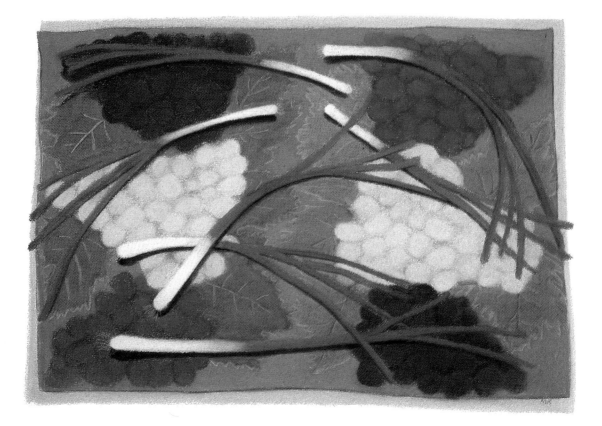

Most of the vegetables in this very satisfying two-dish meal are perennially available, so you can serve it year-round. Mandarin oranges are one of the few fruits that taste good canned. Drain off the syrup, rinse, and serve them in a bowl with a few ice cubes.

Almost everything for this meal can be done ahead. All you have to do the same day is open the can of oranges and complete and heat the soup.

CHINESE VEGETABLE SOUP
COLD HUNAN NOODLES
WITH SESAME AND GREENS
ICED MANDARIN ORANGES

3 DAYS AHEAD: cook noodles for salad; store in water in the refrigerator

2 DAYS AHEAD: cut vegetables for soup / steam greens for salad

1 DAY AHEAD: do steps 1 and 2 of the soup / assemble salad

SAME DAY: heat and complete soup / prepare oranges

CHINESE VEGETABLE SOUP

PREPARATION TIME: 1 HOUR.

YIELD: 4 SERVINGS.

1 medium-sized onion, chopped

6 to 8 large cloves garlic, peeled and halved

2 ounces dried Chinese black mushrooms

4 to 5 thin slices fresh ginger

7 cups water

1½ teaspoons salt

about 10 to 12 fresh mushrooms, cleaned and sliced

1 8-ounce can thinly sliced water chestnuts

2 tablespoons soy sauce

4 to 6 stalks bok choy, stems and leaves separately chopped

½ pound firm tofu, cut in small cubes

1 cup fresh or frozen green peas

approximately ⅓ pound fresh snow peas

3 to 4 scallions, minced (keep whites and greens separate)

small amounts of rice vinegar and Chinese sesame oil for drizzling on top (optional)

This is a simple and mild soup, comforting and filling. It tastes especially good when the weather outside is cold.

You can save on preparation time by getting the vegetables ready (mince the scallions, shell the peas, clean and slice the mushrooms, etc.) while the broth simmers (step 1).

Except for the small amount of sesame oil, which you may or may not choose for garnish, this soup is entirely free of added oil.

1. Combine onion, garlic, black mushrooms, ginger, water, and salt in a soup pot or Dutch oven. Bring to a boil, partially cover, and let simmer for about 45 minutes. Strain the broth and discard the solids,* then return the broth to the soup pot.

2. Add fresh mushrooms, water chestnuts, soy sauce, bok choy stems, and tofu. Bring to a boil again, lower heat, and simmer partially covered, for 8 to 10 more minutes.

3. Heat gently 10 to 15 minutes before serving time. When the soup gets hot, add bok choy leaves, peas, snow peas, and scallion whites. Following those additions, simmer for just 5 minutes, then serve. Top each bowlful with finely minced scallion greens and, if desired, a light drizzle of rice vinegar and/or Chinese sesame oil.

*You may want to save the black mushrooms for use in a stir-fry.

COLD HUNAN NOODLES WITH SESAME AND GREENS

PREPARATION TIME: 1 HOUR.

YIELD: 6 SERVINGS.

2 to 3 stalks celery

5 to 6 stalks bok choy

5 to 6 firm fresh scallions

1 small fennel bulb (optional)

12 ounces thin noodles
(egg or buckwheat)

1 cup sesame seeds or cashews
(or a combination), lightly
ground in a blender

2 tablespoons Chinese
sesame oil

2 tablespoons peanut oil

1 to 3 medium-sized cloves
garlic, minced

1/2 teaspoon ground cinnamon

1/2 teaspoon ground cumin

2 to 3 teaspoons minced fresh
ginger

1/4 cup rice vinegar

2 tablespoons soy sauce

1/2 teaspoon salt

freshly ground black pepper,
to taste

There are some unusual seasonings in here that become more intense as the salad sits around. The flavor is the most subtle on the first day, and by day three or four it will taste as if twice as many seasonings had been added. I like it more and more as the flavor intensifies, and find myself eating it for lunches, dinners, and snacks. All this is another way of saying that this salad is delicious and keeps very well.

The greens can be steamed a day or two ahead. Store in a tightly covered container in the refrigerator. The noodles can be cooked two or three days ahead. Refrigerate in a container of water. Drain thoroughly before using.

1. Slice the celery on the diagonal into thin strips. Remove the leaves from the bok choy and set aside. Cut the bok choy stems into pieces slightly larger than the celery strips, and combine with the celery. Slice the bok choy leaves into strips and place in a separate bowl. Cut the scallion bottoms in half lengthwise, and then at 1½-inch intervals all the way through the tops. (OPTIONAL: Slice the fennel into thin strips.) Group the scallions with the bok choy leaves.

2. Steam the celery and bok choy stems (and optional fennel) together until *almost* tender. Then add the bok choy leaves and scallions and steam for several more minutes, or until everything is just tender and bright green. Rinse immediately in very cold water and set aside in a colander to drain.

3. Cook the noodles in plenty of boiling water until just tender. (Be very careful not to overcook!) Drain and rinse thoroughly under cold water, separating the noodles gently with your hands as you rinse them, so they don't clump together. (It's hard to dress noodles properly when they are riddled with big wads of themselves.) Drain thoroughly after rinsing.

4. Transfer the noodles to a large bowl. Sprinkle with ground sesame seeds and/or cashews, and drizzle with oils. Mix well to be sure all the oil gets well distributed.

5. Add remaining ingredients, taking special care to sprinkle—not dump—in the ground spices, so they can be evenly distributed. Mix gently but well. You may have to use your hands to get things fully combined.

6. Serve cold or at room temperature.

With this light but thorough meal, you can actually feel well fed and celestial at the same time.

If cantaloupe is not in season, serve the most delectable piece of fresh, ripe fruit you can find.

SIMPLEST MISO BROTH
SCATTERED SUSHI RICE SALAD
MARINATED NIGARI TOFU
FRESH CANTALOUPE WITH LIME

1 DAY AHEAD: marinate tofu / for rice salad: cook and season rice (steps 1 through 5), cook egg (step 6), and prepare all the vegetables / store everything in separate containers in the refrigerator

SAME DAY: make broth / assemble salad (NOTE: It should take less than 15 minutes to do both these tasks) / prepare cantaloupe and cut lime

SIMPLEST MISO BROTH

PREPARATION TIME: 3 MINUTES.

YIELD: AN INDIVIDUAL SERVING.
EASILY MULTIPLIED.

PER SERVING:

1½ tablespoons miso
  (any kind)

¾ to 1 cup boiling water

a few small cubes of tofu
  (dice sized)

a few very thin slices scallion

Instant soup! It's hard to imagine how delicious this is just from reading the short list of ingredients. But even though the soup is simple, the miso has a deep and complex flavor that makes a rich broth. It is also very soothing to the digestive tract.

Miso is a paste made from aged fermented soybeans and grains. There are many different varieties of miso (determined by what kind of grain gets added, length of fermentation, etc.), and they are often referred to by their color (red miso, yellow miso, brown, white, etc.). Miso is sold at Japanese groceries and at natural food stores. Experiment and discover your favorite. NOTE: Because it is already fermented, miso keeps indefinitely if stored in the refrigerator.

The recipe below gives proportions for one serving of miso broth. Dissolve the miso in a small amount of water ahead of time. Then add the remaining amount of fresh hot water, as well as the tofu and scallions, right before serving. Prepare additional servings each in its own separate bowl.

1. Place the miso in the serving bowl.

2. Add a small amount of the hot water (about ¼ cup) and mash until the miso is completely dissolved.

3. Add remaining water and tofu. Top with paper-thin slices of scallion.

SCATTERED SUSHI RICE SALAD

PREPARATION TIME: ABOUT
1¼ HOURS.

YIELD: 6 TO 8 PORTIONS.

2 cups uncooked white rice
(long grain or short grain)

2½ cups water

2 tablespoons mirin or sherry
(optional)

6 tablespoons rice or cider
vinegar

½ cup sugar (more or less,
to taste)

1¼ teaspoons salt

6 tablespoons canola or
vegetable oil

1 egg

another splash of mirin or
sherry (optional)

1 medium-sized carrot, minced

1 small cucumber, peeled,
seeded, and minced

2 scallions, minced (whites
and greens)

1 to 2 cups fresh or frozen
green peas, lightly steamed

a few green beans, cut in
½-inch lengths and lightly
steamed (optional)

a handful of snow peas, cut in
½-inch lengths—steamed or
raw (optional)

1 small yellow summer
squash, minced, raw or
lightly steamed (optional)

3 to 4 tablespoons minced
sushi ginger, if available

3 to 4 tablespoons sesame
seeds, plus a little extra for
the top

Serve this special dish to someone you love. The message will be clear.

Sushi rice, or *shari*, as it is called in Japanese, is a white rice preparation lightly seasoned with vinegar and sugar. It is used to make all forms of sushi, for which it is molded or rolled and topped or filled with various tidbits of seafood, eggs, tofu, or vegetables.

In the following delicate and very pretty salad, the rice itself is showcased, adorned with tiny pieces of different colored vegetables and bits of egg. This recipe is so delicious I found myself eating it for breakfast and snacks, as well as for lunch and dinner.

Scattered Sushi Rice Salad calls for sushi ginger (*amazu shoga*). This is thinly sliced pink ginger that has been tenderized and marinated in vinegar. It is a standard condiment to all varieties of sushi, and should be available in most Asian and all Japanese groceries. Mirin (Japanese cooking sake) is also sold at Japanese groceries. If you can't find it, sherry can be substituted.

Steps 1 through 4 can be done, and the vegetables all prepared, a day in advance. Store in separate tightly covered containers in the refrigerator.

1. Place the rice in a strainer and rinse well under cold running water.

2. Combine the rinsed rice with the water and the optional 2 tablespoons mirin or sherry (or not) in a medium-sized saucepan. Bring to a boil, lower heat to the gentlest possible simmer, and cover. Cook undisturbed for 10 to 12 minutes, until tender.

3. Remove the rice from the heat. Uncover and let stand another 10 minutes. Meanwhile, combine the vinegar, sugar, and salt in a small bowl. NOTE: You may wish to heat the vinegar first, to help the sugar dissolve more easily.

4. Spread the hot rice in a long, shallow container (a 9 × 13-inch baking pan is perfect), and sprinkle on half the vinegar mixture. (Cover the remaining mixture and set aside.) Immediately begin mixing the rice very gently with a fork. The goal is to distribute the vinegar mixture as thoroughly as possible without breaking the rice. As you mix, fan the rice with a newspaper or magazine to prevent the rice from becoming sticky. NOTE: I find it practically impossible to mix and fan at the same time, as these two movements seem to cancel each other

out. If you find you have the same problem, alternate a little fanning with a little mixing. Do this for several minutes, or until the rice is uniformly seasoned.

5. Transfer the rice to a medium-large bowl, and set aside.

6. To prepare the egg, heat a medium-sized skillet. Beat the egg well, possibly adding the optional splash of mirin or sherry. Add 1 teaspoon oil to the hot pan and immediately add the beaten egg. Make a thin omelette by tilting the pan in all directions, allowing the egg to run to its limits as you lift the edges of the omelette. When it is set, flip it over and cook briefly on the other side (just long enough to be sure it is dry). Remove the omelette from the pan and transfer to a dinner plate. Allow to cool thoroughly. Slice the cooled omelette into thin strips, then into $1/2$-inch pieces.

7. Add the remaining oil, vegetables, omelette pieces, minced sushi ginger, sesame seeds, and the remaining vinegar mixture to the rice and mix gently.

8. Serve at room temperature or cold, with a few extra sesame seeds sprinkled delicately on top.

MARINATED NIGARI TOFU

PREPARATION TIME: 10 MINUTES
TO PREPARE, SEVERAL HOURS
TO MARINATE.

YIELD: 4 SERVINGS.

2 medium-sized cloves garlic,
minced

2 tablespoons Chinese
sesame oil

2 tablespoons soy sauce

1 tablespoon mirin

1 to 2 teaspoons brown sugar
or honey (to taste)

1 tablespoon fresh lemon juice

1/4 teaspoon salt

crushed red pepper, to taste
(optional)

1 pound nigari tofu

Some people love their tofu plain. Others find it dull unless it is marinated in strong delicious flavors, as in this recipe. Firm tofu marinates beautifully. (Softer varieties contain—and thus expel—more water, causing the marinade to become diluted.)

Nigari tofu is one of the firmest types available. You can find it in some Asian groceries and in many natural food stores. It usually comes vacuum-packed or in a container of water. If you can't get tofu labeled "nigari," just use the firmest you can find. Mirin is Japanese cooking sake, available in most Asian grocery stores. If you can't find it, substitute a sweet wine or sherry.

1. Combine all ingredients except tofu in a shallow pan or bowl. Whisk until well combined.

2. Cut the tofu into $1/2$ x $1^1/2$-inch pieces. Lay them out in the marinade in such a way as to allow maximum contact with the sauce. Marinate at room temperature for several hours (provided the room is not too hot, in which case, cover them and let them marinate in the refrigerator). Turn them and move them around every 20 to 30 minutes or so, and tilt the pan periodically, so the flavors of the marinade can make the rounds and the tofu gets deeply and evenly penetrated.

3. After the tofu has been marinating for several hours you may either serve it at room temperature, or cover it tightly, and refrigerate until serving time. (It will keep for several days if it is fresh to begin with.)

Serve the artichokes as a first course. It looks very nice—and creates a warm, welcoming touch—to have an artichoke waiting at each table setting when everyone first sits down. The Spinach and Mushrooms in Brandy-Cheese Sauce over toast can then be served solo, getting all the undivided attention it deserves. After these two filling courses, Lemon Nut Torte with Orange Glaze will provide the perfect touch. It has a low-keyed fruit flavor, a subtle nutty texture, and is quite light.

COLD ARTICHOKES
WITH CUCUMBER MAYONNAISE
SPINACH AND MUSHROOMS IN
BRANDY-CHEESE SAUCE
TOASTED RICH BAGUETTE SLICES
LEMON NUT TORTE
WITH ORANGE GLAZE

3 DAYS AHEAD: make homemade mayonnaise (optional) / grind nuts for torte and topping / make baguettes (see page 46); store the unbaked loaves in the refrigerator

2 DAYS AHEAD: for sauce: grate cheese, cut onions, prepare garlic / prepare torte ingredients (sift sugar and flour, squeeze lemon juice, separate eggs, etc.)

I DAY AHEAD: assemble and bake torte / bake baguettes / cook artichokes / make Cucumber Mayonnaise / clean spinach and mushrooms

SAME DAY: make glaze and finish torte / assemble and cook Spinach and Mushrooms in Brandy-Cheese Sauce / toast baguette slices

COLD ARTICHOKES WITH CUCUMBER MAYONNAISE

Artichokes are delicious cold, and with Cucumber Mayonnaise they make a stunning first course.

Commercial mayonnaise can be used as the basis for the sauce, but homemade mayonnaise is better. Two recipes for homemade follow: one is standard, the other is made from tofu, and is amazingly good (even to skeptics!).

The artichokes can be cooked several days in advance. Wrap each one tightly in plastic wrap, or store them all together in the refrigerator in a tightly lidded container. The Cucumber Mayonnaise can be made one day ahead.

ARTICHOKES

PREPARATION TIME: 15 MINUTES.

YIELD: PLENTY FOR
   6 ARTICHOKES.

Choose medium-sized artichokes with a solid feel to them and with the petals relatively closed and tight. Trim the stems and the tips, and steam the artichokes over boiling water for about 35 minutes, or until the petals come off without resistance. Cool to room temperature; chill.

CUCUMBER MAYONNAISE

Combine everything, mix well, and chill thoroughly.

1¹/₃ cups of your favorite mayonnaise, commercial or homemade (see following two recipes)

¹/₄ cup each finely minced fresh chives and dill

2 tablespoons minced fresh basil leaves (or 2 teaspoons dried basil)

1 tablespoon Dijon mustard

2 teaspoons fresh lemon juice

1 small firm cucumber (5 to 6 inches long), peeled, seeded, and finely minced

salt and pepper to taste

a few dashes cayenne (optional)

TWO HOMEMADE MAYONNAISES

REAL MAYONNAISE

Quick, easy, ethereal. Making it takes less effort than going to the store and buying a jar.

PREPARATION TIME: 5 MINUTES.

YIELD: 1 1/3 CUPS.

1 egg

3 tablespoons cider vinegar

1/2 teaspoon salt

1/2 teaspoon dry mustard, or 1/4 teaspoon prepared Dijon mustard

1 1/4 cups oil

1. Place the egg, vinegar, salt, and mustard in a blender, along with about 2 tablespoons of the oil. Blend for a few seconds.
2. Keep the motor running as you slowly drizzle in the remaining oil. Stop the blender when all the oil is incorporated. Transfer to a container with a tight-fitting cover, and store in the refrigerator.

TOFU MAYONNAISE

Cholesterol- and oil-free, this tastes surprisingly like real egg mayonnaise. The big test came when I fed this to several different tofu-phobic mayonnaise aficionados, and they loved it.

PREPARATION TIME: LESS THAN 5 MINUTES.

YIELD: ABOUT 1 1/2 CUPS.

2 10-ounce boxes silken tofu (soft or firm)

2 small cloves garlic, minced

2 tablespoons cider vinegar

1 teaspoon salt

2 teaspoons dry mustard (optional)

NOTE: Silken tofu is an ultrasmooth soybean curd that comes in little vacuum-packed boxes. It is sold in natural foods stores and in many supermarkets.

1. Place all ingredients in a blender, and whip until smooth. (You might need to do this in two batches.)
2. Transfer to a container with a tight lid, cover, and refrigerate until use. (It will keep for up to 5 days.)

SPINACH AND MUSHROOMS IN BRANDY-CHEESE SAUCE

PREPARATION TIME: ABOUT
  I HOUR.

YIELD: 4 TO 6 SERVINGS.

about ¹/₄ pound fresh spinach

2 to 3 large cloves garlic, minced

2 cups minced onion

I to 2 tablespoons butter

I teaspoon salt

I pound mushrooms, coarsely chopped (you can use the slicing attachment of a food processor)

freshly ground black pepper

I tablespoon flour

¹/₂ cup brandy or dry sherry

2 tablespoons Dijon mustard

¹/₂ pound medium-sharp cheddar, grated

2 to 3 tablespoons finely minced fresh parsley

toast or English muffins

An elegant variation on the rarebit theme, this is another one of those dishes that tastes a whole lot richer than it actually is. The alcohol content of the brandy dissipates considerably during the cooking, leaving behind its deep and complex flavor. If you have any of this recipe left over, it makes a wonderful omelette filling.

Serve this over toasted baguette slices or English muffins. If you have the time, try baking your own delicious Rich Baguette. The recipe is on page 46.

1. Stem and clean the spinach, and pat dry with paper towels. Chop it very fine (the steel blade attachment of a food processor does this beautifully with a few short pulses), and set aside.

2. In a large heavy saucepan or Dutch oven, cook garlic and onions in butter with salt over low heat until onions are translucent (about 5 to 8 minutes).

3. Add mushrooms. Stir and cook over moderate heat about 5 minutes. Grind in some black pepper.

4. Gradually sprinkle in the flour, stirring constantly. Continue to stir and cook it about 5 more minutes, keeping the heat low.

5. Whisk together the brandy or sherry and mustard. Add this mixture to the saucepan, still stirring. Cook 10 to 15 minutes over medium heat, mixing intermittently.

6. Turn heat down to very low. Let the mixture simmer undisturbed another 10 to 15 minutes. The sauce will thicken somewhat as the liquid evaporates.

7. Add cheese and spinach, and cook another 10 minutes. Serve hot, over toasted bread or English muffins, and top each serving with minced parsley.

LEMON NUT TORTE
WITH ORANGE GLAZE

PREPARATION TIME: I HOUR AND
20 MINUTES, INCLUDING
BAKING AND GLAZING.

YIELD: ABOUT 8 SERVINGS.

Elegant, impressive, delicious…and really easy. It is not necessary to blanch the nuts for this cake, but you may do so if you prefer a more ethereal result. To blanch, spread the whole hazelnuts or almonds on a cookie sheet and bake at 350° for about 15 minutes. Cool, then rub off the skins with your fingers.

NOTE: Up to three of the egg yolks can be deleted.

LEMON NUT TORTE

6 eggs

*I cup confectioners' sugar
(sift before measuring)*

*3 tablespoons fresh lemon
juice*

¹/₄ teaspoon salt

*I tablespoon grated lemon
rind*

*¹/₄ cup unbleached white flour
(sift before measuring)*

*I cup ground hazelnuts or
almonds (use a food processor with steel blade or a
blender with quick spurts)*

TOPPINGS:

*Orange Glaze (next page)
thin lemon slices (rounds)
whole hazelnuts
ground hazelnuts*

1. Separate the eggs, placing yolks and whites in large mixing bowls. Cover and allow to come to room temperature.

2. Preheat oven to 350°. Grease the bottom of a 9-inch or 10-inch springform baking pan.

3. Beat the whites until they form stiff peaks. Set aside.

4. Without cleaning beaters, begin beating the yolks at medium speed. Gradually add sugar, lemon juice, and salt. Continue to beat 8 to 10 minutes.

5. Add rind, flour, and ground nuts to the yolks. Fold until well blended.

6. Add the beaten whites. Fold, using a rubber spatula to scrape the sides of the bowl. Try to blend as uniformly as possible without deflating. (Better to slightly undermix at this point than to overdo it.)

7. Turn the batter into the pan. Bake for 35 minutes (9-inch pan) or 30 minutes (10-inch pan). Remove from the oven, and allow to cool in the pan. Meanwhile, prepare the toppings.

8. When completely cool, remove the rim from the pan. Top the cake with Orange Glaze (recipe follows), lemon slices, and additional hazelnuts.

ORANGE GLAZE

1 tablespoon cornstarch

4 tablespoons orange juice

1 tablespoon orange or berry liqueur (like cassis)

2 tablespoons sugar

1. Place cornstarch in a small saucepan. Gradually add the liquids, whisking constantly. Mix in the sugar.

2. Continue to whisk as you cook it over medium-low heat until thick. This should take approximately 5 minutes.

3. Spread the hot glaze over the top of the cooled torte. Decorate immediately with thin slices of lemon, whole hazelnuts, and a dusting of ground hazelnuts over the top.

This festive menu is influenced by a combination of Central and South American cooking styles. Black Bean Chili is hearty and deep flavored, and its accompanying salsa provides a surprising, refreshing contrast. Banana-Cheese Empanadas are simple and comforting, and at the same time just slightly exotic. These are followed by a cooling salad and fresh watermelon.

BLACK BEAN CHILI
WITH PINEAPPLE SALSA
BANANA-CHEESE EMPANADAS
GREEN SALAD
MINTED CUCUMBER DRESSING
FRESH WATERMELON

3 DAYS AHEAD: soak black beans (unless using canned) / make empanada dough

2 DAYS AHEAD: cook beans (unless using canned) / prepare and sauté vegetables and spices for chili (step 2) / make salad dressing

I DAY AHEAD: assemble chili and partially simmer / assemble empanadas / clean and dry salad greens

SAME DAY: finish simmering chili / cook empanadas / make salsa / assemble salad / prepare the watermelon

BLACK BEAN CHILI WITH PINEAPPLE SALSA

PREPARATION TIME: SOAKED BEANS NEED 1 TO 1½ HOURS TO COOK. CHILI PREPARATION THEREAFTER TAKES 35 MINUTES (MUCH OF WHICH IS SIMMERING TIME).

YIELD: 6 TO 8 SERVINGS.

This highly seasoned chili and tangy fresh salsa make a perfect partnership, especially when topped with small touches of sour cream and cheese.

The beans can be soaked and cooked several days before preparing the chili. The salsa can be prepared—with time to spare—while the chili simmers. Both chili and salsa keep well, and are still exciting as leftovers a few days later.

NOTE: If you don't have time to soak and cook dried black beans, use 3 15-ounce cans. Rinse and drain well before using.

4 cups dried black turtle beans

1 to 2 tablespoons olive oil

5 to 6 medium-sized cloves garlic, minced

2 teaspoons ground cumin

2¼ teaspoons salt

black pepper, to taste

2 teaspoons dried basil

½ teaspoon dried oregano

crushed red pepper or cayenne, to taste

1 tablespoon fresh lime juice

2 medium-sized green bell peppers, chopped

1 to 2 medium Anaheim or poblano chiles, minced, or 2 4-ounce cans diced green chiles

½ cup tomato purée

Pineapple Salsa (recipe follows)

grated cheese and sour cream, for the topping (optional)

squeezable wedges of lime

BLACK BEAN CHILI

1. Soak the beans in plenty of water for several hours or overnight. Drain off the soaking water, and cook in fresh boiling water, partly covered, until tender (1 to 1½ hours). Check the water level during cooking; add more as necessary. Transfer the cooked beans to a large soup pot or saucepan. Include about 2 to 3 cups of their cooking water.

2. Heat the olive oil in a large, heavy skillet. Add garlic, seasonings, lime juice, bell peppers and chiles, and sauté over medium-low heat until the peppers and chiles are tender (10 to 15 minutes).

3. Add the sauté to the cooked beans, along with tomato purée. Simmer, covered, over *very* low heat, stirring every now and then, for about 20 minutes. (Make the salsa during this time.)

4. Serve topped with Pineapple Salsa and, if desired, grated cheese and sour cream. Add a wedge of lime to the side.

PREPARATION TIME: 15 MINUTES
(WITH FRESH PINEAPPLE) OR
5 MINUTES (WITH CANNED).

YIELD: 2 CUPS.

2 cups minced fresh (or
    canned-in-juice crushed)
    pineapple

2 medium-sized cloves garlic,
    minced

2 to 3 tablespoons minced
    fresh mint

2 tablespoons fresh lime juice

¼ teaspoon salt

¼ teaspoon ground cumin

cayenne, to taste

PINEAPPLE SALSA

Combine everything; cover tightly and refrigerate. This keeps a long time.

BANANA-CHEESE EMPANADAS

PREPARATION TIME:
ABOUT 1 HOUR TO
ASSEMBLE, 12 TO 15
MINUTES TO COOK.

YIELD: 8 EMPANADAS.

2 cups unbleached white flour

½ teaspoon salt

½ cup water

1 medium banana, just ripe
    (i.e., firm but not green)

approximately ¼ pound jack
    or mild cheddar cheese, cut
    in small thin slices

approximately 2 tablespoons
    butter or oil for sautéing or
    baking

Empanadas (small pastries, usually stuffed with meat or cheese) are common in many South American countries, where they are considered major snack food. The combination of bananas and cheese is more Central than South American. (I got the idea from a Nicaraguan restaurant in San Francisco.) So this recipe is kind of a regional hybrid. It is a delicious and unusual blend of contrasting flavors and textures, and is surprisingly simple to prepare.

You have a choice of sautéing or baking the empanadas. Either way, you will use about the same amount of butter or oil.

The dough can be made up to two days in advance if stored tightly covered in the refrigerator. Also, the empanadas can be assembled a day or two ahead and stored on a floured plate, tightly wrapped, and refrigerated.

NOTE: If you are going to bake them, preheat oven to 375° and butter or oil a cookie sheet.

1. Combine flour and salt in a medium-sized bowl. Make a well in the center.

2. Pour in the water and stir until reasonably well combined. Then turn out on a floured surface and knead until smooth (5 minutes).

3. Divide the dough into 8 equal parts, and knead each one into a small ball. Set the balls aside.

4. Peel the banana and cut it laterally into quarters. Cut each quarter in half lengthwise.

5. Roll out each ball of dough into a circle approximately 5 inches in diameter. Place a couple of small cheese slices near the center, and cut a piece of banana into several small strips on top of the cheese. Lightly brush the edges of the dough with water, and fold the dough over the filling, as you would a turnover. Crimp the edges securely with a fork. Set the finished empanada aside and repeat until you have 8.

6. *To sauté*: For every 4 empanadas melt 1 tablespoon butter or oil in a heavy skillet and sauté over medium heat for about 5 minutes on each side.

   To bake: Arrange the empanadas on the buttered or oiled cookie sheet, making absolutely sure they are securely closed. (If the cheese creeps out during baking, it will burn.) Brush the tops lightly with melted butter or oil, and bake at 375° for 12 to 15 minutes. Serve hot.

MINTED CUCUMBER DRESSING

PREPARATION TIME: 10 MINUTES.

YIELD: ABOUT 1¼ CUPS (ENOUGH FOR 4 SERVINGS OF GREEN SALAD). EASILY MULTIPLIED.

1 medium-sized cucumber, about 7 inches long

1 scallion

2 tablespoons fresh mint leaves (1 teaspoon dried)

½ cup yogurt

¼ teaspoon salt

After making this and enjoying it tremendously on a salad, I tried putting it on all kinds of leftovers (room-temperature cooked vegetables, cold poached fish, etc.) as a light sauce. It was great! I even found myself eating it plain, with a spoon, for lunch on a hot day. It's actually a simplified version of cold cucumber yogurt soup. Remarkably refreshing, this dressing contains no added oil, and is extremely low in calories.

1. Peel, seed, and coarsely chop the cucumber.

2. Trim the scallion at both ends and chop into ½-inch pieces.

3. Place all ingredients in a blender or food processor (steel blade attachment) and purée until frothy.

4. Chill well before using.

This menu was designed as a Chanukah celebration dinner, but use it for any winter festivity or whenever people's spirits need warming.

TUNISIAN EGGPLANT APPETIZER
WARMED PITA WEDGES
POTATO LATKES; SOUR CREAM; FRIED ONIONS
THREE-FRUIT SAUCE
SPINACH SALAD WITH GREEN GODDESS DRESSING
CHOCOLATE ECLIPSE

3 DAYS AHEAD: grate and parboil potatoes / grate onions for latkes

2 DAYS AHEAD: make Three-Fruit Sauce / make Green Goddess Dressing / assemble latke batter

I DAY AHEAD: make eggplant appetizer / clean spinach for salad / get ingredients ready for Chocolate Eclipse

SAME DAY: assemble and bake Chocolate Eclipse / fry onions to accompany latkes (optional) / assemble salad / fry latkes

TUNISIAN EGGPLANT APPETIZER

PREPARATION TIME: ABOUT
40 MINUTES.

YIELD: APPETIZER FOR 6.

1/4 cup olive oil (or more,
    as needed)

1 medium-sized onion, finely
    chopped

2 to 3 medium-sized cloves
    garlic, minced

1/2 teaspoon salt (or more,
    to taste)

1 large eggplant
    (peeling optional), cut into
    1-inch cubes

3 tablespoons tomato paste

1/4 cup red wine vinegar

1 cup small pitted green olives

1 small jar (6 ounce)
    marinated artichoke hearts
    (drained, each piece cut
    into 2 or 3 smaller pieces)

pinches of dried tarragon,
    basil, and/or oregano
    (optional)

Here is a South Mediterranean version of caponata (the famous Italian eggplant salad) featuring two outstanding guest stars: green olives and marinated artichoke hearts. It is so good it must be served as a course unto itself, accompanied by wedges of pita bread. (If you serve it with anything else, the other dish, no matter how good, might go unnoticed.)

It keeps beautifully, so go ahead and make it three or four days ahead of time, if that is the most convenient for you.

1. Heat the olive oil in a large skillet. Add the onion, garlic and salt, and sauté over medium heat until the onion is soft and translucent (5 to 8 minutes).

2. Add the eggplant cubes, stir, and cover. Cook until the eggplant is very well done (15 to 20 minutes), stirring occasionally. Add small amounts of additional oil, 1 tablespoon at a time, if needed to prevent sticking.

3. Stir in tomato paste and vinegar, and heat to the boiling point. Add the olives and remove from heat.

4. Stir in the artichoke hearts, then cool to room temperature. Taste to adjust seasonings, adding the optional herbs, if desired.

5. Cover tightly and chill. Serve cold or at room temperature.

POTATO LATKES

PREPARATION TIME: 15 MINUTES
TO PREPARE BATTER, ABOUT
10 MINUTES TO FRY EACH
BATCH.

YIELD: 16 TO 20 4-INCH
PANCAKES.

2 large (large-person's-
fist-sized) potatoes

1 medium-sized onion

2 eggs

1/4 cup unbleached white flour

1/2 teaspoon salt

freshly ground black pepper, to
taste (optional)

cayenne, to taste (optional)

7 to 8 tablespoons oil, for
frying

Three-Fruit Sauce
(recipe follows)

sour cream (optional)

fried onions (optional)*

Yet another recipe for potato latkes (also known as potato pancakes), but this one is different.

My own quest for a new potato latke recipe came from a realization that I didn't like the ones I was eating year after year at Chanukah time. I figured out that there were two things wrong with most latkes: they invariably had a raw-potato taste, and they were usually heavy and soggy instead of thin, crisp, and light. This recipe addresses both problems. To alleviate the raw taste, the grated potatoes are precooked just slightly in boiling water. And to assure that they are light and crisp, they are pressed thin and fried in a hot pan with very hot oil.

The potatoes can be grated and parboiled as much as 3 or 4 days ahead. The fully assembled batter also keeps surprisingly well. You can fry a small amount one day, store the batter, then fry some more a few days later. Keep the batter in an airtight container in the refrigerator.

1. Scrub the potatoes (peeling is optional) and grate them. (The food processor's grating attachment does this in seconds!)

2. Heat a medium-sized saucepan of water to boiling. Drop in the grated potato and parboil for 5 minutes. Drain in a colander over a sink and rinse with cold water. Drain thoroughly.

3. Grate the onion. (You can do this with a few quick pulses of a food processor fitted with the steel blade attachment.)

4. Combine the potatoes, onions, eggs, flour, salt, pepper, and cayenne.

5. Place a heavy skillet or griddle over medium-high heat. Add 2 to 3 tablespoons of oil, and wait until the oil is *very* hot (hot enough to sizzle a drop of batter on contact). Spoon in the batter to form pancakes, and press them down to make them thin. Keep the heat medium-high and fry on both sides until uniformly crisp and brown.

   NOTE: It will probably take more than one shift to get all the pancakes fried. Add fresh oil for each batch, making sure it gets very hot each time before you add the batter. Keep the cooked ones warm in a 200° oven on a bed of paper towels. Don't stack the pancakes or they'll get soggy.

6. Serve hot, with Three-Fruit Sauce and sour cream and fried onions, if desired.

*If you need a recipe for fried onions, see Caramelized Onions (page 159).

THREE-FRUIT SAUCE

PREPARATION TIME: 15 MINUTES
TO CUT THE FRUIT, PLUS
30 MINUTES TO COOK.

YIELD: ENOUGH FOR 6 SERVINGS
OF LATKES.

1 large ripe pineapple

5 to 6 tart apples, peeled

4 to 5 ripe pears, peeled

2 sticks cinnamon

a dash of salt

No sugar or honey—just fruit with a touch of cinnamon.

This sauce keeps well for up to a week or more, if stored in a tightly covered container in the refrigerator.

1. Cut fruit into chunks.

2. Place in saucepan with cinnamon sticks and salt.

3. Cover and stew 30 minutes. Serve hot, warm, or cold.

GREEN GODDESS DRESSING

PREPARATION TIME:
10 TO 15 MINUTES.

YIELD: ABOUT 1 CUP OF DRESSING
(ENOUGH FOR AT LEAST 6
SERVINGS OF SALAD).

*1/2 cup (packed) coarsely
chopped fresh parsley*

about 20 leaves fresh basil

*1/2 cup coarsely chopped fresh
dill*

*3 to 4 scallions, coarsely
chopped (whites and
greens)*

1/3 cup olive oil

*1 1/2 tablespoons red wine vine-
gar (or more, to taste)*

*3 to 4 tablespoons mayon-
naise, commercial or homemade (see page 68)*

salt

freshly ground black pepper

Brimming with herbs, this thick green dressing can double as a dip for raw or lightly steamed vegetables. Make it in the heart of the fresh herb season. It goes very well on a simple salad of plain, crisp spinach leaves.

It will keep for three or four days in the refrigerator (depending on how fresh the herbs are to begin with).

1. Place the herbs and scallions in a blender or food processor, and process until very, very finely minced.

2. Add oil and vinegar. Process for just a few seconds longer, then transfer to a bowl or container.

3. Stir in mayonnaise, and add salt and pepper to taste. Taste to adjust vinegar, then whisk until uniformly blended.

4. Cover tightly and chill until use.

CHOCOLATE ECLIPSE

PREPARATION TIME: 15 MINUTES,
PLUS 30 TO 35 MINUTES
TO BAKE.

YIELD: 8 TO 12 SERVINGS,
DEPENDING ON THE PERSON-
ALITIES OF THE EATERS.

2 tablespoons butter

2 ounces (2 squares) unsweetened chocolate

2 cups buttermilk or sour milk
(2 cups milk plus 2 tea-
spoons vinegar)

1 teaspoon vanilla extract

2 1/2 cups unbleached white
flour

2 1/4 cups (packed) brown
sugar

3 teaspoons baking powder

1 teaspoon baking soda

1/2 teaspoon salt

1 cup semisweet chocolate
chips (optional)

1/2 cup plus 2 tablespoons
unsweetened cocoa

2 1/2 cups boiling water

This dessert is fashioned after one of my mother's specialties that she would make about once a year (usually when a grade school teacher came over for lunch). It is a soft, moist chocolate cake with a built-in puddinglike fudge sauce that ends up underneath.

Even though Chocolate Eclipse tastes very rich, it is actually less so than a regular chocolate cake. It has a similar amount of chocolate and sugar, but contains only 2 tablespoons of butter and no eggs.

Chocolate Eclipse tastes best about an hour or two after it has emerged from the oven. For an ultimate experience, serve it with vanilla ice cream.

1. Preheat the oven to 350°. Grease a 9 x 13-inch baking pan.

2. Melt the butter and chocolate together.

3. In a separate saucepan, heat buttermilk or sour milk gently until just a little warmer than body temperature (don't boil or cook it). Remove from heat, and combine with chocolate mixture and vanilla.

4. In a large mixing bowl combine flour, 1 cup of the brown sugar, baking powder, baking soda, and salt. Mix well (use your hands, if necessary) to break up any little lumps of brown sugar, making as uniform a mixture as possible. Stir in chocolate chips, if desired.

5. Pour in the wet ingredients, and stir until well combined. Spread into the prepared pan.

6. Combine the remaining 1 1/4 cups brown sugar with the unsweetened cocoa in a small bowl. Sprinkle this mixture as evenly as possible over the top of the batter.

7. Pour on the boiling water. It will look terrible, and you will not believe you are actually doing this, but try to persevere.

8. Place immediately in the preheated oven. Bake for 30 to 40 minutes, or until the center is firm to the touch.

9. Cool for at least 15 minutes before serving. Invert each serving on a plate so that the fudge sauce on the bottom becomes a topping. Serve hot or at room temperature.

Three distinct courses give this lovely meal a sense of beginning, middle, and end. You can make this menu at any time of the year. The Raspberry-Cheese Dip can be made from fresh or frozen berries; the Fresh Fruit Spears can be made from whatever is in season. The stew ingredients are always available. Applesauce-Cocoa Cake has a complex, wonderful flavor. It is not too terribly sweet and can double as a brunch dish.

FRESH FRUIT SPEARS

RASPBERRY-CHEESE DIP

PEPPER, LEEK, AND MUSHROOM STEW WITH CORNMEAL AND CHEESE DUMPLINGS

APPLESAUCE-COCOA CAKE

2 DAYS AHEAD: grind walnuts for cake / make dip

1 DAY AHEAD: make dumplings; store uncooked in refrigerator / cut vegetables for stew / do steps 2 through 5 of the cake; refrigerate both the butter mixture and the applesauce-yogurt mixture

SAME DAY: assemble and bake cake / cook stew / poach dumplings / cut fruit spears

RASPBERRY-CHEESE DIP

PREPARATION TIME: 10 MINUTES.

YIELD: A LITTLE OVER 2 CUPS.

1¹/₂ cups fresh or frozen, drained raspberries

¹/₄ to ¹/₂ cup sugar or honey (entirely negotiable)

1 8-ounce package Neufchâtel cheese (lowfat cream cheese), softened

1 to 2 tablespoons fresh lemon juice, to taste

This deep pink and festive appetizer flirts seriously with the idea of being a dessert. It is very easy to whip up, and can make an otherwise ordinary weekend supper feel like a special occasion. If you have a craving to make this in the winter, it will work fine with frozen raspberries. Try to find the kind with no added sugar, so you can be the judge of how sweet to make it. If you can find only the frozen-in-syrup variety, drain the berries first, and perhaps increase the lemon juice slightly, so the dip can retain a degree of tartness.

Serve this with any variety of fresh fruit in season. Melon spears are ideal; and tart apples and crisp pears aren't bad either. The dip keeps well for at least several days if stored in an airtight container in the refrigerator.

1. Combine everything in a blender or a food processor with the steel blade attachment. Purée until very smooth.

2. Transfer to a small bowl. Cover tightly and refrigerate until cold.

3. Serve with spears or slices of fresh fruit as an appetizer or snack, or for afternoon tea.

PEPPER, LEEK, AND MUSHROOM STEW WITH CORNMEAL AND CHEESE DUMPLINGS

PREPARATION TIME: 30 TO 40 MINUTES FOR THE DUMPLINGS, 30 MINUTES FOR THE STEW.

YIELD: 4 SERVINGS.

Peppers, leeks, and mushrooms are briefly sautéed and then bathed in yogurt. The dumplings are made from cornmeal, eggs, and three cheeses, and are very, very light.

The vegetables can be cooked up to a day or two in advance, and then reheated. Be sure the yogurt is at room temperature before adding it, so the sauce won't curdle.

The dumplings can also be assembled a day or two in advance. Store them on a floured plate, tightly covered and refrigerated. About 40 minutes before serving time, bring the cooking water to a boil. Poach the dumplings while you heat the stew.

¹/₂ cup grated cheddar cheese

¹/₂ cup grated Swiss cheese

¹/₂ cup yellow cornmeal

¹/₂ cup unbleached white flour

¹/₂ cup cottage cheese

2 eggs, beaten

a pinch of salt

CORNMEAL AND CHEESE DUMPLINGS

NOTE: The cheeses grate most easily when they are very cold.

1. Mix all ingredients together thoroughly in a bowl. Use your hands to form 1-inch balls.

2. In a large pot, bring 4 quarts of water to a rolling boil. Add as many dumplings as possible without crowding. Reduce heat, cover, and allow to simmer for 10 minutes. Remove with a slotted spoon. NOTE: If you have to cook the dumplings in more than one shift, keep cooked ones warm on a tray in a 200° oven, or reheat in a microwave.

1 to 2 tablespoons butter

2¹/₂ cups chopped leeks (white and half the greens)

¹/₂ pound mushrooms, chopped

6 average-sized bell peppers, thinly sliced (any mix of colors)

¹/₂ teaspoon salt

black pepper, to taste

1 cup thick yogurt, room temperature

paprika

PEPPER, LEEK, AND MUSHROOM STEW

1. Melt the butter in a large saucepan or Dutch oven. Cook the vegetables with salt over low heat. After about 10 minutes, turn up the heat and cook, stirring, until most of the liquid evaporates. Be careful not to scorch it! Add black pepper to taste.

2. Stir in the yogurt shortly before serving. Serve immediately without any further cooking. Top each serving with a few of the dumplings and an artful dusting of paprika.

APPLESAUCE-COCOA CAKE

PREPARATION TIME: 25 TO
30 MINUTES TO PREPARE;
45 TO 55 MINUTES TO BAKE.

YIELD: I LARGE CAKE.

³/₄ cup (1¹/₂ sticks) soft butter

1¹/₂ cups (packed) brown sugar

2 eggs

1 teaspoon vanilla extract

¹/₂ teaspoon grated orange rind

3 cups unbleached white flour

¹/₂ cup unsweetened cocoa

¹/₂ teaspoon salt

2 teaspoons baking powder

1 teaspoon baking soda

1 teaspoon cinnamon (optional)

¹/₂ teaspoon allspice (optional)

¹/₄ teaspoon nutmeg (optional)

1 cup finely ground walnuts (use a food processor fitted with a steel blade or a blender, with brief spurts)

1¹/₂ cups unsweetened applesauce

¹/₂ cup yogurt or sour cream

This is a moist, dark dessert—almost a spice cake, understatedly chocolate, with a touch of orange, and the luxurious qualities of an applesauce-nut cake. If you choose to add the spices, the flavor will take on an air of mystery.

This recipe is minimally sweet, so if you prefer a sweeter dessert, you can increase the sugar to 2 cups or use sweetened applesauce.

1. Preheat oven to 350°. Butter a standard-sized tube pan.

2. In a large bowl, cream the butter and sugar. Add eggs, one at a time, beating well after each.

3. Stir in vanilla and orange rind. Set aside.

4. In a separate bowl, sift together all dry ingredients (including the optional spices or not). Stir in the ground walnuts.

5. In a third bowl, whisk together the applesauce and yogurt or sour cream until well blended.

6. Add the dry mixture and the applesauce mixture alternately to the butter mixture (dry-wet-dry-wet). Stir just enough to blend after each addition.

7. Turn the batter into the prepared tube pan. Bake 45 to 55 minutes at 350°. The cake is done when a sharp knife inserted into the center comes out clean.

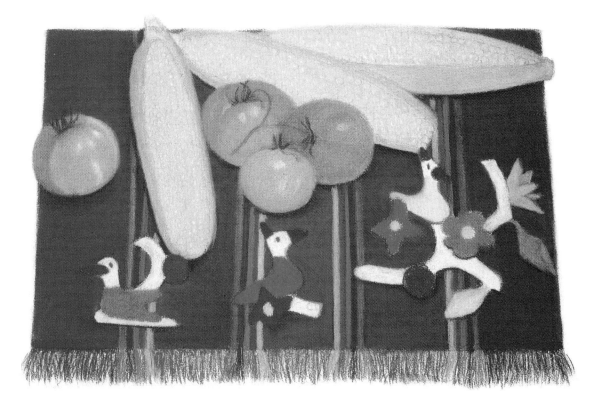

This is a perfect dinner for a warm evening when there are still a few hours of daylight left. Maybe you'll be eating it at a table by a window with a beautiful view. Or you can just imagine that you are.

To heat tortillas: Wrap lightly in foil and heat for about 10 to 15 minutes in the oven. You can put them in with the casserole when it is almost done. NOTE: The casserole and the dessert can be baked at the same time.

INDIAN SUMMER CASSEROLE
HOT BUTTERED FLOUR TORTILLAS
WATERCRESS SALAD
WITH CURRANTS AND WALNUTS
SUMMER FRUIT CRUMBLE

2 DAYS AHEAD: toast walnuts for salad

1 DAY AHEAD: for the casserole: do steps 2, 3, and 4, and make the custard (first half of step 5) / assemble fruit crumble; refrigerate unbaked / clean and dry salad greens

SAME DAY: assemble casserole; bake it along with the fruit crumble / heat tortillas / assemble salad while everything else is in the oven

INDIAN SUMMER CASSEROLE

PREPARATION TIME: 40 MINUTES, PLUS ANOTHER 30 TO 35 TO BAKE.

YIELD: ABOUT 4 SERVINGS. EASILY DOUBLED.

2 cups corn (fresh or frozen)

3 large bell peppers (combined red, yellow, and green, if possible), chopped

2 medium-sized green tomatoes, diced

2 to 3 large cloves garlic, minced

1 cup chopped scallions (whites and greens)

1 tablespoon olive oil

1 teaspoon salt

1 to 2 teaspoons ground cumin, to taste

$^1/_2$ to 1 teaspoon dried oregano, to taste

several leaves fresh basil, minced (or 2 teaspoons dried basil)

$^1/_4$ cup minced fresh parsley

lots of freshly ground black pepper

cayenne, to taste

$^1/_2$ cup chopped olives (black and/or green)

1 small Anaheim or poblano chile, minced, or 1 4-ounce can diced green chiles

$^1/_2$ cup (packed) grated mild white cheese

4 eggs (okay to delete up to 2 yolks)

$^1/_2$ cup yogurt or buttermilk

paprika for the top

Highly seasoned vegetables are combined with olives, chiles, and cheese, and baked in custard.

This recipe is named in honor of that time of year when corn, peppers, and fresh basil are peaking, and late crops of tomatoes are barely ripe. If you can't get green tomatoes, use the firmest and least ripe red ones available.

Steps 2, 3, and 4 of this recipe can be done several days in advance. Cover the pan tightly and refrigerate until an hour or two before finishing and baking.

1. Preheat oven to 375°. Butter or grease the equivalent of a 6 x 9-inch baking pan.

2. In a large skillet, sauté the corn, peppers, tomatoes, garlic, and scallions in olive oil with salt, cumin, and oregano. Sauté quickly over medium-high heat, stirring. After about 8 minutes, remove from heat.

3. Stir in basil, parsley, black pepper, cayenne, olives, and chiles. Stir in the cheese until it melts.

4. Spread the mixture into the prepared pan.

5. Beat the eggs together with the yogurt or buttermilk. Gently pour the custard over the top. Dust modestly with paprika.

6. Bake uncovered 30 to 35 minutes.

WATERCRESS SALAD WITH CURRANTS AND WALNUTS

PREPARATION TIME: LESS THAN 15 MINUTES.

YIELD: 3 TO 4 SERVINGS.

1 medium-sized head butter (Boston) lettuce, or a similar soft lettuce

1 small bunch fresh watercress

1 to 2 perfect scallions

a handful of currants

2 handfuls of lightly toasted walnuts (use a toaster oven or a cast-iron skillet on the stove top)

2 to 3 tablespoons walnut oil

1 scant tablespoon balsamic vinegar

a small amount of salt

a generous amount of freshly ground pepper

This is a subtle and elegant salad, lightly dressed, and with small touches of scallions, walnuts and currants. Balsamic vinegar is the first choice to use here, but champagne vinegar or any fruity variety will be just as effective. Red wine vinegar will also work.

If you clean and dry the greens ahead of time, the salad will take just minutes to prepare. Store the cleaned greens in a bunting of paper towels, sealed in a plastic bag in the refrigerator.

1. Clean the greens and dry them thoroughly. (For best results use several vigorous whirls in a salad spinner, followed by some firm patting with paper towels.) Put them in a salad bowl.

2. Finely mince the scallions. Add them to the greens along with the currants and walnuts.

3. Drizzle in the oil; toss well, then sprinkle in the vinegar and some salt and pepper. Toss again and serve immediately.

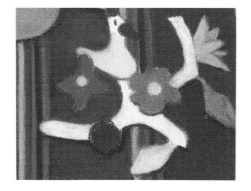

SUMMER FRUIT CRUMBLE

PREPARATION TIME: 20 TO
   30 MINUTES TO PREPARE
   (LESS IF USING FROZEN, PRE-
   SLICED, AND PITTED FRUIT),
   AND ANOTHER 30 TO BAKE.

YIELD: 6 SERVINGS.

*3 to 4 cups sliced fresh
   peaches, apricots, or plums
   (or a combination)*

*2 to 3 cups whole dark cher-
   ries, pitted*

*I cup plus I tablespoon
   unbleached white flour*

2 tablespoons granulated sugar

3 tablespoons brown sugar

¹/₄ teaspoon salt

4 tablespoons melted butter

Here is the dessert to make when the summer fruit season is at its peak. The recipe is very flexible, and almost any combination of soft, ripe fruit will work.

Summer Fruit Crumble can also be made entirely with frozen fruit. If you are blessed with an abundance of fresh fruit, you can freeze the oversupply and make the dessert months past harvest time. To freeze, peel and slice ripe peaches, apricots, and/or plums. Pit the cherries. Spread them out on a tray and place in the freezer for about 20 to 30 minutes. Then wrap them in plastic bags, seal, and return to the freezer, where they can be stored for several months. It's a welcome treat to have a dessert made from peaches, cherries, plums, or apricots in November or February.

NOTE: Thoroughly defrost and drain frozen fruit before using this recipe.

1. Preheat oven to 375°.

2. Combine the fruit in a bowl. Toss with 1 tablespoon flour and granulated sugar. Transfer to a medium-sized baking pan (8 or 9 inches square, or a similar size).

3. Combine brown sugar, 1 cup flour, salt, and melted butter. Distribute this mixture over the panful of fruit, and pat it into place.

4. Bake for 30 minutes, or until the top is lightly browned and the fruit bubbly. Let cool at least 10 to 15 minutes, then serve hot, warm, or at room temperature.

At first glance it might seem like a lot of work to have homemade biscuits and cookies at the same meal, especially with two fairly complex dishes on the same menu. But if you follow the suggestions for advance preparations, you'll find them both highly accessible. Most doughs are quite resilient, and can withstand refrigeration and even freezing without showing a single symptom.

CRISPY BAKED EGGPLANT WITH BLUE CHEESE SAUCE
BAKING POWDER BISCUITS
ROMAINE SALAD WITH BROCCOLI AND APPLES
MRS. BUERSCHAPER'S MOLASSES CRINKLES

3 DAYS AHEAD: make biscuit dough and freeze (detailed instructions in recipe) / make salad dressing

2 DAYS AHEAD: clean and cut broccoli for salad / clean and dry salad greens / make cookie dough and refrigerate

1 DAY AHEAD: bake cookies / steam broccoli / prepare eggplant (steps 2, 3, and 4) / get sauce ingredients ready (chop onions, mince garlic, slice mushrooms, squeeze lemon juice)

SAME DAY: bake eggplant / slice biscuits (while eggplant bakes) / assemble and cook sauce (while eggplant bakes) / bake biscuits / cut apples / assemble salad (while biscuits bake)

CRISPY BAKED EGGPLANT WITH BLUE CHEESE SAUCE

PREPARATION TIME: ABOUT
1 HOUR.

YIELD: 4 TO 5 SERVINGS.

On the following page you'll find a method for making delicious crispy eggplant without frying. The eggplant is coated with herbed wheat germ or bread crumbs and then *baked* until crisp. The sauce is full of mushrooms and yogurt, spiked with blue cheese, and well seasoned with onions, garlic, lemon, and dill. If you prepare the sauce while the eggplant bakes, they will both be ready at approximately the same time.

It's possible to make this recipe in advance and then reheat it (eggplant in the oven, sauce in a microwave or very gently on the stove top), but it tastes best when freshly made.

There are several things you can do in advance to streamline last-minute preparations. Prepare the eggplant—just short of baking it—up to 24 hours in advance. Store the coated slices on a plate or tray, tightly covered, in the refrigerator. Get all the sauce ingredients ready, i.e., chop onions, mince garlic, slice mushrooms, squeeze lemon juice, etc. Doing these things ahead will make it much easier and more enjoyable to accomplish the final preparations, especially if you are making this at the end of a busy workday.

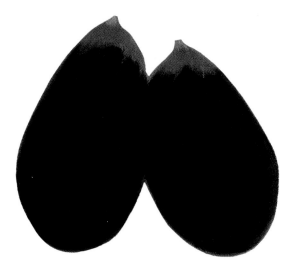

CRISPY BAKED EGGPLANT

oil for the baking tray

1 large eggplant (about
   1 1/2 pounds)

1/2 cup milk (lowfat okay)

1 cup wheat germ or fine
   bread crumbs

1 teaspoon each dried basil
   and dried dill

1/4 teaspoon dried thyme

Blue Cheese Sauce
   (recipe follows)

paprika

minced fresh parsley

1. Preheat the oven to 375°. Lightly oil a baking tray.

2. Slice the eggplant very thin (no more than 1/4 inch). Salt the slices lightly and let them stand about 10 minutes. Then pat dry with paper towels.

3. Place the milk in one bowl; combine the wheat germ and herbs in another.

4. Dip the eggplant slices in the milk, dredge in wheat germ, and arrange on the oiled tray.

5. Bake for 20 to 30 minutes, until the eggplant is crisp on the outside and tender on the inside (test with a fork). Meanwhile, make the sauce.

6. To serve, place several slices of eggplant on each plate and spoon lots of sauce on top. Sprinkle with paprika and minced parsley.

BLUE CHEESE SAUCE

1 1/2 cups minced onion

2 medium-sized cloves garlic,
   minced

2 to 3 tablespoons butter
   or oil

1/2 teaspoon salt

about 3/4 pound sliced
   mushrooms

1 to 2 tablespoons fresh lemon
   juice

1 tablespoon unbleached
   white flour

1 1/2 cups yogurt

3/4 cup crumbled blue cheese

lots of black pepper

2 tablespoons minced fresh dill

1. In a large heavy skillet, cook the onions and garlic in butter or oil with salt until the onions are limp (5 to 8 minutes).

2. Add the mushrooms, lemon juice, and flour (sprinkled rather than dumped in). Cook, stirring, over medium heat another 5 to 8 minutes.

3. Add remaining ingredients, lower heat, and stir. Cover and simmer 10 more minutes, stirring occasionally.

BAKING POWDER BISCUITS

PREPARATION TIME: 20 MINUTES TO PREPARE, 10 TO 15 MIN-UTES TO BAKE.

YIELD: 1 TO 1½ DOZEN, DEPEND-ING ON THE THICKNESS.

3 cups unbleached white flour

a scant ½ teaspoon salt

1 tablespoon baking powder

6 tablespoons cold butter

¾ cup buttermilk, yogurt, or sour milk (¾ cup milk with 1½ teaspoons vinegar added)

Here is a recipe for flaky, buttery biscuits that can be made in minutes in a food processor. The dough can be assembled a day or two ahead of baking time and stored in waxed paper or in a sealed plastic bag in the refrigerator.

The unbaked dough can also be formed in a log shape with a 2- to 2½-inch diameter, wrapped tightly in foil, and frozen. Then you can wake up some morning and have practically instant biscuits. Preheat the oven, let the dough sit at room temperature for 5 to 10 minutes, then slice it at ½-inch (or ¾-inch) intervals. Place the biscuits on a lightly greased baking sheet and bake (see step 5).

1. Preheat oven to 450°. Lightly grease a baking sheet.

2. Place the dry ingredients in a bowl or a food processor fitted with the steel blade. Cut in the butter—either in thin slices or small pieces. Process (or, if using a bowl, cut with a pastry cutter or with two forks) until the butter pieces are uniformly integrated and the mixture has the texture of coarse meal.

3. Add the buttermilk, yogurt, or sour milk, and process or mix for a few more seconds, or until the dough holds together.

4. Turn out and knead briefly. Roll out to ¼-inch thickness for smaller biscuits or to ½- or ¾-inch thickness for heftier ones. Cut with a glass that has a 2- to 2½-inch rim (or you can use a round cookie cutter). Arrange fairly close together on the lightly greased baking sheet.

5. Bake in the middle of a 450° oven for 10 to 12 minutes (thinner ones) or for 12 to 15 minutes (thicker ones).

ROMAINE SALAD WITH BROCCOLI AND APPLES

PREPARATION TIME: 30 MINUTES.

YIELD: 4 TO 6, DEPENDING ON WHAT ELSE IS SERVED.

3 to 4 cups medium-small broccoli spears

1 medium-sized head very fresh, crisp, and beautiful romaine lettuce

1 medium-sized or 2 small tart green apples (for contrast, you can substitute all or part with firm Red Delicious apples)

VINAIGRETTE DRESSING

1/2 cup plus 2 tablespoons combined olive oil and canola or vegetable oil (half and half or maybe a little more than half olive)

2 tablespoons wine vinegar

3 tablespoons fresh lemon juice

a scant 1/2 teaspoon salt

1 tablespoon maple syrup or honey

1 teaspoon Dijon mustard

dried thyme and basil, and black pepper, to taste

This is a simple green salad with lots of refreshing crunch: crisp leaves of romaine, deep green broccoli spears cooked al dente, and fresh slices of tart apple.

The broccoli can be steamed and chilled a day ahead. Make sure it is drained thoroughly and stored in an airtight container in the refrigerator. The vinaigrette dressing can be made as much as a week or more in advance. It keeps practically indefinitely. Slice and add the apple at the very last minute.

1. Steam the broccoli until just tender and bright green. Refresh under cold running water and set aside to drain thoroughly.

2. Clean and thoroughly dry the lettuce. (After spinning it several times, finish off the drying by patting it with clean paper towels.) Wrap in more paper towels, and store in a plastic bag in the refrigerator until just before assembling the salad.

3. Whisk together all the vinaigrette ingredients.

4. Combine lettuce and broccoli in a large bowl. Slice the apples thinly and gently toss everything together with just enough vinaigrette to coat everything lightly. If you have some dressing left over, it keeps indefinitely and lends itself beautifully to any tossed green salad.

MRS. BUERSCHAPER'S MOLASSES CRINKLES

PREPARATION TIME: 25 MINUTES
TO PREPARE, 12 TO 15
TO BAKE.

YIELD: 2¹/₂ TO 3 DOZEN
COOKIES.

¹/₂ cup butter

¹/₄ cup blackstrap molasses

1 cup sugar

1 egg

¹/₄ teaspoon salt

2 teaspoons baking soda

1 teaspoon cinnamon

1 teaspoon allspice

1 teaspoon ground ginger

2 cups unbleached white flour

1 to 2 tablespoons additional
sugar

When I was a child, my next door neighbor, Mrs. Buerschaper, used to make these cookies on special occasions. The neighborhood children would sniff them out from blocks away, and come to hover fetchingly on the doorstep, waiting to be offered some. When Mrs. B. finally gave the recipe to our mother, my brothers and I knew we had it made! I think these cookies were my earliest experience of loving a dessert that had no chocolate in it. That felt very sophisticated.

1. Preheat oven to 350°. Lightly grease a cookie sheet.

2. Melt the butter over low heat. Transfer to a medium-sized mixing bowl.

3. Beat in molasses and 1 cup sugar. Beat the egg by itself in a small bowl first, then beat this into the molasses mixture.

4. Sift together the dry ingredients (except the additional sugar). Then add them to the wet mixture, stirring until well combined.

5. Use your hands (flour them, if necessary) to form 1¹/₂-inch balls of dough. Place the additional 1 to 2 tablespoons sugar on a small plate, and roll each ball in the sugar before arranging on the cookie sheet. (This coating provides the crinkle factor.)

6. Bake for 12 to 15 minutes, until firm to the touch. Cool on a rack.

Make this dinner for a special occasion when you have a long evening and can eat slowly, taking a breather between courses. You won't feel too full of food this way, just full of contentment.

RACHELI'S DELUXE CHALLAH

EGG, GREEN ONION, PARSLEY, AND WATERCRESS APPETIZER WITH RAW VEGETABLES

CREAM OF MUSHROOM SOUP

SWEET AND TART CABBAGE WITH COTTAGE CHEESE-DILL DUMPLINGS

CREAM CHEESE-WALNUT COOKIES

3 DAYS AHEAD: make dumpling batter / make and freeze cookie dough

2 DAYS AHEAD: boil eggs for appetizer / make challah (refrigerate the unbaked loaves) / cut vegetables for the cabbage and the soup

1 DAY AHEAD: poach dumplings / assemble and cook the cabbage / assemble soup through step 4 / assemble the appetizer

SAME DAY: bake challah / bake cookies / finish and heat soup / reheat cabbage / sauté dumplings

RACHELI'S DELUXE CHALLAH

PREPARATION TIME: 4½ TO 5½ HOURS, MOST OF WHICH IS EITHER RISING OR BAKING TIME.

YIELD: 2 SUBSTANTIAL LOAVES.

2½ cups lukewarm water

1 package active dry yeast

½ cup sugar or honey

3 eggs

1 tablespoon salt

¼ cup vegetable oil (plus a little extra to oil the bowl, dough, and baking sheet)

1 cup (packed) raisins (optional)

8 to 9 cups unbleached white flour

poppy and/or sesame seeds, to sprinkle on top

Here is yet another recipe for challah (braided egg bread). I thought there was nothing new under the sun in the challah department, having tasted thousands of them in my lifetime. But then my friend Racheli brought this one over for dinner one Friday night, and I knew that the case on challah had not yet been closed. This one is the best I've had yet!

The loaves can be put together several days in advance of baking. Store them airtight in the refrigerator (details in step 7).

NOTE: You can make one huge loaf instead of two normal-sized ones. Divide the dough into two unequal parts, and make both a large, fat braid and a smaller, skinnier one. Place the smaller one on top, and pinch them together. Baking time might be up to 10 minutes longer.

1. Place the water in a very large bowl. (Make sure the water is no warmer than wrist temperature!) Sprinkle in the yeast, and let stand 5 minutes until foamy.

2. Add the sugar or honey, 2 of the eggs, salt, oil, and optional raisins, and beat with a wire whisk for several minutes.

3. Begin adding the flour 1 cup at a time, stirring with a wooden spoon after each addition. When you reach about the seventh cup of flour, start slowing the additions, adding ¼ cup at a time, mixing and kneading in the flour with your hand. Stop adding flour when the dough is quite firm and no longer feels sticky.

4. Turn the dough out onto a floured surface, and knead vigorously—as though you mean it—for 5 to 10 minutes, or until you've had enough. (The more kneading the better, but on the other hand, bread dough is very adaptable and will accommodate you.)

5. Oil the bowl and the top surface of the dough, and place the dough in the bowl. Cover with a clean tea towel, and place in a draft-free place to rise until double in bulk (1½ to 2 hours).

6. Punch down the dough, return to the floured surface, and divide in half. Knead each half for at least 5 minutes, then divide each into thirds. Roll each third into a long rope about 1½ inches in diameter, and form 2 braided loaves (3 strands per braid).

7. Oil a baking sheet, and place the braids on the sheet at least 4 inches apart. Cover with the towel, return to the draft-free spot, and let rise again, this time for only about 45 minutes. (Alternatively, you can let the braids rise in the refrigerator for up to three days before baking. Be sure they are sealed airtight in a large, loose-fitting plastic bag. You can then put them directly from the refrigerator into a preheated oven.)

8. Preheat oven to 350°. Beat the remaining egg, and brush it onto the risen loaves. Sprinkle generously with poppy and/or sesame seeds. Bake for 35 to 45 minutes, or until the breads give off a hollow sound when thumped resolutely on the bottom. Remove from the sheet immediately, and cool on a rack.

EGG, GREEN ONION, PARSLEY, AND WATERCRESS APPETIZER

PREPARATION TIME: AFTER THE EGGS ARE COOKED, 15 MINUTES WITH FOOD PROCESSOR, 30 MINUTES BY HAND.

YIELD: 2 CUPS.

1/2 cup (packed) chopped fresh parsley

1 small bunch fresh watercress

6 hard-boiled eggs (okay to delete some or all yolks)

4 medium-sized scallions, minced (whites and greens)

1/4 teaspoon salt

1 to 2 teaspoons prepared white horseradish, to taste

1 to 2 tablespoons sour cream (lowfat okay)

black pepper

One of my mother's standard Friday night appetizers was something we called simply "Chopped Egg and Onion." It was served on lettuce on small individual plates, eaten with a fork, and washed down with chicken soup and challah. This recipe is my own expanded version of that theme. Spread it on crackers or bread, or use it as a dip for raw vegetables. This can be made with a food processor or by hand, allowing one the choice of dwelling either in the present or in the past.

NOTE: This is especially lovely if served on a bed of fresh spinach and garnished with oil-cured or Greek olives.

FOOD PROCESSOR METHOD:

1. Mince the parsley and watercress separately using the steel blade with the motor running steadily until fine and feathery. Transfer to a medium-sized bowl.

2. Process the eggs and scallions separately using the steel blade attachment, pulsing on and off until the eggs and onions are each finely grated. Add them to the bowl.

3. Add salt, horseradish, sour cream, and pepper, and gently fold everything together with a rubber spatula. Mold into a mound in an attractive serving dish, cover tightly with plastic wrap, and chill at least several hours before serving.

OLD-FASHIONED METHOD:

1. Grate the eggs.

2. Mince the parsley, watercress and scallions as finely as possible.

3. Proceed as described above (step 3).

CREAM OF MUSHROOM SOUP

PREPARATION TIME: 45 MINUTES.

YIELD: 4 SERVINGS (EASILY
   DOUBLED).

1 1/2 pounds mushrooms

2 tablespoons butter or canola
   or vegetable oil

1 bay leaf

1 1/4 teaspoons salt (or more or
   less, to taste)

2 small cloves garlic, minced

1/4 cup dry vermouth or sherry

freshly ground black pepper
   and white pepper, to taste

1 cup water

1 teaspoon soy sauce

1 cup milk (lowfat or soy
   okay), room temperature

1 scallion

1/2 cup half-and-half or evaporated skim milk, room temperature (optional)

Cream of mushroom soup is usually assumed to be ultrarich, so many people watching their fat intake consider it off-limits. Yet you can get a delicious result from this recipe without including *any* butterfat! Oil can be used in place of butter, the milk can be lowfat or soy, and the optional half-and-half can be substituted with evaporated skim milk. You'll be amazed by how good this is!

1. Pick out the 5 or 6 nicest mushrooms and put aside. Coarsely chop the rest.

2. In a heavy saucepan, melt 1 1/2 tablespoons of the butter or heat the oil. Add the chopped mushrooms and stir. Add bay leaf, salt, garlic, and vermouth or sherry. Cover and cook over low heat for about 10 minutes.

3. Add black and white pepper, water, and soy sauce. Cover and simmer 10 to 15 minutes. Let cool to room temperature. Remove the bay leaf.

4. Purée in blender or food processor until smooth. Return to the saucepan. Add milk.

5. Thinly slice the reserved mushrooms and the white of the scallion. (Reserve the scallion greens.) Sauté these in the remaining 1/2 tablespoon butter or oil over medium heat for about 5 minutes, then add to the soup.

6. Heat gently just before serving. Don't cook it or let it boil. Add the half-and-half or evaporated milk, if desired, at the very end.

7. Serve topped with thin slices of scallion greens.

SWEET AND TART CABBAGE WITH COTTAGE CHEESE-DILL DUMPLINGS

PREPARATION TIME: ABOUT
1 HOUR (A LITTLE LONGER IF
YOU SAUTÉ THE DUMPLINGS).

YIELD: 6 MAIN-DISH SERVINGS.

Sweet and sour cabbage is a classic East European dish, often served alongside a hunk of pot roast. This tart version features oranges in addition to the standard apples, and cumin seed in place of the more traditional (but more bitter) caraway. When topped with a batch of light, golden Cottage Cheese-Dill Dumplings, this dish becomes a full-blown main course, making it highly unlikely that anyone will miss the pot roast.

The dumplings can be made and poached a day or two in advance, wrapped tightly, and stored in the refrigerator. The final sautéing of the dumplings can be done while the cabbage cooks. The cabbage can also be made in advance. It reheats very well on top of the stove.

COTTAGE CHEESE-DILL DUMPLINGS

2 eggs

½ cup cottage cheese

1 cup unbleached white flour

1 teaspoon salt (seems like a lot, but some of it will dissipate in the poaching water)

2 tablespoons fresh dill, finely minced (or 2 teaspoons dried dill—as new a jar as possible)

4 tablespoons butter

1. Beat together the eggs and cottage cheese in a medium-sized bowl.

2. Stir in the remaining ingredients (except butter) and mix well. NOTE: The dough may be stored at this point for up to 24 hours before poaching. Cover tightly and refrigerate.

3. Boil a large kettleful of water (about 3 quarts). Add rounded tablespoonfuls of dumpling dough, being careful not to crowd them. (As you will see, they expand a LOT.) Poach the dumplings for 15 minutes in gently simmering water, then remove them with a slotted spoon to a large plate or a medium-sized tray or shallow pan. (You might have to cook the dumplings in several batches if the kettle gets too crowded.) Put the poached dumplings aside, and prepare steps 1 and 2 of the Sweet and Tart Cabbage.

4. About 20 to 30 minutes before serving, melt 4 tablespoons butter in a large heavy skillet. Add the dumplings and sauté over medium heat until golden. (Depending on just how golden you like them, this will take anywhere from 10 to 20 minutes.) Serve hot on Sweet and Tart Cabbage.

NOTE 1: If your skillet can't accommodate all the dumplings at once, you can sauté them in two batches, keeping the earlier ones warm in a covered dish in a 200° oven. Use 2 tablespoons butter for sautéing each batch.

NOTE 2: For daintier-sized dumplings (and twice as many), slice them in half before sautéing.

SWEET AND TART CABBAGE

1 to 2 tablespoons butter or oil

4 medium-sized onions, thinly sliced or chopped

8 to 10 cups shredded cabbage (mixed red and green—about 1 small head each)

1 1/2 teaspoons salt

1 teaspoon whole cumin seeds (lightly toasted, if desired)

4 medium-sized tart green apples, sliced (peeling is optional)

4 navel oranges, peeled and sectioned

1/2 cup granulated sugar, brown sugar (packed), or honey

a generous amount black pepper

up to 3 tablespoons cider vinegar (optional)

1. Melt the butter or heat the oil in a large deep skillet or Dutch oven. Add the onions and cook for about 5 minutes over medium heat, stirring frequently until onions are softened.

2. Add cabbage and salt, and continue to cook in the same fashion for another 8 to 10 minutes or until the cabbage is well on its way to becoming tender. NOTE: Depending on the size of the skillet, you may have to add the cabbage several cups at a time, waiting each time for the previous batch to cook down enough to make room.

3. Add remaining ingredients. Stir well, cover, and continue to cook over medium-low heat with occasional stirring, until everything is very well mingled. This will take about 20 to 30 minutes, during which time you can sauté the dumplings.

4. Transfer to a large, shallow serving bowl or platter, top with sautéed Cottage Cheese-Dill Dumplings, and serve hot.

CREAM CHEESE-WALNUT COOKIES

PREPARATION TIME: 15 MINUTES TO PREPARE, FOLLOWED BY AT LEAST 30 TO 40 MINUTES TO CHILL AND 8 TO 10 MINUTES TO BAKE.

YIELD: ABOUT 4 DOZEN.

½ cup butter

½ cup (packed) brown sugar

½ cup (half an 8-ounce package) softened cream cheese

1 egg

1 teaspoon vanilla extract

1½ cups unbleached white flour

¼ teaspoon salt

½ teaspoon baking soda

1 cup ground walnuts (ground to a coarse meal in a food processor or blender, using quick spurts)

½ teaspoon cinnamon

These thin, crisp, not-too-sweet rounds are hard to stop eating. The dough can be frozen indefinitely, and you needn't defrost it before slicing and baking. In fact, it's easier to cut the cookies into elegantly slender wafers when the dough is frozen.

1. Cream together butter, sugar, and cream cheese at high speed with an electric mixer. When the mixture is light and fluffy, add the egg and beat for a few more minutes.

2. Stir in the remaining ingredients and mix well.

3. Cut a piece of aluminum foil approximately 10 x 13 inches. Place the dough in a strip down the center of the foil, and mold it with your hands (flouring them if necessary) to form a log approximately 12 inches long and 2 inches in diameter. Roll up the dough with the foil, wrapping tightly as you roll. Refrigerate for several hours, or, if you are in more of a hurry, put it in the freezer, where it will chill adequately in about 30 to 40 minutes.

4. Preheat the oven to 400°. Slice the cold dough at ⅛-inch intervals (or as close to that as possible), and place the cookies fairly close together on an ungreased cookie sheet. Bake for 12 to 15 minutes, and remove immediately to a cooling rack for ultimate crispness.

Plan to serve this hearty meal at the end of a day filled with vigorous activity or when the weather outside is blustery and cold. It is a filling, warming dinner that can satisfy even the most cavernous appetites.

MARINATED MINIATURE ARTICHOKES
GREEK STUFFED EGGPLANT
WITH BÉCHAMEL SAUCE
CRUSTY SESAME RING
GREEK RICE PUDDING WITH LEMON

3 DAYS AHEAD: make the artichokes

2 DAYS AHEAD: make the bread; refrigerate the unbaked loaves / chop onions and mince garlic for the stuffing

1 DAY AHEAD: make stuffing and fill eggplants / make rice pudding (or make it the same day, whichever fits your schedule)

SAME DAY: bake the bread and eggplant at the same time / make Béchamel Sauce while they bake

MARINATED MINIATURE ARTICHOKES

PREPARATION TIME: ABOUT
15 MINUTES TO PREPARE,
45 MINUTES TO COOK, AND
AT LEAST 1 HOUR TO COOL.

YIELD: ENOUGH FOR 6 APPETIZER
OR SALAD PORTIONS.

1½ pounds small artichokes
(2-inch diameter or less)

3 cups water

juice from 1 medium-sized
lemon

⅓ cup wine vinegar

⅓ cup olive oil

1½ teaspoons salt

1 tablespoon whole pepper-
corns

4 medium-sized cloves garlic,
peeled and halved

One of the nice things about small artichokes is that with just a touch of trimming, the entire globe is edible. The choke has not had a chance to develop yet, so there is mostly just tender heart.

This recipe is very easy to make and keeps extremely well (for weeks!).

1. To trim the artichokes, cut off the tips and the ends of the stems. Use a scissors or paring knife to shave off any extraneous outer leaves (ones that look like they would rather not be there anyway). You may either leave the artichokes whole, or halve or quarter them, depending on their size and your preference.

2. Place the artichokes in a saucepan with all other ingredients. Bring to a boil, and lower heat to medium. Continue to boil gently another 40 minutes, or until liquid reduces to approximately 1 cup. (This does not have to be exact!)

3. Remove from heat and cool to room temperature. You can eat them at this point or refrigerate them (include all the liquid) in a tightly covered container. If stored this way, they should keep at least two weeks. (On the other hand, they might not last that long, simply because they make such good snack food.)

GREEK STUFFED EGGPLANT WITH BÉCHAMEL SAUCE

Eggplants are stuffed with themselves, plus lots of onion and garlic, tomatoes, herbs, sesame, pine nuts, feta, and lemon. The flavor is savory and tart; the texture is varied, with soft, crunchy, and juicy components. Béchamel Sauce, smooth and comforting, balances and completes this dish. (Note that the sauce can be made with lowfat milk. It will still taste rich enough!)

The stuffing can be prepared and the eggplants filled a day ahead. The sauce takes only 20 minutes to prepare, and can be made while the eggplant is baking.

PREPARATION TIME: 1½ HOURS.

YIELD: 4 TO 6 MAIN-DISH SIZED
SERVINGS.

2 large or 3 medium-size
   eggplants

3 tablespoons olive oil

5 cups minced onion

5 cloves garlic, minced

2 teaspoons salt

4 cups chopped fresh tomatoes

2 teaspoons dried basil

freshly ground black pepper,
   to taste

3 cups good bread crumbs
   (from good bread)

½ cup ground sesame seeds
   (use a blender; grind in
   quick spurts until the seeds
   are flourlike)

1 cup toasted pine nuts

1 cup crumbled feta cheese

2 tablespoons fresh lemon
   juice

Béchamel Sauce

cinnamon

nutmeg

paprika

a small amount of fresh
   parsley, well minced

GREEK STUFFED EGGPLANT

1. Preheat oven to 375°.

2. Cut the eggplants in half lengthwise. Using a plain teaspoon, scoop out the innards, leaving a shell approximately ¼ inch thick. Set the shells aside; finely chop the innards.

3. Heat the olive oil in a deep skillet. Sauté the onions and garlic with the salt. Cook over medium heat, stirring intermittently. When the onions are very soft and translucent (10 to 15 minutes), add the chopped eggplant. Cover and let cook another 8 to 10 minutes.

4. Add tomatoes, basil, and pepper. Cover and cook another 10 to 15 minutes over medium heat.

5. In a large bowl, combine bread crumbs, ground sesame seeds, pine nuts, and crumbled feta. Stir this mixture, along with the lemon juice, into the cooked vegetables. Mix well.

6. Stuff the eggplant shells. Arrange them in a shallow baking pan, and cover with foil. Bake for 30 minutes. Prepare the sauce during the baking.

5. Ladle some Béchamel Sauce over each individual portion. Garnish with a dash each of cinnamon, nutmeg, and paprika, and a sprinkling of minced parsley.

3 tablespoons butter

3 tablespoons unbleached
   white flour

2½ cups hot milk (lowfat or
   soy okay)

a dash each of salt and white
   pepper

BÉCHAMEL SAUCE

1. In a medium-sized saucepan, melt butter over low heat.

2. Whisk in the flour. Cook over low heat, whisking steadily for several minutes.

3. Drizzle in the hot milk. Keep whisking and slowly cooking until thick and smooth (5 to 8 minutes).

4. Add salt and white pepper.

CRUSTY SESAME RING

PREPARATION TIME: ABOUT 2½ HOURS, START TO FINISH (MUCH OF WHICH IS RISING OR BAKING TIME).

YIELD: 2 MEDIUM-SIZED RINGS.

1⅓ cups lukewarm water

1 package active dry yeast

1 tablespoon sugar or honey

1 teaspoon salt

4½ to 5 cups unbleached white flour

oil for the bowl and the dough

water

½ cup sesame seeds, plus extra for the baking sheet

This is a simple, crusty, sesame-coated bread with very little sugar and no oil in the dough. It's perfect served within one hour of baking, and very good thereafter. Leftovers are excellent for sandwiches, toast, or snacks. When it is three or four days old (if it ever lasts that long), try slicing it thin, brushing each side with olive oil, and toasting it until crisp on both sides, either in the oven or on the stove top in a heavy skillet. Cut each piece in half, and serve as croutons in a green leaf salad.

1. Place the lukewarm water in a large bowl. Sprinkle in the yeast, and let it sit for 5 minutes until it gets foamy. Stir in sugar and salt.

2. Beat in the flour, 1 cup at a time. (Begin with a wire whisk, then switch to a wooden spoon as it thickens.) When you get to about 4 cups of flour, slow down, and begin adding only ¼ cup flour at a time. At this point, switch to mixing with one hand, while adding flour with the other. Knead the dough for a minute or two after each addition. You've added enough flour when the dough becomes firm and ceases feeling sticky.

3. Turn the dough out onto a floured surface, and knead for about 5 minutes. If the dough suddenly becomes a little sticky again, just knead in a small amount of flour.

4. Clean or wipe out the mixing bowl, and oil it lightly. Add the kneaded dough, and lightly oil its top surface. Cover with a clean tea towel, and set in a warm (or at least draft-free) place to rise for 1 hour or until doubled in bulk, whichever comes first.

5. Punch down the risen dough and return it to the floured surface. Knead for another 5 to 8 minutes. Divide the dough in half. Roll each half into a snake about 16 inches long and 1½ inches in diameter. Brush each snake lightly with water, then sprinkle liberally with sesame seeds. Roll each snake around on the work surface to distribute the seeds all over and help them adhere to the dough. Form each snake into a ring, and pinch the ends together (they will look like large, slim bagels).

6. Sprinkle a large baking tray with more sesame seeds, and place the rings on top, several inches apart. Cover with the tea towel again, and return to the rising place. Let rise again for about 45 to 50 minutes. (You can also let the dough rise in the refrigerator. Wrap the baking tray loosely in a large plastic bag and seal it with a bag tie. It can stay in the refrigerator up to three days before baking. The tray can go directly from the refrigerator into a preheated oven.)

7. Place a panful of water on the floor of the oven or on a lower rack. Preheat the oven to 375°. Spray the sesame rings liberally with water from a plant mister, then place them in the oven. Bake for 25 minutes, interrupting every 8 to 10 minutes to spray with more water. The loaves are done when they are golden brown and give off a hollow sound when thumped on the bottom. Remove from the tray, and cool on a rack.

8. Cool for at least 10 minutes before slicing.

GREEK RICE PUDDING WITH LEMON

PREPARATION TIME: 30 MINUTES.

YIELD: 3 TO 4 SERVINGS.

1²/3 cups water

1 cup uncooked white rice

1 tablespoon butter (optional)

¹/2 teaspoon salt

2 eggs, well beaten

¹/3 cup (packed) brown sugar

³/4 teaspoon freshly grated
    lemon rind

2 tablespoons fresh lemon
    juice

¹/4 teaspoon vanilla extract

cinnamon

This authentic Greek dessert is almost like a lemon custard with rice. You'll be impressed by its creaminess, especially considering that it has no milk in it.

1. Combine water, rice, optional butter, and salt in a small saucepan. Bring to a boil, lower the heat to a very quiet simmer, cover, and cook until the rice is tender. This will take approximately 20 minutes.

2. Remove the rice from the stove, and beat in the eggs. Continue to beat well for a minute or two.

3. Stir in sugar, lemon rind and juice, and vanilla. Transfer to a bowl.

4. Sprinkle the top generously with cinnamon, and cool to room temperature. Then cover tightly and refrigerate until cold. Serve cold or at room temperature.

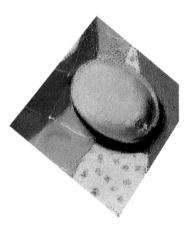

This is another menu that is always in season. The pilaf and the carrot salad seem like they were made to go together (actually they were created separately, but it was love at first sight). The dark green, freshly sautéed, lightly marinated Swiss chard is a perfect complement. Cheesecake Bars (which are lower in fat than one would think) add a nice balance to the meal.

TURKISH BULGUR PILAF
LEVANTINE CARROT SALAD
WARM MARINATED SWISS CHARD
CHEESECAKE BARS

3 DAYS AHEAD: soak white beans or chick-peas for salad

2 DAYS AHEAD: cook beans (chick-peas) / make Cheesecake Bars (also can be made 1 day ahead) / for pilaf: cut apricots; chop and toast walnuts; chop onions and celery / cut and steam carrots for salad

1 DAY AHEAD: sauté bulgur with onion, celery, etc. (steps 1 and 2); chop parsley for pilaf / marinate carrots and beans or chick-peas (when you make the marinade, mince enough garlic for the salad topping and the Swiss chard) / make salad topping / cut Swiss chard

SAME DAY: finish the bulgur / sauté and finish the Swiss chard

TURKISH BULGUR PILAF

PREPARATION TIME: 50 MINUTES.

YIELD: 4 TO 5 SERVINGS.

1 to 2 tablespoons olive oil

1 1/2 cups minced onion

2 medium stalks celery,
    minced

1 teaspoon salt

2 cups uncooked bulgur

2 1/2 cups boiling water

1/2 cup dried currants

1 cup sliced dried apricots

1 cup chopped, toasted
    walnuts (a toaster
    oven works best for this)

1/2 cup finely minced fresh
    parsley

3 Tablespoons minced
    fresh dill

lemon wedges for garnish

Bulgur's naturally nutty flavor is enhanced by being sautéed first with onion, celery, and dill in olive oil. The finished pilaf is adorned throughout with currants, slices of dried apricot, toasted walnuts, and flecks of parsley.

Step 1 can be done a few hours in advance. Also, the entire pilaf (except for the walnuts, parsley, and lemon garnish) can be made a day or two in advance. Reheat very gently, either in a microwave or in an oiled casserole, tightly covered, in a 300° oven for about 45 minutes.

1. Heat the oil in a large heavy saucepan. Add the onion, celery, and salt and sauté over medium heat until the vegetables are tender (8 to 10 minutes). Stir intermittently.

2. Add the bulgur. Continue to sauté, and stir fairly attentively over medium-low heat until the bulgur is lightly browned and everything is well coated and integrated (about 5 minutes).

3. Add water, currants, and apricots. Cover and remove from heat. Let stand for about 25 minutes, or until the bulgur is tender and the water is absorbed.

4. Mix in the walnuts, parsley, and dill just before serving. Garnish with generous, squeezable wedges of lemon.

LEVANTINE CARROT SALAD

PREPARATION TIME: THE SOAKED CHICK-PEAS OR BEANS TAKE ABOUT 1½ HOURS TO COOK. PREPARATION THEREAFTER IS ABOUT 35 MINUTES, FOLLOWED BY SEVERAL HOURS' CHILLING TIME.

YIELD: 4 TO 6 SERVINGS.

³/₄ cup dried chick-peas or white pea beans (optional)

1½ pounds carrots

¹/₃ cup olive oil

¹/₄ cup red wine vinegar

2 tablespoons fresh lemon juice

1 large clove garlic, minced

¹/₄ cup finely minced fresh parsley

3 to 4 slender scallions, minced

¹/₃ cup minced fresh dill (or 2 teaspoons dried)

1 teaspoon salt

freshly ground black pepper, to taste

¹/₂ teaspoon ground cumin

TOPPING:

¹/₂ cup sesame seeds

³/₄ cup yogurt

2 tablespoons minced fresh parsley

1 tablespoon honey

1 teaspoon fresh lemon juice

1 small clove garlic, minced (optional)

a dash or two of salt

up to ¹/₃ cup water (optional)

Strips of carrot are cooked until tender, then combined with chick-peas or white beans, marinated thoroughly, and finished off with a yogurt-sesame topping.

The beans, which are optional, need to be soaked and cooked before the salad is assembled. You can do this several days ahead. You can also make both the salad and the topping a day or two in advance. Refrigerate them in separate tightly covered containers. Put the topping on the salad just before serving.

1. OPTIONAL STEP: Soak the dried chick-peas or white pea beans in plenty of water for at least 4 hours, but preferably overnight. Cook in plenty of gently boiling water until tender (about 1½ hours). Drain well.

2. Peel or scrub the carrots, and cut them into thin, flat matchstick pieces about 1½ inches long and ¹/₄ inch wide. Steam until just tender (5 to 10 minutes), then refresh them under cold running water, and drain well.

3. Combine all ingredients in a large bowl. Mix well, cover tightly, and refrigerate for several hours. Meanwhile, prepare the following topping.

TOPPING:

1. Whirl the seeds in a blender at high speed for about 25 seconds until they are ground to a meal.

2. Combine all ingredients except water in a small bowl, mixing well.

3. Thin with water to desired consistency. (You can also leave it thick.) Chill until serving time.

4. Place a healthy dollop of topping on each serving.

WARM MARINATED SWISS CHARD

PREPARATION TIME: 20 MINUTES.

YIELD: 4 SIDE-DISH-SIZED
    SERVINGS.

Here is a quick and easy side dish that tastes good warm, at room temperature, or cold.

NOTE: Due to the bulkiness of the uncooked chard, you may have to cook this in two batches so the skillet or wok won't get overcrowded.

*1½ pounds fresh Swiss chard
    (ruby or green)*

1 tablespoon olive oil

*6 medium-sized cloves garlic,
    minced*

salt and pepper, to taste

*2 tablespoons vinegar (prefer-
    ably balsamic, but red wine
    vinegar is also fine)*

1. Cut the leaves off the chard and discard the stems. Coarsely chop the leaves.

2. Heat a wok or a large heavy skillet (cast iron is ideal). When it is hot, add the olive oil and the chard. Stir and cook for about 2 minutes over high heat.

3. Add the garlic, and stir-fry several minutes more until the chard is limp.

4. Sprinkle lightly with salt and pepper. Toss with vinegar, and serve.

CHEESECAKE BARS

PREPARATION TIME: 25 TO
30 MINUTES TO PREPARE, 30
TO 40 TO BAKE.

YIELD: 25 SQUARES.

½ cup (1 stick) butter

½ cup (packed) brown sugar

1½ cups unbleached white flour

1½ cups cottage cheese

½ cup softened cream cheese

2 eggs

1 teaspoon vanilla extract

½ teaspoon grated orange or lemon rind

1 tablespoon fresh lemon juice

strawberry slices (optional)

If you love cheesecake but feel guilty going after it in a big way, you can go after it in a small way instead. These bars hit that same indescribable spot (over which cheesecake lovers wax euphoric), yet they do it on a miniature scale. In addition, they accomplish that *je ne sais quoi* with mostly cottage cheese (regular *or* lowfat), and without compromise.

Cheesecake Bars keep beautifully up to a week in an airtight container in the refrigerator.

1. Preheat oven to 350°.

2. Melt the butter, and place it in a bowl with ¼ cup of the brown sugar and the flour. Mix with a spoon or with your hand until uniformly combined.

3. Press the mixture firmly into the bottom of an ungreased 8 x 8-inch square baking pan (or a pan of equivalent size). At this point, you have the option of prebaking the crust for about 10 to 12 minutes, if you like a crispier bottom layer. (You don't need to cool it before adding the filling.) Or you can leave it alone and just bake the whole thing at one time.

4. Purée the cottage cheese for several minutes in a blender or a food processor fitted with a steel blade. Add remaining ingredients (including remaining brown sugar) and process for a few minutes more.

5. Spread the cheese mixture over the partially baked or unbaked crust. Bake for 30 to 40 minutes or until the top feels firm to the touch.

6. Wait until it is cool before garnishing with strawberry slices and cutting into 2½-inch squares.

You can plan to serve this informal supper on a winter weekend when you'll have a lot of people around the house. The eggplant relish can be late afternoon snack food, and the hot spiced cider can be simmering and available all day long.

If you make this when there *aren't* a lot of people around, freeze the leftover chili for later use, and serve the leftover muffins throughout the week for breakfasts and lunches.

SOUTHWEST EGGPLANT RELISH WITH ROASTED PEPPERS AND GROUND PEPITAS

ASSORTED RAW VEGETABLES

LENTIL CHILI

CORN AND RED PEPPER MUFFINS

HOT SPICED APPLE AND BERRY CIDER

CHOCOLATE CHIP-PEANUT BUTTER COOKIES

2 DAYS AHEAD: bake eggplant; roast and peel peppers; peel tomatoes / prepare onions and garlic for chili; get other ingredients ready / make cookie batter

I DAY AHEAD: assemble eggplant relish / cut raw vegetables / combine dry ingredients for muffins; sauté peppers; prepare muffin cups / make chili (this can also be done the same day)

SAME DAY: bake cookies / assemble and heat cider / assemble and bake muffins / reheat chili

SOUTHWEST EGGPLANT RELISH WITH ROASTED PEPPERS AND GROUND PEPITAS

PREPARATION TIME: 40 TO 45 MINUTES (PLUS CHILLING TIME IF SERVING COLD).

YIELD: APPETIZER FOR 4 TO 5; LUNCH FOR 2.

a little oil for the baking tray

1 medium-sized eggplant

2 medium-sized Anaheim or poblano chiles, or bell peppers

2 medium-small ripe tomatoes

1 cup shelled pepitas (pumpkin seeds), lightly toasted

1 to 2 medium-sized cloves garlic, minced

2 tablespoons fresh lime juice

1/2 teaspoon salt

freshly ground black pepper

crushed red pepper

a few sprigs fresh cilantro for garnish (optional)

It seems there is no limit to the number of cold eggplant variations one can compose. This one celebrates the cooking of the Southwest United States, a cuisine in which pumpkin seeds achieve new status as pepitas and are deservedly considered a real food (not just something school children buy in a box at the candy store). Pepitas are available in bulk at most natural food stores.

If you are lucky enough to have access to fresh chiles, try Anaheim or poblano in this recipe. Anaheim chiles, also called "mild green chiles" (although sometimes they are slightly hot), are beautiful long, slim, light-green peppers that are often available in supermarkets with large, thorough produce departments. Poblano chiles are smaller, wider, and darker green. They have a deeper flavor, especially when roasted. Plain bell peppers (green or red) will also work well in this recipe. I've made it all three ways and enjoyed it each time.

You can streamline the preparation time by getting all the other ingredients ready while the eggplant and peppers are in the oven. This relish keeps well for several days, and won't suffer at all from being made a few days ahead.

As an alternative to serving this as an appetizer, try it for lunch, surrounded by chips and assorted cut-up raw vegetables.

1. Preheat oven to 350°. Lightly oil a baking tray.

2. Slice the eggplant in half lengthwise and place the halves open side down on the baking tray. Place the whole peppers on the same tray.

3. Bake the eggplant and peppers together, turning the peppers every 5 to 8 minutes to help them blister evenly. When the eggplant is tender (test with a fork) and the pepper skins are blistered all over, remove from the oven. This should take about 30 minutes. If the peppers get done a little sooner, remove them first.

4. As soon as the peppers come out of the oven, place them in a paper bag for about 3 minutes. This will assist them in sweating off their skins. Then take them out, wait until they are cool enough to handle, and scrape off and discard their skins.

Remove the tops, seeds, and inner membranes, and dice the peppers. Place them in a medium-sized bowl.

5. Bring a small saucepan of water to a boil. Core the tomatoes and plunge them into the boiling water for a slow count of 10. Remove and peel the tomatoes under cold running water. Cut them open and squeeze out and discard the seeds. Dice the tomatoes, and add them to the peppers in the bowl.

6. Use a blender or food processor with the steel blade attachment to grind $1/2$ cup of the pepitas to a powder. Add this to the peppers and tomatoes.

7. Scoop out the eggplant pulp and add it to the food processor or blender (no need to clean the machine first). Purée until quite smooth, then add it to the pepita-vegetable mixture in the bowl.

8. Add garlic, lime juice, salt, and the other $1/2$ cup of whole pepitas, season to taste with black and red peppers, and mix until well combined. Dust the top lightly with crushed red pepper if desired, and garnish with a few small sprigs of fresh cilantro. Serve at room temperature or cold.

LENTIL CHILI

PREPARATION TIME: ABOUT
1/2 HOUR FOR THE INITIAL
PREPARATION; 2 HOURS
TOTAL, INCLUDING THE
COOKING TIME.

YIELD: EASILY SERVES 8.

4 cups dried lentils

6 to 7 cups water (tomato juice can be substituted for about 2 cups water)

1 1-pound can tomatoes, or 3 to 4 large ripe fresh tomatoes (peeling optional), chopped

2 teaspoons ground cumin

1 teaspoon paprika

1/2 teaspoon dried thyme (or about 2 teaspoons minced fresh)

10 to 12 (that's right!) medium-sized cloves garlic, minced

2 medium-sized onions, finely chopped (about 1 2/3 to 2 cups chopped)

2 teaspoons salt

lots of freshly ground black pepper

4 to 6 tablespoons tomato paste

1 to 2 tablespoons red wine or balsamic vinegar

crushed red pepper, to taste

OPTIONAL TOPPINGS:

thin slices of sharp cheddar

a handful of toasted cashews

minced fresh parsley and/or cilantro

Lentils make great chili. Unlike beans, they don't need to be soaked first, so you can make this dish more spontaneously than traditional chili. If cooked long enough, lentils achieve a consistency similar to ground beef, and can give a similar satisfaction (for those who are nostalgic for beef barbecue and sloppy Joes).

This chili is full-bodied and richly seasoned. The seemingly huge amount of garlic blends in well, mellowing with the length of the cooking.

You can make lentil chili on a day when you are home doing other things. (Rainy Sunday mornings are especially conducive.) Much of the preparation time allotted is for simmering, which the chili does on its own.

The yield is for at least 8 servings, but if you are cooking for fewer, keep in mind that it freezes beautifully.

1. Place lentils and 6 cups of water in a large soup pot or Dutch oven. Bring to a boil, partially cover (*mostly* cover, but leave an air vent), and lower the heat to a simmer. Leave it this way for about 30 minutes, checking it every now and then to be sure it isn't cooking any faster than a gentle simmer. (You can chop the vegetables during this time.)

2. Add tomatoes, cumin, paprika, thyme, garlic, and onions. Stir, mostly cover again, and let it cook for another 45 to 60 minutes until the lentils are tender. Check the water level as it cooks, and add water or tomato juice in 1/4-cup increments as needed, to prevent dryness. Stir from the bottom every 10 to 15 minutes during the cooking.

3. Add salt, black pepper, and tomato paste. Stir and continue to simmer slowly, partially covered, until the lentils are very soft (up to 30 minutes more).

4. About 10 to 15 minutes before serving, add vinegar and red pepper. Adjust seasonings to taste, and serve with some or all or none of the optional toppings.

CORN AND RED PEPPER MUFFINS

PREPARATION TIME: 10 TO
15 MINUTES TO PREPARE,
15 TO 20 TO BAKE.

YIELD: 1 DOZEN MEDIUM-SIZED
MUFFINS.

1 cup minced red bell pepper
(approximately 1 medium-
sized pepper)

2 tablespoons butter

1 cup unbleached white flour

$\frac{1}{2}$ teaspoon salt

$1\frac{1}{2}$ teaspoons baking soda

$\frac{1}{2}$ teaspoon baking powder

$\frac{1}{4}$ cup (packed) brown sugar

$1\frac{1}{4}$ cups cornmeal

1 egg

1 cup buttermilk or yogurt

These delicious muffins are easy to make and very pretty.

If red bell peppers are out of season, try using $\frac{1}{2}$ cup drained, minced pimientos. (Still include the butter. Melt it first, and add it with the liquid.)

These muffins make great lunch fare. Split and toast them, then melt some cheddar cheese over each half. Possibly habit forming.

1. Preheat oven to 400°. Grease—or line with muffin papers—12 muffin cups.

2. In a small skillet, sauté the minced pepper in butter over low heat, stirring occasionally for about 8 to 10 minutes, or until soft. Set aside.

3. In a medium-sized bowl sift together flour, salt, baking soda, and baking powder. Stir in brown sugar and cornmeal, and mix until quite uniform. (You may have to use your hands to break up and distribute the brown sugar.)

4. Beat together the egg and buttermilk or yogurt. Stir this into the flour mixture along with the sautéed pepper. (Be sure to include all the butter it was cooked in!)

5. Spoon the batter into the prepared muffin cups, filling them until just even with the top surface of the pan.

6. Bake for 15 to 20 minutes, or until a knife inserted into the center comes out clean and the tops are beginning to brown. Cool in the pan for about 10 minutes before removing.

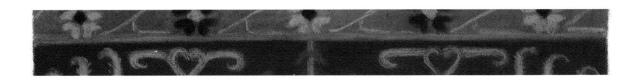

HOT SPICED APPLE AND BERRY CIDER

PREPARATION TIME: 10 TO
15 MINUTES.

YIELD: 4 CUPS. VERY EASILY
MULTIPLIED.

*I quart cranberry-apple juice
(or any variation of cran-
berry-apple-berry juice)*

*I to 2 teaspoons whole pep-
percorns*

I stick cinnamon

*a few whole cardamom pods
(optional)*

*¹/₂ teaspoon whole cloves
(optional)*

*I to 2 tablespoons fresh lemon
juice*

orange wedges for garnish

When people first taste hot spiced cider made with peppercorns, they tend to do a double take. The bite of the pepper sneaks up at the tail end of the sip. Everything else about the drink is homey and familiar, and then, a gentle but definite little zap.

The amount of peppercorns (as well as the other spices) can be played with according to your preferences. Consider the proportions below a suggested ratio. The smaller amount of pepper is intended for the average palate, and can be increased, decreased, or even omitted (for those who are not in the mood for anything even a little unusual).

1. Combine cranberry-apple juice and spices in a heavy, nonaluminum saucepan. (If you prefer, the peppercorns, cardamom pods, and whole cloves can be placed inside a tea ball first. This way you won't have to make detours around them or fish them out later.)

2. Bring to a boil and cover. Turn off the heat and let sit about 5 minutes.

3. Stir in the lemon juice, and serve garnished with a squeezable-sized wedge of orange perched on the edge of each mug.

CHOCOLATE CHIP-PEANUT BUTTER COOKIES

PREPARATION TIME: 35 MINUTES (INCLUDES BAKING).

YIELD: ABOUT 3 DOZEN.

1/2 cup (1 stick) soft butter

1 cup peanut butter (smooth or crunchy, preferably unadulterated)

3/4 to 1 cup sugar (to taste)

1 egg

1 teaspoon vanilla extract

2 cups unbleached white flour

1/2 teaspoon salt (if peanut butter is not too salty)

1 teaspoon baking soda

1/4 cup water

1 cup semisweet chocolate chips

a little extra flour for your hands

I made up this recipe on one of those days when I felt that just about *anything* would taste better with chocolate chips added. (Do you have days like that?) Anyway, as it turned out, with this recipe I was right.

For a nuttier-tasting, heartier cookie, try substituting 1 cup of the white flour with whole wheat. It's surprisingly good.

1. Preheat oven to 375°. Lightly grease a cookie sheet.

2. In a large bowl, beat together the butter, peanut butter, sugar, and egg. Continue to beat well (high speed with an electric mixer is the best way) for 5 minutes.

3. Stir in vanilla.

4. Sift in the dry ingredients, then add the water and the chocolate chips. Stir by hand until well blended.

5. Flour your hands, and form the dough into 1 1/2-inch balls. Place each ball on the cookie sheet, and press with a fork to flatten.

6. Bake 12 to 15 minutes. Cook on a rack for ultimate crispness.

Here is an example of how a simple vegetable and grain dinner, when carefully prepared and served with just the right accoutrements, can be elegant enough for any range of occasions.

MILLET AND VEGETABLE PILAF
ALMOND-ORANGE SAUCE
SWEET AND HOT FRUIT RELISH
GREEN SALAD
CREAMY VINAIGRETTE
LINZER TEA SQUARES

3 DAYS AHEAD: make fruit relish

2 DAYS AHEAD: prepare vegetables for pilaf / make Creamy Vinaigrette

I DAY AHEAD: do steps I and 2 of the pilaf / clean greens for salad / assemble Linzer Tea Squares and refrigerate unbaked

SAME DAY: bake tea squares / cook pilaf / assemble Almond-Orange Sauce / assemble and dress salad

MILLET AND VEGETABLE PILAF

PREPARATION TIME: 20 MINUTES
TO PREPARE, 30 MORE MIN-
UTES TO COOK.

YIELD: 4 TO 6 SERVINGS.

¹/₂ pound mushrooms, coarsely chopped

3 medium leeks, coarsely chopped (whites and about half the greens) or 2 medium-sized onions, chopped

2 tablespoons canola or vegetable oil

1 teaspoon salt

2 cups uncooked millet

2 cups boiling water

1 large carrot, diced or quartered lengthwise and thinly sliced

¹/₂ pound fresh green beans, trimmed and cut in 1¹/₂-inch pieces

1 cup sunflower seeds, lightly toasted

Sautéing the millet before simmering gives it a nuttier, more interesting flavor. The light coating of oil helps to keep each grain distinct and unmushy throughout the cooking. The vegetables are added at different times to take into account their varying cooking requirements. Attention to such details rewards you with a perfectly textured pilaf.

The weights and amounts of vegetables in this recipe are approximate and somewhat flexible, so don't panic and run to the store if you have only ¹/₃ pound green beans. The pilaf is resilient and will forgive you.

1. In a large deep skillet or Dutch oven, sauté mushrooms and leeks (or onions) in oil with salt for about 5 minutes. Use medium heat.

2. Add the millet. Continue to cook over medium heat, stirring often for another 5 minutes.

3. Add boiling water, cover, and keep cooking.

4. Five minutes later, add carrots and green beans. Simply lay them on top—don't mix them in at this point. Reduce heat, cover again, and allow the pilaf to cook undisturbed another 15 minutes.

5. Remove from heat and fluff the millet with a fork, mixing in the carrots and green beans at the same time.

6. Mix in the toasted sunflower seeds. Serve hot, topped with warm or room temperature Almond-Orange Sauce (recipe follows).

ALMOND-ORANGE SAUCE

PREPARATION TIME: 10 MINUTES.

YIELD: 2 CUPS.

1 cup almond butter
½ cup boiling water
½ cup orange juice
1 tablespoon soy sauce
1 teaspoon minced fresh ginger
½ teaspoon orange rind
salt, to taste (optional)

Orange, almond, and ginger mingle delicately in this sauce. It's good enough to eat with a spoon all by itself, but it's especially good on millet pilaf. (Also try it on baked or grilled fish.)

If you can't find almond butter in the store, make some by grinding toasted or raw almonds to a paste in a blender. Or you could substitute peanut butter. The taste will be altered somewhat, but it will still be good.

1. Place the almond butter in a medium-small bowl.

2. Add boiling water, and carefully mash with a spoon until the mixture is uniform.

3. Add remaining ingredients and mix well. Salt to taste.

4. Serve warm or at room temperature over hot pilaf.

SWEET AND HOT FRUIT RELISH

PREPARATION TIME: 30 MINUTES
TO ASSEMBLE; 55 MINUTES TO
COOK, 5 TO 10 MINUTES TO
PURÉE (PLUS AN OPTIONAL
HOUR OR TWO TO LET IT
MACERATE).

YIELD: 2 TO 2½ CUPS.

1 medium-sized tomato (okay
    if not completely ripe)

2 medium-sized tart apples

1 seedless orange

1 cup chopped onion

3 to 5 medium-sized cloves
    garlic, minced

1 heaping tablespoon minced
    fresh ginger

½ teaspoon salt

1 teaspoon crushed red pepper

¼ cup cider vinegar

5 tablespoons (packed) brown
    sugar or honey

This is an exotic combination of tomatoes, apples, and oranges, with bold spices. It keeps for weeks, and can be used as a condiment for just about anything. If you are not a vegetarian, try it with grilled chicken or fish.

1. Fill a small saucepan with water, and bring to a boil. Core the tomato, and blanch it in the boiling water for a slow count of 10. Remove, and peel off the skin under cold running water. Cut in half, and squeeze out as many of the seeds as you can. Chop what's left, and place in a medium-sized nonaluminum saucepan.

2. Peel, core, and chop the apples. Add them to the chopped tomato.

3. Cut the entire orange into small pieces—rind and all—and add to the saucepan.

4. Add all remaining ingredients. At this point, you may choose to let it stand for an hour or two to macerate. Or you can proceed right away with the cooking.

5. Bring to a boil over medium heat. Lower to a simmer, and cook gently, stirring occasionally for 45 minutes. Cool to room temperature.

6. Purée all or some of the relish in a blender or food processor. Taste, and adjust the seasonings if necessary.

7. Store in an airtight container in the refrigerator. It should keep for several weeks.

CREAMY VINAIGRETTE

PREPARATION TIME: 5 MINUTES.

YIELD: ABOUT ³/₄ CUP, ENOUGH FOR ABOUT 6 SERVINGS OF SALAD.

1 to 2 medium-sized cloves garlic, finely minced or crushed

¹/₃ cup extra virgin olive oil

1¹/₂ to 2 tablespoons red wine vinegar (to taste)

¹/₄ teaspoon salt (or more, to taste)

3 tablespoons yogurt

1 tablespoon mayonnaise

¹/₂ teaspoon dried basil

¹/₄ teaspoon dried dill

¹/₄ teaspoon dried thyme

This garlicky vinaigrette, smoothed by yogurt and a touch of mayonnaise, goes especially well on romaine, spinach, and other firm-bodied salad greens. It keeps for about a week in the refrigerator. Just spoon out however much you need, and put the rest back for sometime later.

NOTE: Recipes for homemade mayonnaise appear on page 68.

1. Whisk together all ingredients in a small bowl. Taste to adjust seasonings.

2. Transfer to a small lidded jar, and store in the refrigerator.

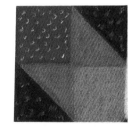

LINZER TEA SQUARES

PREPARATION TIME: 30 MINUTES,
PLUS 40 TO 45 MINUTES TO
BAKE.

YIELD: 2¹/₂ TO 3 DOZEN.

³/₄ cup (1¹/₂ sticks) soft butter

*¹/₂ cup (packed) light brown
   sugar*

I egg

I teaspoon vanilla extract

I cup unbleached white flour

¹/₄ teaspoon salt

*I cup finely ground almonds
   (use a food processor with
   steel blade or blender in
   quick bursts)*

*¹/₄ teaspoon each cinnamon
   and allspice*

¹/₂ teaspoon grated orange rind

¹/₂ teaspoon grated lemon rind

*¹/₂ to ²/₃ cup raspberry pre-
   serves (you may also use
   peach or apricot)*

This is like a junior version of linzer torte. It is more homespun and easier to make than its elegant mentor, but it is really just as delicious. These cookies are only about 2 inches square, so if you chew slowly you'll get as much pleasure as you would from a whole piece of torte, while you are actually consuming quite a bit less.

1. Preheat oven to 350°. Lightly grease a 9 x 13-inch baking pan.

2. Using an electric mixer at high speed, beat the butter and sugar until light. Add the egg and vanilla and beat a few minutes more.

3. Stir in the remaining ingredients except the preserves. Mix by hand until well blended.

4. Flour your hands and pat half the dough into the prepared pan.

5. Spread the top of the dough with preserves.

6. Place spoonfuls of remaining dough on top, here and there. Flour your hands again and try to pat the dough into place as evenly as possible, covering the preserves. (Don't worry if it isn't perfect. It will smooth itself out as it bakes.)

7. Bake 40 to 45 minutes (until medium brown—not too dark). Cut into 1¹/₂- or 2-inch squares while still hot. Remove each square and cool on a rack.

In this menu, the smooth, custardy casserole pairs up beautifully with the highly-textured bean salad.

For a winter fruit salad, use frozen unsweetened berries and/or cherries (available in most grocery stores), pineapple chunks canned in their own juice, apples, pears, and bananas. (Add the bananas just before serving.)

CHILAQUILE CASSEROLE
SOUTHWEST SALAD
WITH BLACK BEANS AND CORN
WINTER FRUIT SALAD
CHOCOLATE CHIP-MINT COOKIES

3 DAYS AHEAD: grate the cheese / soak black beans for salad / make cookie dough and refrigerate

2 DAYS AHEAD: cook the beans / get other salad ingredients ready (cook corn, prepare onion and garlic, squeeze lime juice)

1 DAY AHEAD: assemble salad / bake cookies

SAME DAY: fix tortillas for salad / assemble and bake casserole / make fruit salad

CHILAQUILE CASSEROLE

PREPARATION TIME: 20 MINUTES
TO PREPARE, 35 MINUTES TO
BAKE.

YIELD: 4 TO 6 SERVINGS.

12 uncooked corn tortillas
(if using frozen, be sure
they are defrosted)

I medium Anaheim or
poblano chile, minced, or
2 4-ounce cans diced green
chiles

2 to 3 cups grated jack cheese

a few dashes each salt and
pepper

4 eggs

2 cups buttermilk

OPTIONAL ADDITIONS:

I to 2 cups cooked pinto
beans

$^{1}/_{2}$ pound firm tofu, cut into
thin slices

small touches of cumin, and
dried basil and/or oregano

I cup chopped onion, sautéed
until soft in I tablespoon
butter or olive oil

I to 2 medium-sized cloves
garlic, minced and lightly
sautéed in butter or
olive oil

I small zucchini, sliced or
cubed, and lightly sautéed
in butter or olive oil

Chilaquile Casserole is a thick, puddinglike combination of soft tortillas, cheese, and custard, plus a few chiles to liven things up a bit. It is a comforting and filling lunch or supper dish, which tastes as good reheated as it does freshly baked. The basic recipe is simple, but a variety of additions is possible. A few suggestions are included in the recipe. Use all, some, or none—or make up your own. It is also delicious plain, especially if served with an energetic companion dish, like Southwest Salad.

This is one of the easiest main-dish recipes in this book. It can be whipped up in less than 20 minutes, especially if you have all the ingredients ready and the cheese grated in advance. (A food processor fitted with the grating attachment will take care of the cheese in seconds.)

If you have some stale tortillas sitting around, this is the way to employ them. They'll rejuvenate when combined with the other ingredients.

1. Preheat oven to 375°. Butter or oil a 2-quart casserole or a 9 x 13-inch pan.

2. Tear 6 tortillas into bite-sized pieces and spread them evenly in the greased casserole.

3. Distribute half the chiles and half the cheese over the layer of tortillas. (At this point, spread, sprinkle, or place any optional additions on top of the cheese.)

4. Tear the remaining tortillas and spread them on top. Follow with the remaining chiles and cheese.

5. Beat the eggs and buttermilk together with salt and pepper. Slowly pour this custard over the casserole.

6. Bake uncovered for 35 minutes. Serve hot, warm, or at room temperature.

SOUTHWEST SALAD
WITH BLACK BEANS AND CORN

PREPARATION TIME: 1¼ TO 1½ HOURS TO COOK THE SOAKED BEANS. 40 MINUTES AFTER THAT.

YIELD: 6 TO 8 SERVINGS.

2 cups dried black beans

2 cups cooked corn

2 to 3 medium-sized cloves garlic, finely minced

a heaping ½ cup well-minced red onion

1 medium-sized red bell pepper, minced

1 medium-sized carrot, minced (optional)

1 teaspoon salt

½ cup extra virgin olive oil (plus an optional 1 to 2 tablespoons for the tortillas)

½ cup fresh lime juice (3 to 4 limes)

2 to 3 teaspoons whole cumin seeds

½ cup minced fresh cilantro

½ cup minced fresh parsley

½ cup minced fresh basil (if available)

1 teaspoon crushed red pepper (adjust this to your taste)

a moderate amount of freshly ground black pepper

3 to 4 corn tortillas (optional)

Black beans and corn are marinated in olive oil and lots of lime juice and seasoned with garlic, peppers, onion, roasted cumin seeds, and cilantro. Partly chewy, partly crunchy tortilla strips provide textural contrast.

This salad keeps extremely well (up to five days or more) if stored in a tightly covered container in the refrigerator. If you are making it a day or two in advance of serving, leave out the fresh cilantro and parsley until a few hours before serving. Also, prepare the tortilla strips as close to serving time as possible.

Leftover Southwest Salad makes a wonderful lunch or light supper served cold or at room temperature over hot rice with fresh tortilla chips or quick nachos (see page 231) on the side.

1. Soak the beans for at least 4 hours, but preferably overnight. Drain off any excess soaking water, place the soaked beans in a soup pot, and cover with fresh water. Bring *just* to a boil, then cover and turn the heat way down. Cook at a very slow simmer—with no agitation in the water—until the beans are tender. This should take 1¼ to 1½ hours. Check intermittently to be sure there is enough water, and add more if necessary. When the beans are cooked, drain them well. Then rinse them thoroughly in cold water, and drain them well again.

2. In a large bowl, combine beans, cooked corn, minced garlic, red onion, bell pepper, optional carrot, salt, ½ cup olive oil, and lime juice.

3. Roast the whole cumin seeds, either in a cast-iron skillet over medium heat, stirring for several minutes, or very carefully in a toaster oven. Add the toasted seeds to the salad, along with the cilantro, parsley, basil, and red and black pepper, and mix thoroughly but gently.

4. Lightly brush both sides of each tortilla with olive oil, and cut the tortillas into strips approximately ¼ inch wide and 1½ inches long. Cook the strips slightly by toasting them in an oven (350°) or a toaster oven for only about 2 minutes, or in a heavy skillet over medium heat for 2 to 3 minutes. Ideally, they should be partly crispy and partly chewy. Stir these into the salad shortly before serving, or, if you prefer, scatter them on top as a garnish.

CHOCOLATE CHIP-MINT COOKIES

PREPARATION TIME: 20 MINUTES
TO PREPARE, 12 TO 15 MIN-
UTES TO BAKE.

YIELD: 2¹/₂ DOZEN.

³/₄ cup (1¹/₂ sticks) butter

¹/₂ cup (packed) brown sugar

¹/₂ cup granulated sugar

1 egg

1 teaspoon vanilla extract

1 teaspoon peppermint extract

*1¹/₂ cups unbleached white
   flour*

¹/₄ cup unsweetened cocoa

1 teaspoon baking soda

¹/₄ teaspoon salt

1 cup chocolate chips

This is the only recipe in which I have ever used peppermint extract, but these cookies are worth the price of several bottles. They freeze beautifully stored in a tin, and they even taste good frozen.

I tested this recipe midway through working on the book, and I can't tell you how many of these I consumed while sitting here at my desk writing recipes. Tofu, grains, and vegetables have their place, but Chocolate Chip-Mint Cookies are creative soul food.

1. Preheat oven to 350°. Lightly grease a cookie sheet.

2. Cream together butter and sugars with an electric mixer at high speed.

3. Beat in egg. Stir in vanilla and peppermint extracts.

4. Sift together the dry ingredients, and add this to the butter mixture along with the chocolate chips. Stir until well combined.

5. Drop by rounded teaspoons onto a lightly greased cookie sheet. Bake 12 to 15 minutes at 350°. Remove from the sheet immediately after baking, and cool on a rack.

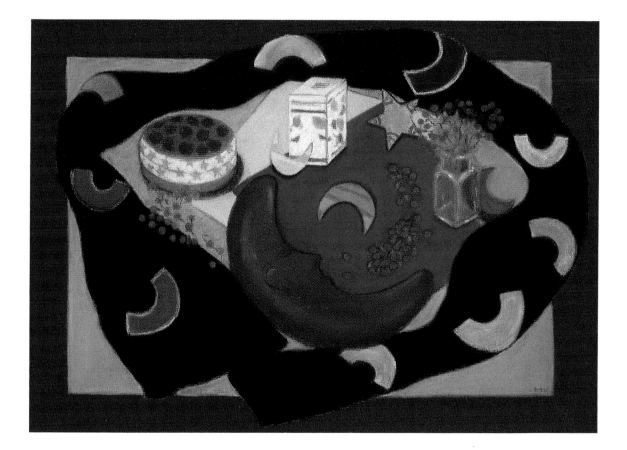

The noodle and cucumber salad is a light first course in the Japanese tradition. The broiled vegetables, covered by exquisite Misoyaki Sauce, are a moderately filling and humble entrée. This quietly delicious dinner is then set off dramatically by the more flamboyant Lunar Eclairs, which are *wildly* delicious.

SUNOMONO (JAPANESE NOODLE AND CUCUMBER SALAD)
BROILED EGGPLANT, MUSHROOMS, TOFU, AND RED ONIONS WITH MISOYAKI SAUCE
BROWN RICE
LUNAR ECLAIRS

2 DAYS AHEAD: cook noodles for salad; store in water in the refrigerator / make eclair filling; mince pistachios for topping

1 DAY AHEAD: assemble salad, leaving out cucumbers; prepare cucumbers and store separately / make eclair pastry (if not too humid) / Misoyaki Sauce can be made today or tomorrow

SAME DAY: make sauce if not done yesterday; if already made, bring to room temperature / cook rice; cook and broil vegetables / add cucumbers to salad / finish eclairs (step 4) within an hour of serving

SUNOMONO (JAPANESE NOODLE AND CUCUMBER SALAD)

PREPARATION TIME: 15 MINUTES, PLUS CHILLING TIME.

YIELD: 4 TO 5 SERVINGS.

5 to 6 ounces dry vermicelli noodles (Japanese saifun or Chinese bean thread noodles are best, but regular vermicelli will work)

6 tablespoons rice vinegar

4 teaspoons sugar

2 teaspoons soy sauce

1 teaspoon salt

1 to 2 tablespoons sesame seeds

1 medium-sized cucumber

extra sesame seeds for the top

scallion greens, thinly sliced (optional)

This salad is subtle and very refreshing. There is a variety of textures—chewy cold noodles, crunchy sesame seeds, and smooth cucumber slices. Sweet, salt, and vinegar combine harmoniously, each understated but very much present.

Everything except the cucumbers and toppings can be combined several days ahead of time. The cucumbers can be prepared ahead also, and kept separate until serving.

NOTE: The dressing contains no oil.

1. Cook the noodles in boiling water until just tender. Drain and rinse in cold water. Drain thoroughly, and transfer to a medium-sized bowl.

2. Add vinegar, sugar, soy sauce, salt, and sesame seeds. Mix well. Cover and chill until cold.

3. Peel and seed the cucumber. Cut into quarters lengthwise, then into thin pieces. If not serving right away, wrap the cucumber pieces in a plastic bag or plastic wrap and refrigerate.

4. To serve, divide noodles among 4 or 5 serving bowls. Top with a small handful of cucumber slices, a light sprinkling of sesame seeds, and, if desired, a few very thin slices of scallion greens. Serve cold.

BROILED EGGPLANT, MUSHROOMS, TOFU, AND RED ONIONS WITH MISOYAKI SAUCE

PREPARATION TIME: 25 MINUTES. (BEGIN TO COOK RICE 30 MINUTES AHEAD.)

YIELD: 4 TO 5 SERVINGS.

Certain vegetables lend themselves very well to broiling. If you cut them right, brush them with oil to prevent their drying out, and keep careful watch over them as they cook, as described on the following page, broiled vegetables can be a very special event. Experiment with vegetables not mentioned in this recipe. Try zucchini or yellow squash (sliced lengthwise, $1/2$ inch thick, or halved, if small), strips of carrot, parboiled slices of sweet potato, etc. If you think of it, broil some extra for use on pizza (page 226) or for marinating (page 45).

Miso is an aromatic, potent, and often salty paste made from aged and fermented soybeans and grains. Mirin is Japanese cooking sake, sweet and full-bodied. Mixed together they create a delicious sauce for broiled vegetables and tofu. (Also try this on grilled fish!) It is so easy and satisfying, you will find yourself making it over and over again.

There are many varieties of miso that can be found at most Asian groceries and natural food stores. Mirin is also usually available at Asian grocery stores. If you can't find it, substitute a fruity white wine or some light, relatively sweet sherry.

About 20 to 30 minutes before you begin preparations, place 2 cups brown rice in a medium-sized saucepan with 3 cups water. Bring to a boil, cover, and simmer very slowly. It will be done in about 35 to 45 minutes.

Meanwhile, prepare the sauce, and then begin work on the vegetables. This way, everything will be ready at the same time.

MISOYAKI SAUCE

½ cup yellow, barley, or
  Hatcho miso

I cup water

I cup mirin

2 tablespoons cornstarch

1. Place miso in a medium-sized bowl. Heat ½ cup water, add to miso, and mash together with a spoon to make a uniform paste.

2. Add ½ cup mirin to the paste and mix it thoroughly.

3. Place cornstarch in a small saucepan. Whisk in remaining ½ cup water and ½ cup mirin until smooth.

4. Heat cornstarch mixture over medium heat, whisking constantly. When it gets hot, cook it, still whisking, until thickened (5 to 8 minutes after it gets hot). Remove from heat and stir into miso mixture. Mix thoroughly. Set aside while you prepare the broiled vegetables.

5. Serve at room temperature or warm (heat gently—without cooking!—in a microwave or on the stove top) over hot broiled vegetables, tofu, and rice.

BROILED EGGPLANT, MUSHROOMS, TOFU, AND RED ONIONS

I medium-sized eggplant

salt

I pound firm tofu

I large or 2 not-so-large red
  onions

15 to 20 large mushrooms

a mild oil (canola works well)

Misoyaki Sauce (recipe above)

1. Peel the eggplant, cut off the ends, and slice into ½-inch thick rounds. (Better to err on the thick side in this case.) Salt lightly, and set aside on a plate or tray, to sweat out its bitter juices. Meanwhile, prepare the other items.

2. Cut the tofu into squares or rectangles, approximately ½ inch thick.

3. Peel onions, and cut them lengthwise into ½-inch wedges.

4. Remove mushroom stems and discard. Clean the caps.

5. Preheat broiler to 500°, and oil a 9 × 13-inch square baking pan.

6. Pat the eggplant slices dry with a paper towel. Arrange the vegetables and tofu flat in the baking pans. Brush their top surfaces lightly with oil.

7. Broil for 5 to 8 minutes on each side (length of broiling time depends on how close the rack is to the heat)—or until the vegetables are tender and lightly browned. Serve hot over steaming hot brown rice and under a blanket of Misoyaki Sauce.

LUNAR ECLAIRS

PREPARATION TIME: 20 MINUTES
TO PREPARE, 40 MINUTES TO
BAKE. MAKE THE FILLING
WHILE THE PASTRY BAKES.

YIELD: 6 SUBSTANTIAL YET
ETHEREAL PASTRIES (LARGE
ENOUGH TO SHARE).

$^1\!/_4$ teaspoon salt

1 cup unbleached white flour
(sift before measuring)

1 cup water

6 tablespoons butter

4 eggs, room temperature

Puffs of pastry are filled with ricotta cheese and white chocolate, and topped with more white chocolate and minced pistachios.

The baked pastries may be stored—uncovered and at room temperature (provided the kitchen is not too humid)—for up to 24 hours. The filling will also keep for 24 hours if covered tightly and refrigerated. Fill and decorate the eclairs within a few hours of serving.

PASTRY:

1. Preheat oven to 400°. (Oven temperature is critical in this recipe, so check your oven with a thermometer.) Lightly grease a rectangular baking sheet.

2. Add salt to the flour and set aside.

3. Combine water and butter in a medium-sized saucepan. Bring to a boil, lower heat, and simmer until all the butter is melted. Turn heat back up to medium-high, and dump in the dry ingredients all at once, stirring vigorously with a wooden spoon. The mixture will smooth itself out as you stir—keep up the pace. Very shortly the dough will become smooth, separating itself from the spoon. At this point, remove from heat, and let it rest for a couple of minutes.

4. Beat in the eggs, one at a time. (As each egg is incorporated, the dough goes from slippery to cake-batter-like.) When the final egg has been integrated into the batter, stir a little bit longer until the dough is stiff enough to make a small peak on the end of the spoon.

5. Use a spoon to form 6 eclairs (long ovals) or 6 crescent shapes on the greased baking sheet. Each eclair or crescent should be at most 3 inches wide at the center. Bake at 400° for 10 minutes, then at 350° for another 30 minutes. Cool completely on a rack.

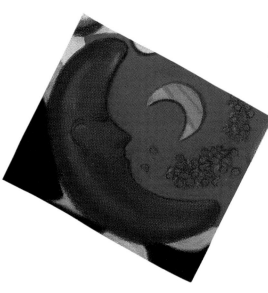

1 pound ricotta cheese

*about ¹/₂ pound white
chocolate*

1 teaspoon vanilla extract

*1 to 3 tablespoons sugar or
honey, to taste*

*juice and rind of 1 medium-
sized lime*

¹/₄ teaspoon salt

*¹/₂ cup blanched pistachio
nuts, very finely chopped
(optional)**

FILLING AND ASSEMBLY:

1. Place the ricotta in a medium-sized bowl and beat until smooth, using a whisk or electric mixer.

2. Set aside about ¹/₃ of the chocolate. Grate the other approximate ²/₃, either by hand or with a food processor (steel blade attachment) or a blender.

3. Add the grated chocolate to the ricotta, along with vanilla, sugar or honey, juice, rind, and salt. Mix well. At this point, the filling may be stored, covered and refrigerated, until use. It will keep for 24 hours.

4. Fill the eclairs within an hour of serving. Melt the remaining chocolate, slice the pastries in half lengthwise, and place ¹/₆ of the filling inside each. Spread it evenly, put the other pastry half back on, and drizzle the top elegantly with melted white chocolate. A sprinkling of minced pistachio nuts is a glorious final touch.

*To blanch pistachio nuts, toast them in a 350° oven for about 15 minutes. Cool until comfortable to handle, then gently rub off the skins with your fingers. Please note that blanching is not crucial, it just takes this dish a step further esthetically by showcasing the pistachios' exquisite green color.

In traditional Indian cooking there are no courses. Everything—including soup and dessert—gets served at once. So in this menu, there is no one entrée, but rather a chorus of what might otherwise be considered secondary dishes, all combining to make one very complete meal. You can also expand the dinner into a banquet by adding a curry or two from your own repertoire.

INDIAN TOMATO SOUP WITH COCONUT
YELLOW SPLIT PEA DAL
RICE WITH NUTS AND RAISINS
SPINACH-CILANTRO RAITA
CHAPPATIS
ALMOND-STUFFED DATES

3 DAYS AHEAD: do steps 1 and 2 of the soup

2 DAYS AHEAD: prepare Chappatis through step 3; store uncooked, as described in recipe / assemble soup, short of adding yogurt and mint / make stuffed dates

1 DAY AHEAD: prepare garlic for dal and rice / prepare onion, ginger, and nuts for the rice / make raita (can also be made same day)

SAME DAY: cook rice / cook dal / reheat soup / cook Chappatis

INDIAN TOMATO SOUP
WITH COCONUT

PREPARATION TIME: 40 MINUTES.

YIELD: 4 SERVINGS.

1 cup shredded unsweetened
  coconut

2 cups boiling water

⅓ cup sesame seeds

½ teaspoon whole or ground
  cumin seed

½ teaspoon mustard seeds

¾ teaspoon each cinnamon
  and ground coriander

1 tablespoon butter

½ teaspoon salt
  (increase to taste if using
  fresh tomatoes)

3 cups puréed cooked
  tomatoes

OPTIONAL GARNISHES:

yogurt

a little cayenne

minced fresh mint leaves

This recipe calls for puréed cooked tomatoes. You can purée canned tomatoes in the blender or food processor, or cook fresh peeled ones and then purée them. (Don't use canned tomato purée. It will be too thick and intense.) Approximately 2 pounds or 3 large tomatoes will yield 3 cups of purée.

The sesame and mustard seeds can be left whole or, for a finer-textured soup, ground (before cooking) to a powder in a spice mill or a clean coffee grinder.

1. Lightly toast the coconut, either by stirring it in a cast-iron skillet over medium heat or in a toaster oven. Watch very carefully to prevent burning.

2. Place the toasted coconut in a bowl, pour the boiling water over it, and let it soak for about 15 minutes. Strain through a fine strainer or sieve into another bowl, pressing out and reserving all excess liquid. Discard the coconut.

3. In a medium-sized cast-iron skillet, sauté sesame, cumin, and mustard seeds with cinnamon and coriander in butter over medium heat, stirring frequently, for 8 to 10 minutes, or until they give off a deeply toasted smell (and the whole seeds start popping). Remove from heat and add salt.

4. Combine the sautéed seeds and spices with the coconut liquid in a soup pot or Dutch oven. Add the tomatoes.

5. Heat just to boiling, then reduce heat and simmer very gently 15 to 20 minutes. Correct and adjust seasonings to taste. Serve topped with yogurt, cayenne, and a few sprigs of fresh mint.

YELLOW SPLIT PEA DAL

PREPARATION TIME: JUST A FEW MINUTES OF PREPARATION; 2¹/₂ HOURS OF SIMMERING (DURING WHICH YOU CAN DO OTHER THINGS).

YIELD: 6 TO 8 SERVINGS.

2 cups dried yellow split peas

10 cups water (possibly more later)

1 to 2 tablespoons cumin seeds, lightly toasted

2 tablespoons ground coriander

2 tablespoons mustard seeds, lightly toasted

2 teaspoons turmeric

1 teaspoon cinnamon

10 to 12 medium-sized cloves garlic, minced

2 teaspoons salt

3 tablespoons fresh lemon juice (or more, to taste)

black pepper

crushed red pepper

"Dal" in Indian cooking refers to porridgelike dishes made from dried legumes—usually split peas or lentils. Dal is often served in a thinned state as a soup, but equally often it will be a thick, hearty side dish. This is a thick dal, comprehensive and highly spiced enough to be the focus of a meal. Leftovers can be thinned with a little water and served as soup.

In this dish, yellow split peas are cooked slowly as seasonings are gradually added. Cumin and mustard seeds can be lightly toasted in a small skillet or a toaster-oven (watch them carefully!).

1. Place split peas and 10 cups water in a soup pot or Dutch oven. Cover and heat to the boiling point. Reduce heat and simmer very slowly, partially covered—stirring intermittently—for about 2¹/₂ hours, or until very soft.

2. About 45 minutes into the simmering add the cumin seeds, ground coriander, mustard seeds, turmeric, and cinnamon. Stir well, and continue to simmer.

3. Add half the garlic about 45 minutes later. Stir, and continue to simmer. As the dal gets thicker, you may want to place a heat diffuser under the pot to prevent sticking on the bottom.

4. When the dal is just about ready, add the remaining garlic, salt, lemon juice, and black and red pepper to taste. If desired, thin it to taste with small amounts of additional water. Simmer for about 10 minutes longer. Serve hot.

RICE WITH NUTS AND RAISINS

PREPARATION TIME: 45 MINUTES.

YIELD: 6 SERVINGS.

This is a highly textured pilaf that harmonizes beautifully with many variously seasoned other dishes. It also tastes wonderful served with just a little plain yogurt on top and a green salad or steamed green vegetables on the side.

2 cups uncooked brown rice (plain or basmati)

3 cups water

1 to 2 tablespoons peanut or canola oil or butter

1 1/2 cups finely chopped onion

2 large cloves garlic, minced

1 tablespoon minced fresh ginger

1 to 2 teaspoons fennel seeds (optional)

1 teaspoon salt (or more, to taste)

1 cup raisins

1 teaspoon grated orange or lemon rind (or a combination)

1 1/2 cups chopped nuts (any combination of almonds, cashews, walnuts, pecans) lightly toasted

1. Place the rice and water in a pot with a tight-fitting lid. Bring to a boil, then cover, and simmer undisturbed over the lowest possible heat until tender (35 to 45 minutes).

2. Meanwhile, heat the oil or melt the butter in a medium-sized skillet. Add the onion, garlic, ginger, fennel seeds, and salt. Sauté over low heat for about 10 to 12 minutes, or until the onion is very soft. Remove from heat.

3. When the rice is completely cooked, transfer to a serving bowl, and fluff gently with a fork. Stir in the sautéed mixture, along with the raisins and orange or lemon rind. Sprinkle the nuts over the top, and serve.

SPINACH-CILANTRO RAITA

PREPARATION TIME: 10 MINUTES.

YIELD: CONDIMENT FOR 6 TO 8.

2 cups (packed) finely minced
    fresh spinach leaves (about
    ¹/₄ pound)

¹/₃ cup minced fresh cilantro

3 cups firm yogurt

¹/₂ teaspoon fennel seeds

¹/₂ teaspoon cumin seeds

¹/₄ teaspoon salt (or more or
    less, to taste)

cayenne

Raita is a lightly spiced yogurt preparation, graced with small amounts of minced vegetables. In Indian cuisine, it is commonly served as a side dish or condiment, intended to complement (and provide cooling relief from) the hotter, more dominant dishes.

The spinach should be very finely minced. A food processor with the steel blade attachment does the job perfectly in just a few pulses. In fact, process the cilantro and the spinach together and this dish will take less time to assemble than it's taking me to write this paragraph!

If you can't get fresh cilantro, substitute parsley and/or ¹/₄ teaspoon ground coriander.

The raita can be assembled up to a day in advance if the spinach is very fresh to begin with. Cover it tightly and refrigerate.

1. Combine everything except the cayenne, and mix well. Transfer to an attractive small bowl.

2. Lightly dust the top with cayenne. Cover tightly and chill until serving.

CHAPPATIS

PREPARATION TIME: 20 MINUTES
TO PREPARE, 5 TO 10 MIN-
UTES TO COOK.

YIELD: 8 LARGE BREADS.

¹/₂ cup whole wheat flour

*1¹/₂ cups unbleached white
flour (plus a little extra for
kneading)*

¹/₂ teaspoon salt

1 cup water

2 tablespoons melted butter

Chappatis are a special and exciting addition to an Indian dinner cooked at home. At first glance they may seem like a lot of work, but they really aren't. Chappati dough is a simple flour-and-water combination that needs no rising and requires very little kneading. Rolling out the Chappatis is also quite easy. Unlike that of pie crust and certain other roll-outables, this dough is sturdy and untemperamental. It is guaranteed not to fall apart or give you a hard time in any way.

Make the dough as much as several days in advance. You can roll it out a day or two ahead also; just be sure you store the Chappatis in a stack with plenty of flour between the layers, so they won't stick together. Wrap tightly in plastic wrap and refrigerate. Cook them as close to serving time as possible.

1. Combine flours and salt in a medium-sized bowl.

2. Make a well in the center and add the water. Stir to combine, then turn the dough out on a floured surface and knead for about 5 minutes.

3. Divide the dough into 8 equal parts. Make each into a ball, then roll into a thin circle with a floured rolling pin.

4. Heat a griddle or cast-iron skillet and brush with melted butter. Add as many Chappatis as you have room for. Brush the top surface of the Chappatis with more butter. Cook on each side over medium heat for just a minute or two, or until light brown blisters appear. Wrap cooked Chappatis in a clean tea towel to keep warm while you cook the rest. Serve as soon as possible. If you can't serve them immediately, place them (still wrapped in the tea towel) in a 200° oven until serving time.

ALMOND-STUFFED DATES

PREPARATION TIME: 10 MINUTES.

YIELD: 12 STUFFED DATES.

12 whole dates

12 almonds

approximately ¹/₂ cup unsweetened shredded coconut

1 tablespoon fennel seeds

This is a potent little dessert, the perfect ending to a meal that is filling and good but just needs a final punctuation mark.

You can prepare stuffed dates in minutes; there is no mixing, no baking, and practically nothing to clean up. (Your hands might be just a little sticky. Deliciously so.)

1. Make a lengthwise slit in each date, and pop out the pit.

2. Slip 1 almond into each date, pushing it in as far as possible and wrapping the date around it.

3. Combine the coconut and fennel seeds on a small plate. Press the stuffed dates into this mixture, rolling them until coated.

4. Arrange on a small serving platter, and serve.

These are not the sidekick type of home fries—they are a meal unto themselves. This menu makes a great brunch or lunch, but don't rule it out as a dinner as well. Oaxaca Bean Salad is a perfect partner, and you won't need or want anything else, except perhaps a small serving of refreshing Piña Colada Fool.

MEXICAN HOME FRIES
OAXACA BEAN SALAD
PIÑA COLADA FOOL

3 DAYS AHEAD: soak beans for salad / for the home fries: peel garlic, chop onions, chop olives, squeeze limes, grate cheese / toast coconut for the Fool

2 DAYS AHEAD: slice and cook potatoes for home fries (step 1) / cook beans / prepare pineapple for the Fool (and if desired, soak it in rum)

1 DAY AHEAD: assemble salad / chop peppers and tomatoes for both home fries and salad garnish

SAME DAY: assemble and cook home fries / complete the Fool

MEXICAN HOME FRIES

PREPARATION TIME: 1 HOUR.

YIELD: 4 TO 6 MAIN-DISH-SIZED SERVINGS.

6 to 7 small potatoes (half-fist-sized)

4 to 6 corn tortillas

1/3 to 1/2 cup olive oil

3 to 4 large cloves garlic (you can also use smaller ones and more of them)

1 heaping cup minced onion

1 teaspoon ground cumin

3/4 teaspoon salt (or more, to taste)

a generous amount of freshly ground black pepper

1 medium-sized red, yellow, or green bell pepper, or a combination, cut in small strips

1/2 cup chopped, pitted black olives (you may also leave them whole, for texture)

1 medium-sized ripe tomato, chopped

1/2 to 3/4 teaspoon crushed red pepper

2 tablespoons fresh lime juice

1 heaping cup (packed) grated jack cheese

sour cream for garnish

minced fresh cilantro and/or parsley for garnish

Much more than just potatoes, these highly seasoned home fries feature whole garlic cloves, peppers, tortillas, olives, tomatoes, cheese, and more. This is hearty main-course fare.

If you pay careful attention to each process (i.e., slice the potatoes thin enough, get the oil hot enough, etc.), the texture will be as exquisite as the flavor.

Step 1 of this recipe (as well as all the chopping, tearing, and grating) can be done a day ahead. Store all components separately, in airtight containers in the refrigerator, until you begin final preparations.

1. Scrub the potatoes and boil them whole for 10 to 15 minutes, or until just tender. They should give just a little resistance when stabbed with a fork. Drain and rinse the potatoes under cold water until cool enough to handle. Slice thin. NOTE: You can prepare the other ingredients while the potatoes boil.

2. Tear the tortillas into small pieces (1 or 2 inches) or cut them into wedges. Set aside.

3. Heat the oil in a large skillet or Dutch oven. When it is very hot, add sliced potatoes. Cook for about 10 minutes, stirring over medium-high heat, then add garlic cloves and onions. Keep the heat medium-high, and shake the pan frequently until the potatoes are quite brown and crisp. This will take about 15 to 20 more minutes.

4. Add cumin, salt, and pepper. Stir until seasonings are well distributed.

5. Add bell pepper strips, tortilla pieces, olives, and tomato. Cook and stir about 10 to 15 minutes—until everything is blended and tender.

6. Stir in crushed red pepper and lime juice. Taste to correct seasonings. You can serve it at this point or, if you prefer, cook it longer until the dish is browner and crisp. Just be sure you keep stirring from the bottom of the pan. Add cheese during the last few minutes of cooking and stir it in until it melts.

7. Serve hot, with sour cream and minced cilantro and/or parsley.

OAXACA BEAN SALAD

PREPARATION TIME: THE SOAKED BEANS TAKE 1 TO 2 HOURS TO COOK; SALAD PREPARATION AFTER THAT IS ABOUT 15 MINUTES, PLUS TIME TO CHILL.

YIELD: 8 SERVINGS.

2¹/₂ cups dried kidney beans

5 tablespoons olive oil

5 tablespoons red wine vinegar

³/₄ to 1 teaspoon salt

3 tablespoons fresh lime juice

1 cup finely minced red onion

2 to 3 medium-sized cloves garlic, finely minced

1 stalk celery, finely minced

1 small cucumber, peeled, seeded, and chopped (a small zucchini may be substituted)

1 small red bell pepper, minced

lots of coarsely ground black pepper

crushed red pepper, to taste

¹/₂ cup (packed) minced fresh or frozen basil leaves (or 1 tablespoon dried)

¹/₄ cup (packed) finely minced fresh parsley

lime wedges and tomato slices, for garnish

The texture of the cooked beans is crucial to the success of this salad. Ideally the beans should be intact and perfectly tender after cooking, not mushy or exploded. This can be achieved by keeping the cooking water down to a gentle simmer and preventing any frantic boiling activity.

The fresh basil is also important, as it gives the salad a personality all its own. If fresh basil is unavailable, use frozen. If you forgot to freeze some when it was in season, remind yourself to do it next year. Meanwhile, use the freshest dried basil available. (Remember, dried herbs fade over time. Buy a new bottle and keep it refrigerated.)

1. Soak the beans in plenty of water for several hours or overnight. Rinse and place in a large saucepan. Cover the beans with water and bring to a boil under medium-high heat. As soon as the water boils, cover, and turn the heat down, so the beans can cook gently until tender (1 to 1¹/₂ hours—keep checking them and add water if needed).

2. As soon as the beans are as tender as you desire, remove the pan from the heat and drain its contents in a colander. Rinse the beans under cold water and drain well. Transfer to a medium-large mixing bowl.

3. Add remaining ingredients except fresh basil (if using dried, add it now), parsley, and garnishes. Mix thoroughly but gently, cover tightly, and chill for at least 3 hours. Add the fresh herbs, mix, cover, and refrigerate another hour. Serve garnished with wedges of lime and slices of ripe red tomato.

PIÑA COLADA FOOL

PREPARATATION TIME: ABOUT 20
MINUTES (METHOD II ALSO
NEEDS 30 MINUTES EXTRA TO
CHILL).

YIELD: 4 TO 6 SERVINGS.

1 medium-sized perfectly ripe
   pineapple

3 to 4 tablespoons rum
   (or more, to taste)

1/2 pint heavy cream
   (make sure it's cold)

2 to 3 tablespoons sugar or
   honey (optional)

2/3 cup lightly toasted coconut
   (use toaster oven or
   a heavy skillet on the
   stove top)

The drink is a legendary and inspired creation. Why not expand it into a *dessert* that you can actually sink your teeth into?

This dish will be as good as the fresh pineapple you choose, so search for one that is perfectly ripe and very sweet. (It should give a little when squeezed, and smell intensely pineapple-y at the base.) If you have a chance, cut up the pineapple at least an hour or two in advance of serving time. It will taste even better for having had a little time to sit around.

There are two different ways to put this together. In Method I, the pineapple is simply put into individual bowls, topped with whipped cream and coconut, and served immediately. In the second method, the fruit, whipped cream, and coconut are all folded together and then chilled before serving, like a mousse.

NOTE: Firm yogurt can be substituted for the whipped cream. Increase the sugar or honey to taste.

METHOD I

1. Skin the pineapple, remove the core, and cut the fruit into small chunks (1 inch or less). Place in 4, 5, or 6 individual serving bowls. Drizzle each bowlful with rum, to taste.

2. Whip the cream to whatever consistency you prefer, beating in sugar or honey (or not) to taste.

3. Sprinkle each portion with a small amount of coconut, top generously with whipped cream, and garnish with additional coconut.

METHOD II

1. Within 1 hour of serving, skin the pineapple and chop it into very small (1/4- to 1/2-inch) pieces. Place in a large bowl and drizzle with rum, to taste.

2. Whip the cream to a fairly stiff consistency, adding sugar or honey as desired.

3. Reserve a few tablespoons of the coconut, and stir the remainder into the pineapple. Add the whipped cream and fold until well combined. Cover and chill about 30 minutes.

4. Sprinkle the reserved coconut over the top and serve.

This menu pays homage to the cuisine of the American South. Serve Black-eyed Peas and Greens, yams, and corn bread together, followed by Sliced Fresh Fruit with Sweet and Hot Seed Dressing as a second course. The cookies are appropriately small and compact, as you won't have room after this meal for anything much bigger.

BLACK-EYED PEAS AND GREENS
BAKED YAMS
SIMPLE CORN BREAD
SLICED FRESH FRUIT WITH SWEET AND HOT SEED DRESSING
CHOCOLATE GINGER SNAPS

2 DAYS AHEAD: make cookie dough

I DAY AHEAD: make Sweet and Hot Seed Dressing / cut garlic, greens, and leeks for black-eyed peas / mix together dry ingredients for corn bread / bake cookies (this can also be done the same day)

SAME DAY: bake yams / assemble and cook black-eyed peas / assemble and bake corn bread / slice fruit

BLACK-EYED PEAS AND GREENS

PREPARATION TIME: JUST A FEW MINUTES TO PUT TOGETHER, 35 MINUTES TO SIMMER.

YIELD: AT LEAST 6 SERVINGS, ESPECIALLY IF SERVED WITH YAMS AND CORN BREAD.

3 cups dried black-eyed peas

6 cups water

6 medium-sized cloves garlic, minced

1 1/2 teaspoons salt

6 to 8 cups (packed) chopped mixed greens (recommended: collard, mustard, and dandelion)

2 medium-sized leeks, cleaned well and chopped

freshly ground black pepper

Even the bitterest, sternest-seeming greens soften their disposition in the company of naturally sweet black-eyed peas and soothing leeks. This dish might seem pedestrian at first glance, but you will be amazed by how delicious such sturdy and inexpensive fare can be. (And your body will thank you for honoring it with such good nutrition!)

NOTE: This recipe is fat free!

1. Place the black-eyed peas and water in a very large soup pot or a Dutch oven. Bring to a boil, lower the heat to a simmer, and mostly cover (i.e., cover but leave an air vent). Cook gently until tender, checking the water level every now and then. If it appears to be getting dry, add water, 1/2 cup at a time. About 15 minutes into the cooking, add the garlic. The peas will take 30 to 35 minutes to cook.

2. When the black-eyed peas are just about tender, stir in the salt, greens, and leeks. Cover and continue to simmer just a few more minutes. (The greens and leeks will cook very quickly.)

3. Season to taste with freshly ground black pepper, and serve hot.

SIMPLE CORN BREAD

PREPARATION TIME: 10 MINUTES
TO ASSEMBLE, 25 TO
30 MINUTES TO BAKE.

YIELD: 6 TO 8 SERVINGS.

1 cup cornmeal

1 cup unbleached white flour

$^{1}/_{2}$ teaspoon salt

2 tablespoons brown or
granulated sugar

1 teaspoon baking soda

1 cup buttermilk (or 1 cup
milk with $^{1}/_{2}$ teaspoon
vinegar)

1 egg

2 tablespoons melted butter

Here is a standard, straightforward corn bread recipe, about as easy as you can get. Yet no matter how commonplace plain, unadorned corn bread might be, it is always inexplicably exciting when it comes to the table, fresh from the oven.

1. Preheat oven to 350°. Butter a 9-inch square baking pan or a 10-inch diameter cast-iron skillet.

2. In a medium-sized bowl, combine all dry ingredients. It's not necessary to sift, but make sure that the sugar and the baking soda are well distributed.

3. Beat together buttermilk, egg, and melted butter. Make a well in the center of the dry ingredients, pour in the wet ingredients, and mix with a few quick strokes.

4. Pour the batter into the prepared pan and bake 25 to 30 minutes, or until a knife probing the center comes out clean.

SLICED FRESH FRUIT WITH SWEET AND HOT SEED DRESSING

PREPARATION TIME: 10 TO
15 MINUTES TO MAKE THE
DRESSING, 10 TO 20 MINUTES
TO ASSEMBLE THE FRUIT.

YIELD: 6 TO 8 SERVINGS.

3 tablespoons poppy seeds

3 tablespoons sunflower seeds

3 tablespoons sesame seeds

1 tablespoon mustard seeds

1 teaspoon cumin or fennel
seeds

a pinch of celery seed

$^2/_3$ cup pineapple juice

1 cup firm yogurt

2 tablespoons orange juice
concentrate

3 to 4 pounds assorted fresh
fruit (any combination; see
introduction above)

a few sprigs fresh mint and/or
watercress for garnish.

As an elegant alternative to fruit salad, try an arrangement of sliced fruit on a platter, garnished with sprigs of mint and watercress, and accompanied by a small pitcher of creamy dressing. Depending on your selection and the quantity, this platter can be a salad course for dinner or a main course for lunch.

The following dressing is unusual and substantial. It is full of ground seeds, with a hint of hotness, a suggestion of sweetness, and a modest amount of creaminess. This goes especially well with a composition of avocado, grapefruit, ripe papaya, and pear slices. Other winning combinations: peaches, cherries, and cantaloupe; mango, honeydew, strawberries, and kiwifruit. Or if it is the dead of winter and/or you don't have access to all these fancy designer fruits, try a platter of plain apple and banana slices. They will rise to the occasion.

The dressing is quick to make, and can be prepared up to a day ahead. The fruit should be sliced as close to serving time as possible.

1. Toast the seeds in a heavy skillet over low heat, stirring intermittently, until they give off a roasted aroma (up to 5 minutes).

2. Remove from the heat, and transfer the seeds to a blender. Grind to a coarse meal, using quick spurts. Transfer to a small bowl.

3. Whisk in all remaining ingredients except fruit and garnish. Mix well, cover, and refrigerate until serving time.

4. To serve, slice the fruit and arrange it artfully on a platter or on individual plates. Garnish exquisitely with sprigs of mint and/or watercress. Drizzle some dressing over the top, or pass it in a small pitcher, or both.

CHOCOLATE GINGER SNAPS

PREPARATION TIME: 30 MINUTES TO PREPARE, 12 TO BAKE.

YIELD: 3¹/₂ TO 4 DOZEN COOKIES.

¹/₂ cup (I stick) butter

I square (I ounce) unsweetened chocolate, melted

³/₄ cup granulated sugar

6 tablespoons brown sugar

3 tablespoons molasses

I egg

I teaspoon vanilla extract

2 cups unbleached white flour

³/₄ teaspoon baking soda

I¹/₂ to 2 teaspoons ground ginger

¹/₄ teaspoon salt

Some things, no matter how good, are just a little better with chocolate added.

1. Preheat oven to 350°. Grease a cookie sheet.

2. Cream the butter in a large mixing bowl. Drizzle in melted chocolate, and beat well. (Ideally, use an electric mixer at high speed.) Add sugars, molasses, and egg. Beat several more minutes. Stir in vanilla.

3. In a separate bowl, sift together flour, baking soda, ginger, and salt. Stir this into the first mixture. Mix thoroughly but briefly (just enough to combine). Do not beat.

4. Lightly flour your hands, and form 1-inch balls. Place them about 2 inches apart on the greased cookie sheet. Bake for 12 minutes at 350°. Cool on a rack.

The soup is fragrant and surprisingly mild. The salad is sweet, pungent, and sharp. Pad Thai is a spectacular peanut-flavored noodle dish, full of crunchy bean sprouts, soft tofu, and bits of egg. Make your own coconut ice cream by mashing together softened vanilla ice cream with lightly toasted unsweetened coconut. All the ingredients for this authentic Thai dinner can be found in American supermarkets.

THAI GARLIC SOUP
PAD THAI
THAI CUCUMBER SALAD
COCONUT ICE CREAM

3 DAYS AHEAD: cook noodles for Pad Thai; store in water in the refrigerator

2 DAYS AHEAD: cut vegetables for soup / make cucumber salad

I DAY AHEAD: make soup / for Pad Thai: cut scallions, garlic, and tofu; make sauce (step 2); cook egg (step 3)

SAME DAY: reheat soup / assemble and cook Pad Thai

THAI GARLIC SOUP

PREPARATION TIME: 45 MINUTES.

YIELD: 6 SERVINGS.

Don't be scared off by the amount of garlic in here! It mellows amazingly as it cooks. The result is a light and gentle first course that can either precede a dramatic entrée or be a soothing small meal all by itself.

4 to 5 tablespoons minced garlic

2 tablespoons peanut or canola oil

6 cups light stock or water

4 to 5 teaspoons soy sauce

1 scant teaspoon salt

3 cups coarsely shredded cabbage

2 medium-sized carrots, cut on the diagonal in 1-inch lengths

1 stalk celery, chopped (optional)

a few mushrooms, sliced (optional)

crushed red pepper, to taste (if you go lightly on this it lends an intriguing and subtle touch)

1. In a deep saucepan or Dutch oven, sauté the garlic in oil over medium heat until it starts to turn brown. (This will take only a few minutes.)

2. Add remaining ingredients, and bring to a boil. Lower the heat and simmer, covered, about 10 minutes, or until all the vegetables are tender.

3. Taste and adjust seasonings. Serve immediately or store for reheating later. (Unlike many other soups, this one is not delicate, and reheats readily.)

PAD THAI

PREPARATION TIME: 45 TO
50 MINUTES.

YIELD: 4 TO 6 SERVINGS.

6 ounces uncooked rice
  noodles (enough to make
  3 cups cooked)

5 tablespoons soy sauce

2 tablespoons peanut butter

1 tablespoon brown sugar

3 tablespoons peanut or
  canola oil

3 eggs, beaten

6 scallions, cut in 1-inch
  lengths (whites and greens)

1 pound fresh mung bean
  sprouts

3 medium-sized cloves garlic,
  minced

up to 1½ teaspoons crushed
  red pepper (to taste)

1 pound firm tofu, cut in
  small cubes

⅓ cup cider vinegar

1½ cups chopped toasted
  peanuts (use a toaster oven
  or a heavy skillet on the
  stove top)

wedges of lime (large enough
  to really squeeze)

Translation: Rice Noodles with Tofu and Eggs in Spicy Peanut Sauce. This is a very popular dish, served in many Thai restaurants. The traditional version calls for several imported exotic ingredients, and contains fish sauce and shrimp. The following adaptation is completely vegetarian, and uses only familiar, easily obtainable items.

Rice noodles are the only unusual ingredient in this recipe. They are sold in most Asian grocery stores, imported either from Thailand or China. If you can't find them, you can substitute plain vermicelli. You will need 3 cups cooked noodles, and they can be made a day or two ahead and stored in a container of water in the refrigerator. Drain well before using.

1. Cook the noodles 3 to 5 minutes in boiling water. Drain, rinse in cold running water, and drain thoroughly again. Set aside.

2. Combine the soy sauce, peanut butter, and brown sugar in a small bowl, and stir—or mash—until it becomes a uniform paste. Set aside.

3. Heat a wok or a large skillet. Add a tablespoon of oil, wait a minute, then add the beaten eggs. Cook, stirring, until the egg is dry. Remove the cooked egg and set aside.

4. Heat the wok (or skillet) again, allowing it to get quite hot. Add 2 tablespoons oil, scallions, bean sprouts, garlic, and red pepper. Stir-fry for a minute or so. Add tofu and stir-fry a few more minutes.

5. Add the cooked, drained noodles to the wok or skillet. (It may be useful to use a large fork in addition to the wok shovel at this point, as the stirring gets cumbersome.) Stir-fry, attempting to combine everything as uniformly as possible, about 5 more minutes.

6. Add the peanut butter paste (from step 2), along with the vinegar. Stir and cook several more minutes.

7. Stir in the cooked egg. Serve immediately, topped with peanuts and accompanied by generous wedges of lime.

THAI CUCUMBER SALAD

PREPARATION TIME: 10 MINUTES
TO PREPARE, AT LEAST
4 HOURS TO CHILL.

YIELD: 4 TO 6 SERVINGS.

2 medium-sized cucumbers

½ cup very finely minced red
onion

½ teaspoon salt

2 teaspoons sugar

¼ cup cider vinegar

¼ cup minced fresh cilantro

OPTIONAL:

½ cup finely minced red or
green bell pepper

1 small red serrano chile,
seeded and cut into very
thin strips, or crushed red
pepper, to taste

sprigs of cilantro

This is a simple dish with a cool, clean taste. You also have the option of spicing it up with a touch of hot chiles.

If you decide to add the serrano chile, be very careful handling it, as it is very hot. Wash your hands with soap and warm water *immediately* after contact to avoid severe irritation to your eyes or mouth.

NOTE 1: This salad contains no oil.

NOTE 2: Marinated cucumber salads improve with age, so I recommend that you make this a day or two ahead.

1. Peel and seed the cucumbers. Cut into quarters lengthwise, then into thin slices.

2. Combine everything except the serrano chile and cilantro sprigs in a medium-sized bowl. Mix gently. Cover tightly, and let marinate in the refrigerator at least 4 hours.

3. Serve cold. Top with thin strips of red serrano chile and sprigs of fresh cilantro, if desired, shortly before serving.

COCONUT ICE CREAM

PREPARATION TIME: 5 MINUTES

YIELD: 4 TO 6 SERVINGS.

1 pint vanilla ice cream or
frozen yogurt (softened)

1 cup (or more) lightly toasted
unsweetened shredded
coconut

1. Place the ice cream or yogurt in a large-enough bowl. Add the coconut and stir until well combined. Refreeze or eat right away.

2. That's it!

~

The flavors of Thailand and Java have much in common (peanuts and coconut; sweet, pungent, and hot seasonings; etc.) and in this menu they intermingle. Serve everything at the same time, with a cup of strong jasmine tea for a wonderfully exotic dinner.

TOFU AND SWEET POTATOES WITH SWEET AND PUNGENT PEANUT SAUCE
CARAMELIZED ONION CONDIMENT
JAVANESE VEGETABLE SALAD
RICE

3 DAYS AHEAD: make onion condiment / trim green beans for salad / cut sweet potatoes; store in water in the refrigerator

2 DAYS AHEAD: for the salad: make marinade; cook green beans and sprouts (steps 3 and 4); clean spinach / cook sweet potatoes and tofu; drain and store (steps 1 and 2)

1 DAY AHEAD: make peanut sauce; mince cilantro and store separately for the topping / cook spinach and assemble salad

SAME DAY: take out onion condiment to come to room temperature / make rice / sauté sweet potatoes and tofu / gently heat sauce

TOFU AND SWEET POTATOES WITH SWEET AND PUNGENT PEANUT SAUCE

PREPARATION TIME: 1 HOUR.

YIELD: 4 SERVINGS.

1/2 pound very firm tofu

2 medium-sized sweet potatoes or yams

1 1/2 cups peanuts, coarsely ground in a food processor or blender

4 tablespoons cider vinegar

3 tablespoons sugar or honey

grated rind of 1 lime

2 tablespoons fresh lime juice

1/2 to 1 teaspoon salt (to taste, depending on salt content of peanuts)

1/2 teaspoon crushed red pepper (more or less, to taste)

1/3 cup hot water

cornstarch for dredging

peanut oil for sautéeing

3 tablespoons minced fresh cilantro

Small cubes of tofu and sweet potato are cooked until lightly brown and crisp, and served with a lively, spicy peanut sauce for dipping.

Steps 1, 2, and 3 can all be done up to several days in advance. Store tofu, sweet potatoes, and sauce in separate airtight containers in the refrigerator. Reheat the sauce either in a microwave or very gently on the stove top. (The sauce does not have to be piping hot, as long as the tofu and sweet potato cubes are.)

About 45 minutes before serving time, put up 2 cups brown rice to cook in 3 cups water. Bring to a boil, cover, and lower heat to a very slow simmer. Cook undisturbed for about 35 minutes, or until tender.

1. Cut tofu into 1-inch cubes. Scrub or peel sweet potatoes, and cut them into slightly smaller than 1-inch cubes.

2. Fill a medium-sized saucepan with water and bring to a boil. Add tofu and boil for about 5 to 8 minutes. Remove with a slotted spoon. Then add sweet potato chunks and cook until just tender (about 8 to 10 minutes). Drain everything well, and set aside, keeping tofu and potatoes separate.

3. Combine peanuts, vinegar, sugar or honey, lime rind and juice, salt, red pepper, and water in a small saucepan, and cook uncovered over low heat for about 5 to 8 minutes. Set aside.

4. Place the cornstarch on a large plate, and lightly dredge the tofu and potatoes. Use a strainer to shake off any excess.

5. Heat a medium-large skillet, and add 2 tablespoons oil. Sauté the tofu chunks until lightly brown and crisp. Remove with a slotted spoon and place on paper towels to drain. Then cook the potato chunks in the same manner. After draining both tofu and potatoes on paper towels, arrange them next to each other in a serving bowl or on a platter.

6. Transfer the sauce to a small serving bowl and sprinkle the top with cilantro.

7. Serve the chunks with the dipping sauce, and Caramelized Onions (recipe follows) on the side as a heavenly condiment.

CARAMELIZED ONION CONDIMENT

PREPARATION TIME: 5 MINUTES TO PREPARE, 30 MINUTES TO COOK.

YIELD: ENOUGH FOR 5 AS A CONDIMENT. VERY EASILY MULTIPLIED.

1 medium-sized yellow onion

2 tablespoons peanut oil

1. Peel the onion, and cut it in half, then in very thin slices.

2. In a heavy skillet cook the onion slices in oil over low heat for 20 to 30 minutes, stirring occasionally.

3. When the onions are very, very well done, remove with a slotted spoon, and drain on paper towels to absorb excess oil. Place in an attractive small dish, and serve at room temperature.

JAVANESE VEGETABLE SALAD

PREPARATION TIME: 30 TO 40 MINUTES.

YIELD: 4 TO 6 SERVINGS, DEPENDING, AS MANY THINGS DO, ON WHAT ELSE IS SERVED.

6 tablespoons fresh lime juice

2 large cloves garlic, finely minced

1/2 teaspoon salt

2 tablespoons sugar or honey

1/2 teaspoon crushed red pepper (or to taste)

1 cup shredded unsweetened coconut, lightly toasted in a toaster oven or cast-iron skillet

2 teaspoons dried mint

1 to 2 teaspoons minced or grated fresh ginger

1 bunch fresh spinach (approximately 3/4 pound)

1/2 pound fresh green beans, trimmed

3/4 pound fresh mung bean sprouts

This dish features three quite modest vegetables (spinach, green beans, and mung bean sprouts), which become transformed by a marinade of garlic, lime, coconut, mint, and ginger into an exotic salad.

The marinade can be made and the green beans and sprouts cooked up to several days in advance. Store separately in airtight containers in the refrigerator. Complete and assemble the salad at least several hours before serving.

1. In a medium-large bowl combine lime juice, garlic, salt, sugar or honey, crushed red pepper, coconut, mint, and ginger. Stir until well blended. Set aside.

2. Place cleaned, stemmed whole spinach leaves in a heavy skillet and cook quickly over high heat without any additional liquid until wilted. Add immediately to the marinade.

3. Cook the green beans in boiling water for 5 minutes, or until just tender. Drain and refresh under cold running water. Drain again very thoroughly, and add to the marinade.

4. Drop the mung sprouts into boiling water and blanch for about 2 minutes. Drain well, and add to remaining ingredients.

5. Stir until everything is nicely combined. Cover and chill.

Here is another menu that blends two different Southeast Asian cuisines. The soup is Vietnamese and the other dishes are Thai. The flavor combinations—and the juxtaposition of ingredients—are unusual and exciting, even though at first glance they might rattle Western sensibilities. My own range of cooking has expanded dramatically since being exposed to these Southeast Asian cooking styles. I think the same will be true for you.

SWEET AND SOUR SOUP
WITH PINEAPPLE AND BASIL
SPINACH ROLL-UPS WITH LIME CHUTNEY
EGGPLANT WITH GARLIC,
MINT, AND CHILES
RICE

3 DAYS AHEAD: make chutney

2 DAYS AHEAD: make soup, leaving out basil and bean sprouts

I DAY AHEAD: clean spinach, and get all the little doo-dads ready for the roll-ups (step 2) / for the eggplant: slice eggplant, mince garlic and mint, cut chiles

SAME DAY: cook rice / cook eggplant / heat soup; add basil and bean sprouts / assemble roll-ups

SWEET AND SOUR SOUP WITH PINEAPPLE AND BASIL

PREPARATION TIME: 30 MINUTES.

YIELD: 4 TO 6 SERVINGS.

3 medium-sized fresh ripe
   tomatoes

1¹/₂ tablespoons peanut or
   canola oil

1 cup coarsely chopped onion

2 tablespoons minced garlic

2 stalks celery, thinly sliced on
   the diagonal

1 teaspoon salt

4 cups water

1 20-ounce can pineapple
   chunks (packed in juice)

the equivalent of 20 to 25
   large leaves of fresh basil,
   coarsely chopped

approximately ¹/₃ pound fresh
   mung bean sprouts

This lively soup abounds with contrasts in flavor and texture: juicy, soft pineapple chunks, crunchy celery slices, barely cooked mung bean sprouts, tart fresh tomato, pungent basil leaves, a generous amount of fried garlic, and more.

The whole soup can be made, short of adding the basil and bean sprouts, several days in advance.

NOTE: Frozen or dried basil leaves will also work in this recipe, although the result will be less intense.

1. Bring a saucepan of water to a boil. Core the tomatoes and add to the boiling water for a slow count of 10. Remove from the saucepan and rinse under cold running water. As you rinse them, gently pull off the skins. Chop the peeled tomatoes into 1-inch chunks and set aside.

2. Heat the oil in a Dutch oven or large saucepan. Add onion, garlic, celery, and salt, and sauté over medium heat for about 5 minutes.

3. Add water and bring to a boil. Lower the heat, cover, and simmer for about 5 minutes.

4. Add pineapple chunks with all their juice, and the chopped tomatoes. Cover again, and simmer about 15 more minutes.

5. Just before serving, add basil and bean sprouts to the hot soup. Simmer, covered, for just a few minutes, then serve.

SPINACH ROLL-UPS
WITH LIME CHUTNEY

PREPARATION TIME: 20 TO
30 MINUTES.

YIELD: ABOUT 4 SERVINGS
(POSSIBLY MORE, DEPENDING
ON HOW MANY EACH
PERSON EATS).

*1/2 pound fresh spinach
(the most attractive and
intact leaves possible)*

1/4 onion, cut into 1/4-inch dice

*1/2 lime, cut into 1/4-inch pieces
(include rind, but discard
any seeds)*

*a 1-inch piece of ginger, cut
into 1/8-inch-thick slices*

*3 to 4 tablespoons shredded
unsweetened coconut*

*3 to 4 tablespoons whole
peanuts (preferably roasted,
unsalted)*

*1 batch Lime Chutney
(recipe follows)*

PREPARATION TIME: 10 MINUTES.

YIELD: A GENEROUS CUP,
AT LEAST.

*1 small lime, seeded and cut
into eighths*

*1 tablespoon coarsely chopped
fresh ginger*

1/2 cup chopped onion

*1/3 cup (packed) brown sugar
or honey*

*1/2 cup peanuts (preferably
roasted, unsalted)*

*1/4 cup shredded unsweetened
coconut*

Crisp spinach leaves cradle a mixture of toasted coconut, peanuts, and tiny chunks of fresh ginger, lime, and onion. Top each unit with a little lime chutney (sublime!), roll it up, and, as the waitress in my favorite Thai restaurant says, "The secret is: one bite!"

This might be the world's most exotic and exciting appetizer yet. In Thailand it is a ubiquitous snack food called *Miang Kum*, and contains tiny dried shrimp and fish paste. This is my vegetarian adaptation that can be made entirely with familiar ingredients, available in ordinary U.S. supermarkets.

The chutney can be made days ahead. The spinach should be very crisp and fresh. You can clean and prepare it a day ahead if it is kept very dry and airtight in the refrigerator. The bits of onion, lime, and ginger can be cut a day ahead. Wrap them separately in airtight containers (or in plastic wrap) and refrigerate.

1. Remove and discard spinach stems. Clean the leaves well and spin dry. Wrap snugly in paper towels and refrigerate until use.

2. Prepare onion, lime, and ginger as described above. Place each item in a small individual dish, cover, and refrigerate until serving time.

3. Just before serving, arrange the spinach leaves on a large plate or a platter. Place 1 piece each of onion, lime, and ginger on the lower center of each leaf. Add a pinch of coconut and 1 or 2 peanuts. Place the chutney in a small bowl, with a small spoon, at the center of the platter.

4. To eat, place a delicate mound of chutney on top of the little pile of stuff in the center of the leaf. Roll it up, tucking in the sides, and, if possible, pop it into your mouth all at once. You will be amazed at how wonderful this is!

LIME CHUTNEY

1. Combine all ingredients in a blender or a food processor fitted with the steel blade. Process until it acquires the consistency of a thick sauce (it need not be perfectly smooth).

2. Cover and refrigerate until serving time.

EGGPLANT WITH GARLIC, MINT, AND CHILES

PREPARATION TIME: 40 TO 45 MINUTES.

YIELD: 4 SERVINGS.

2 tablespoons peanut or canola oil

4 large cloves garlic, minced (approximately 1 heaping tablespoon)

2 red serrano chiles, cut in thin strips or rounds (with all, some, or none of the seeds—see above note)

1 1/2 pounds eggplant, cut in 1/8-inch-thick slices (if using a large eggplant, cut in quarters lengthwise, then slice thin)

1/2 teaspoon salt

3 tablespoons mirin (Japanese cooking sake) or sherry

2 tablespoons brown sugar or honey

1 tablespoon soy sauce

1 tablespoon fresh lime juice

2 tablespoons water

1/4 cup fresh mint leaves, coarsely chopped (if using dried, use less)

extra mint and minced cilantro for the top (optional)

Garlic, mint, and chile are frequent companions in Thai cooking. Eggplant, with its unique capacity to absorb strong flavors and become meltingly tender, is an ideal meeting ground for this trio.

I like to use the small, slim Japanese eggplants for this dish. They slice beautifully into neat little rounds. But if this type of eggplant is unavailable to you, go ahead and use the regular size. It will work just fine.

About the serrano chiles: These small and brightly colored chiles are extremely hot. Most of the heat is concentrated in the seeds. Depending upon your tolerance, you may choose to seed (or partially seed) the chiles before slicing them. In any case, wash your hands with soap and warm water immediately after handling the chiles—especially before touching your face or eyes. If you don't have access to fresh chiles, you can use crushed red pepper to taste.

About 45 minutes before serving time, put up 2 cups brown rice to cook in 3 cups water. Bring to a boil, cover, and lower heat to a very slow simmer. Cook undisturbed for about 35 minutes, or until tender.

1. Heat the oil in a large, heavy skillet or Dutch oven, and cook the garlic and chiles over medium heat for 1 or 2 minutes.

2. Add eggplant and salt. Cook and stir for about 5 minutes.

3. Add mirin or sherry, cover, and cook for 5 minutes more.

4. Combine sugar or honey, soy sauce, lime juice, and water. Add this mixture to the eggplant, cover again, and let cook over medium heat another 10 to 15 minutes, stirring occasionally.

5. When the eggplant is very tender, add 1/4 cup chopped mint, stir, lower the heat, and let simmer just a few more minutes.

6. Serve over rice, topped with a light sprinkling of mint and cilantro, if desired.

With Indonesian cuisine, rice (usually yellow) is the centerpiece, and everything else is served over or around it. In designing an Indonesian menu, it is especially fun to pair relatively extreme tastes: hot with creamy, sweet with tart. The rice serves to mediate and harmonize, and the result is stimulating and deeply satisfying.

CABBAGE SALAD WITH PEANUTS
COCONUT CREAMED VEGETABLES
YELLOW RICE
PECELI (SPICY PINEAPPLE RELISH)
FRIED BANANAS

3 DAYS AHEAD: make Peceli / make batter for Fried Bananas

2 DAYS AHEAD: cut cabbage for salad (store in plastic bag in refrigerator) / for creamed vegetables: cut garlic, ginger, onions, green beans, and broccoli (refrigerate in separate airtight containers)

1 DAY AHEAD: make cabbage salad (leave out peanuts) / for creamed vegetables: prepare coconut milk, peel and chop tomatoes

SAME DAY: make rice / assemble Coconut Creamed Vegetables / add peanuts to cabbage salad just before serving / assemble and sauté Fried Bananas (do this after the meal)

CABBAGE SALAD WITH PEANUTS

PREPARATION TIME: 20 MINUTES,
PLUS AT LEAST 4 HOURS TO
CHILL.

YIELD: 4 TO 6 SERVINGS.

¹/₄ cup peanut butter

¹/₂ cup hot water

*¹/₂ cup plus 1 tablespoon rice
vinegar or cider vinegar*

*3 tablespoons brown sugar
or honey*

1¹/₂ teaspoons salt

1 tablespoon soy sauce

1 teaspoon Chinese sesame oil

*7 to 8 cups shredded green
cabbage (1 small head)*

crushed red pepper, to taste

GARNISHES:
¹/₂ cup peanuts
grated carrots
minced fresh cilantro

Sweet and sour—and slightly creamy from the peanut butter—this is a nice way to eat cabbage. The salad benefits from sitting around for 12 to 24 hours, so feel encouraged to make it up to a day ahead. Just hold off on adding the peanuts until the very last minute. Their crunch is a large part of this salad's charm, and they lose it if they sit too long in the marinade.

1. In a large bowl, mash together the peanut butter and hot water until they form a uniform mixture.

2. Mix in vinegar, sugar or honey, salt, soy sauce, and sesame oil.

3. Add the cabbage in 2-cup increments, mixing well after each addition. Add red pepper to taste.

4. Cover the bowl tightly, and refrigerate for at least 4 hours (but preferably 12 to 24), visiting it every hour or two to give it a good stir.

5. Sprinkle the peanuts on top right before serving. Serve with a slotted spoon.

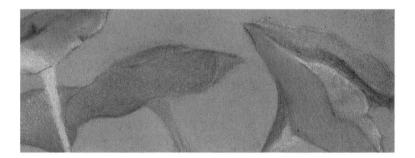

COCONUT CREAMED VEGETABLES

PREPARATION TIME: 1 HOUR.

YIELD: 4 SERVINGS.

2 cups grated unsweetened coconut

2 cups milk (lowfat or soy okay)

2 medium-sized fresh ripe tomatoes

2 medium-sized cloves garlic, minced

1 to 2 tablespoons minced fresh ginger

2 cups chopped onion

1 tablespoon peanut or canola oil

1 1/2 teaspoons salt

1/2 teaspoon turmeric

1 2-inch piece bruised lemon grass (or 1 teaspoon dried, crumbled)

1 teaspoon chile powder

1/2 pound firm tofu, diced

crushed red pepper, to taste

1/2 pound fresh green beans, trimmed and cut in 1 1/2-inch lengths

1/4 to 1/2 cup water, as needed

3 to 4 cups (approximately 1/2 pound) chopped broccoli

Ordinary vegetables (green beans, broccoli, tomatoes) become extraordinary in a richly flavored, creamy yellow sauce that combines coconut, ginger, garlic, onion, lemon grass, and chile.

The one exotic ingredient in this dish is lemon grass, which is a hard, aromatic grass used in most Southeast Asian cuisines. Usually the lower section of the stalk is bruised and added in 1- to 2-inch pieces to soups and sauces. (Like bay leaves, lemon grass is virtually inedible in its hard form, and should be either fished out or eaten around.) Lemon grass is also available in powdered form, although it is less potent when ground. Look for either form in Asian groceries. If you can't find it, use lemon grass tea right out of a teabag. This form is available wherever herb teas are sold.

The coconut-milk mixture can sit up to 24 hours. The longer it steeps, the more the milk becomes infused with the coconut flavor. The tomatoes can be peeled and seeded in advance, and the vegetables, garlic, and ginger can be prepared ahead as well. Just make sure everything is tightly wrapped and refrigerated.

About 45 minutes before serving time, put up 2 cups of white or brown rice to cook in 3 cups water with 1/2 teaspoon turmeric. Bring to a boil, cover, and simmer until tender (20 minutes for white; 35 to 45 for brown).

1. In a toaster oven, or in a heavy skillet on the stove top, lightly toast 1 cup of the coconut and set aside. Place the other cup of coconut in a saucepan with the milk. Heat slowly until it almost reaches the boiling point. Remove from heat just before it boils, and allow to cool to room temperature. Purée in a blender, then strain, reserving the milk. Discard the coconut after pressing out all the liquid.

2. Heat a small saucepan of water to boiling. Core the tomatoes and drop them into the boiling water for a slow count of 10. Remove and peel under cold running water. Cut the tomatoes open and squeeze out and discard the seeds. Then chop the tomatoes into cubes and set aside.

3. In a deep skillet or Dutch oven, sauté garlic, ginger, and onion in oil with salt. Add turmeric, lemon grass, chile powder, tofu, and crushed red pepper to taste. Sauté over medium heat for about 5 minutes.

4. Stir in the green beans and $^1/_4$ cup water. Cover and cook 5 to 8 minutes, stirring occasionally. If it seems dry, add another $^1/_4$ cup water.

5. Add the chopped broccoli, tomatoes, and coconut milk; mix well and cover. Continue to cook over medium heat, stirring now and then, for 5 minutes, or until the broccoli and green beans are bright green and just tender.

6. Serve in bowls, alongside plates of yellow rice. Top the rice with the reserved toasted coconut (from step 1).

PECELI (SPICY PINEAPPLE RELISH)

PREPARATION TIME: 15 MINUTES TO PREPARE, 20 TO 30 MINUTES TO COOK.

YIELD: ABOUT 2$^1/_2$ CUPS.

3 cups fresh, ripe pineapple chunks

1 cup water or fruit juice (orange, apple, pineapple)

$^1/_4$ teaspoon salt

freshly ground black pepper

$^1/_2$ teaspoon ground cumin

$^1/_2$ teaspoon ground coriander

$^1/_2$ teaspoon ground cloves

$^1/_2$ teaspoon cinnamon

$^1/_2$ teaspoon crushed red pepper (or less, to taste)

$^1/_4$ teaspoon nutmeg

2 tablespoons brown sugar or honey

2 tablespoons fresh lemon juice

$^1/_2$ cup finely minced onion

Chutney, Indonesian style. Cutting the pineapple is 90 percent of the work.

This keeps for weeks if stored in an airtight container in the refrigerator.

Serve as a condiment to Coconut Creamed Vegetables, with plain or fried rice, or as an accompaniment to Steamed Vegetables with Miso-Almond Sauce (page 170-171).

1. Combine everything in a heavy saucepan. Bring to a boil. Reduce heat to moderate. Cook 20 to 30 minutes uncovered, or until reduced to a chutneylike thickness.

2. Cool and refrigerate until use.

FRIED BANANAS

PREPARATION TIME: 15 TO 20 MINUTES.

YIELD: 4 TO 6 SERVINGS.

2 eggs

1 tablespoon canola or vegetable oil

2 tablespoons milk (lowfat or soy okay)

1 cup unbleached white flour

¼ teaspoon salt

2 medium-sized or 3 small bananas (firm and not too ripe)

2 to 3 tablespoons butter or additional oil for frying

confectioners' sugar, for dusting (optional)

Chunks of banana are served hot, coated in tender, flaky batter. The bananas cook just enough to acquire a buttery—but not mushy—texture.

The batter keeps well for at least several days, as long as it is wrapped well and refrigerated. Once the batter is put together, the remaining preparation time is brief.

1. Beat together eggs, 1 tablespoon oil, and milk.

2. In a medium-sized bowl, combine flour and salt. Make a well in the center, and pour in the wet mixture. Stir with a few swift strokes until well blended. (Don't overmix.)

3. Peel the bananas. You may leave them whole or cut them in half widthwise.

4. Begin heating a medium-sized skillet over medium-low heat. Add 2 to 3 tablespoons butter or oil.

5. Meanwhile, place the bananas in the batter, and use a large spoon to gently roll them around until they are generously coated.

6. When the melted butter or oil is hot enough to sizzle a fleck of batter on contact, use a spoon to lift the bananas out of the bowl of batter, and gently place them in the hot pan. (Spoon on extra batter as needed to cover up any bald spots.) Fry the bananas over medium heat, turning frequently to make sure all surfaces get lightly brown. This will take about 5 to 8 minutes, perhaps a little longer, depending on the size of the bananas and the thickness of the coating layer. Remove, and blot on paper towels. Transfer to individual serving plates, and dust with confectioners' sugar, if desired. Serve immediately.

MISO-ALMOND SAUCE
STEAMED FRESH VEGETABLES AND TOFU
WITH SOBA NOODLES

People assume that we eat fancy meals all the time at our house. After all, I write cookbooks. But to tell you the truth, what we mostly eat is this: Steamed Fresh Vegetables and Tofu with Soba Noodles and Miso-Almond Sauce, usually with toasted nuts sprinkled on top. And not only do we never get tired of it, we get excited about it each time (and sometimes that means getting excited three times a week). It just feels so good to eat this simple, wholesome food. And if the vegetables are steamed just right, so that they are bright and vital and slightly crunchy, this kind of eating never becomes dull.

You can vary the vegetables according to what is in season. Softer vegetables (summer squash, peppers, leafy greens) cook more quickly than harder ones (carrots, cauliflower, broccoli, etc.), and thick cuts of vegetable cook more slowly than thin. Keep this in mind when steaming, and put softer, more thinly cut vegetables in later than harder, thicker pieces. This way, nothing will be overcooked or undercooked.

Soba noodles are available at natural food stores and Japanese grocery stores. There are also many other types of whole-grain noodles available, and you can experiment with different kinds. Try *udon* noodles, made from brown rice, or *somen* noodles, made from whole wheat. (Of course, you can also serve steamed vegetables with any kind of grains, plain or fancy.)

Vegetables for steaming can be cut the night before and stored in plastic bags in the refrigerator. Then you can come home from work, put the noodle and steaming waters up to boil, pop in the vegetables and noodles, whip up the sauce, and voilá! Instant good food!

MISO-ALMOND SAUCE

PREPARATION TIME: 5 MINUTES.

YIELD: ABOUT 2 CUPS (ENOUGH TO AMPLY COVER 4 SERVINGS OF STEAMED VEGETABLES AND NOODLES).

4 tablespoons yellow, Hatcho, or barley miso
6 tablespoons almond butter
1 1/2 cup boiling water

This is a very simple sauce containing no dairy products and requiring no cooking.

Miso is a strongly flavored fermented paste made from soybeans and grains. You can find many varieties of it in Japanese grocery stores and natural food stores. Experiment with different types (made from different grains and aged to varying degrees) to discover your own preferences.

You can alter this recipe in several ways. Try using different kinds of nut butters, or several in combination. (My current favorite is a combination of almond butter and toasted sesame tahini.) Try substituting apple juice for the water. Spice it up by adding small amounts of garlic and/or freshly grated ginger. But try it plain before you begin your variations. It's reassuring to know that something so simple can be so good.

This sauce keeps for at least a week, so make it as far ahead of time as you need to for your convenience. If you're using it straight from the refrigerator, heat it gently either on the stove or in a microwave, but be careful not to cook it.

1. Place the miso and almond butter in a medium-sized bowl.

2. Add a small amount of hot water (about 1/2 cup) and mash with a spoon until it becomes a uniform paste.

3. Add the remaining water, and mix until well combined.

4. Serve warm or at room temperature over hot steamed vegetables and tofu, or mixed into hot soba noodles (or both!).

STEAMED FRESH VEGETABLES AND TOFU WITH SOBA NOODLES

PREPARATION TIME: ABOUT 30 MINUTES (ASSUMING MISO-ALMOND SAUCE IS ALREADY MADE).

YIELD: 4 SERVINGS.

1 large bunch broccoli (approximately 1 1/2 pounds)

2 large carrots

1 medium-sized red or yellow onion

1 small head cauliflower

12 to 15 large mushrooms

about 3/4 pound firm tofu

8 ounces uncooked soba noodles

Miso-Almond Sauce (preceding recipe)

toasted cashew pieces or chopped almonds for the top (optional)

1. Fill a medium-large saucepan with water, and put it up to boil.

2. Arrange a vegetable steamer over water in another saucepan, and put this up to boil also.

3. Cut off 3 inches from the base of the broccoli stalks and discard. Shave off the tough outer skin from the remainder of the stalks, and cut the broccoli into approximately 2-inch spears. Set aside.

4. Peel or scrub the carrots, and cut into diagonal slices about 1/4 inch thick. Set aside.

5. Cut the onion into 1-inch chunks, and break the cauliflower into 1-inch florets. Set aside in separate bowls.

6. Clean the mushrooms and trim off the bottoms of the stems. Quarter the mushrooms and set aside.

7. Cut the tofu into 1-inch cubes.

8. Arrange the vegetables in the steamer (over the water, which should be boiling by now), and cover. Begin cooking over medium heat.

9. About 3 to 4 minutes later, add the soba noodles to the boiling water in the first saucepan (step 1), partially cover, and turn heat to medium.

10. The vegetables and the soba noodles should be done at about the same time (6 to 8 minutes after the noodles hit the water). Drain the noodles in a colander over the sink, and transfer to a bowl. Add about 1/2 cup Miso-Almond Sauce and mix well. Remove the vegetables from the steamer, either by lifting the entire basketful out from the saucepan or by picking the vegetables out with tongs.

11. Serve the vegetables on top of the lightly sauced noodles. Ladle additional sauce all over the vegetables, and top with toasted nuts if desired.

VEGETARIAN BARBECUE

RICOTTA-SPINACH DIP WITH CHIPS

CHILE MAYONNAISE, GARLIC OIL, GARLIC-BASIL OIL

GRILLED DELICACIES:

POLENTA / MARINATED TOFU AND MUSHROOMS / EGGPLANT AND ZUCCHINI OR YELLOW SUMMER SQUASH / PEPPERS / POTATOES AND / OR SWEET POTATOES / ONIONS / MEXICAN-STYLE CORN

SOME OTHER FOODS TO CONSIDER GRILLING:

BREAD, ARTICHOKES, PEARS, BANANAS, PINEAPPLE, PEACHES

It's hard to be a non-meat-eater at a barbecue. Everyone else is running around smacking their lips, busily fussing over their steaks, hamburgers, or chicken wings, and you are sitting in the corner next to the dips and salads, trying to look enthusiastic and feeling like something is missing.

But not any more!

With the following recipes even the most devout vegetarian can enter the domain of barbecuephilia as a full participant. Many kinds of vegetables lend themselves exquisitely to grilling, and meat lovers will also want to make room on their plates for marinated charcoal-grilled eggplant, peppers, tofu, summer squash, corn, sweet potatoes, etc. I tested these recipes alongside some barbecued chicken. People ate the vegetarian part of the meal first (it gets done a *lot* sooner), and everyone was so full and satisfied with the mixed vegetarian grill that most of the chicken went untouched.

Here is a description of the Vegetarian Barbecue:

Begin heating the coals. In the meantime, serve Ricotta-Spinach Dip with chips and perhaps a few crisp vegetables. (Emphasize vegetables that won't be on the grill, to avoid duplication. Choose from jicama, carrots, celery, radishes, and maybe some very lightly steamed, chilled broccoli spears.)

When the coals are glowing and white ash has formed, place the corn, potatoes, and sweet potatoes right down in there, around the edges of the coals. Everything else gets cooked on top of the grill. (Actually, so can the corn and both kinds of potatoes. I've done it both ways with equal success.) As each vegetable or piece of tofu or polenta is cooked, it can be taken off the grill and eaten right away. Or everything can be piled onto a couple of platters and served all at once. Grilled vegetarian food tastes good at just about any temperature! In fact, you may wish to cook extra of everything so you'll have leftovers for snacks, lunches, pizza toppings, pasta sauces, etc.

While you are enjoying your dinner, put some slices of fresh fruit on the grill to cook slowly over the coals. Recommended: pears, bananas, and pineapple. If the season is right, also try firm ripe peach halves.

You will be impressed by how much fun this event is, and by how satisfied everyone will feel afterward. One need never be a wallflower at a barbecue again!

The following guidelines should help you coordinate your Vegetarian Barbecue, enabling you to enjoy yourself throughout the process, and sparing any last-minute panic. The amounts suggested should feed at least six people, and can easily be adjusted to accommodate a larger or smaller gathering.

↭ Ricotta-Spinach Dip and its accompaniments (chips and optional vegetables) should be prepared by the very beginning of the event, so they can be available for a first course while the coals are heating.

↭ All the sauces (Chile Mayonnaise, Garlic Oil, and Garlic-Basil Oil) should be made ahead.

↭ The polenta should be made well in advance, so it can solidify before being cut into wedges and grilled.

↭ The tofu and mushrooms should be marinated for at least 12 (and preferably 24) hours before grilling.

↭ Larger potatoes and sweet potatoes need to be parboiled until tender before grilling. (Smaller ones can cook right on the grill.)

↭ The corn should be prepared for grilling, and lime wedges cut and ready.

↭ Oil the grill well while it is still cold. If you forget to oil it, the outermost, crispiest, most interesting and delicious part of whatever will get left behind when you lift the morsel off the grill. This is especially disappointing with chunks of tofu and wedges of polenta, not normally known for their textural personalities. Acquiring those telltale black barbecue marks, along with a fantastically crispened exterior, is one of the high points of their career, and gives them a whole new status in the world. Don't let them—or yourself—down by forgetting to oil the grill. An alternative is to use a nonstick grilling surface, which you can buy at good kitchenware stores.

↭ Light the fire a good 20 to 30 minutes before you intend to start cooking. You're going to need an evenly hot set of coals, red and glowing and with a white ash beginning to form. This takes a little bit of time. The Ricotta-Spinach Dip helps it to go faster.

↭ Be sure you have proper equipment—most importantly a set of grilling tongs with an extra-long handle and a flexible heatproof mitt. A long-handled fork comes in handy as well.

RICOTTA-SPINACH DIP WITH CHIPS

PREPARATION TIME: 15 TO
20 MINUTES.

YIELD: A LITTLE OVER 2 CUPS.

1 bunch fresh spinach
(approximately ³/₄ pound)

1 pound ricotta cheese

3 to 4 scallions, very finely
minced, or a handful of
minced fresh chives

5 to 6 healthy radishes, finely
minced

salt and freshly ground black
pepper, to taste

1 to 2 tablespoons fresh dill,
minced (optional)

¹/₂ cup finely minced water
chestnuts (optional)

OPTIONAL GARNISHES:
fresh parsley, olives, and/or
cherry tomatoes

This tastes just as rich and creamy as if it were made with cream cheese or sour cream. But since ricotta is much lower in fat and higher in protein than both cream cheese and sour cream, this dip can be extravagant and serious at the same time.

Scoop it up with any combination of steamed and raw vegetables, or just serve it with chips. If you have any left over, use it to fill sandwiches or omelettes, or as a baked potato topping.

This dip can be made up to one day in advance.

1. Stem the spinach, and clean it thoroughly in several changes of cold water. Dry completely using a salad spinner followed by paper towels, and mince fine. (A few whirls in the food processor with the steel blade attachment accomplishes this perfectly.)

2. Place the ricotta in a medium-large bowl. Use a wire whisk or a wooden spoon to beat it until quite smooth.

3. Stir in the spinach and all other ingredients, except garnishes, including (or not) the optional dill and minced water chestnuts. Cover tightly, and chill until very cold.

4. Garnish or not as you wish, and serve with chips, raw vegetables, or good crackers.

CHILE MAYONNAISE

*I cup mayonnaise, commercial
or homemade (page 68)*

2 tablespoons chile powder

1. Combine in a small bowl, and beat until uniform with a small whisk.

2. Cover tightly and refrigerate until use. (It will be an amazing color!)

NOTE: If you have any left over, spread it on bread before making cheese sandwiches, or use it for artichoke dipping.

GARLIC OIL

½ cup olive oil

*3 to 4 large cloves garlic,
minced*

1. Combine the oil and garlic in a small saucepan. Heat gently until very hot (3 to 4 minutes over medium heat).

2. Remove from heat, and brush onto polenta wedges, sweet potatoes, and bell peppers while the oil is still hot (or at least still warm).

NOTE: Leftover Garlic Oil can be spread onto thin baguette slices before baking them to make croutons. It can also be used in salad dressing.

GARLIC-BASIL OIL

Same as above, but with a handful or two of minced fresh basil leaves added.

GRILLED DELICACIES

POLENTA

PREPARATION TIME: 10 MINUTES, PLUS SEVERAL HOURS TO SIT AND SOLIDIFY.

YIELD: SERVES 8.

4 cups water

2 cups coarse cornmeal

1 teaspoon salt

Garlic Oil or Garlic-Basil Oil
  (preceding recipes)

This is an extra-thick polenta, suitable for cutting into solid wedges that will hold together on the grill.

1. Place the water in a medium-sized saucepan and bring to a boil.

2. Slowly sprinkle in the cornmeal and salt as the water boils rapidly.

3. Whisk and cook over medium heat for 5 minutes, or until very thick.

4. Divide the polenta between two standard-sized dinner plates and spread each mound into a circle about ³/4 inch thick.

5. Chill until solid (at least several hours). Cut into wedges, brush both sides of each piece liberally with the seasoned oil, and place over indirect heat (glowing or white ash-covered coals). Grill more slowly and for a longer time than the vegetables (about 8 minutes or more on each side), so it heats through and becomes crispy on the outside. (You may wish to finish it off over a hotter area of coals to make sure the outside gets crisp enough.) As an extra precaution against possible sticking, brush each wedge of polenta with a little extra Garlic Oil or Garlic-Basil Oil before turning or moving it.

MARINATED TOFU AND/OR MUSHROOMS

6 tablespoons cider or rice vinegar

3 tablespoons soy sauce

3 tablespoons molasses

5 to 6 medium cloves garlic, minced

salt and black pepper to taste

NOTE 1: This delicious marinade is oil-free.

NOTE 2: The recipe makes enough for 1½ pounds firm tofu or for about 2 to 3 medium portobello mushrooms, or about a pound of large, fresh domestic mushrooms. If you want to grill all three, just double the marinade recipe.

NOTE 3: Make sure the grill is well oiled, unless it's nonstick.

1. Combine all marinade ingredients in a 9 x 13-inch glass pan or its equivalent.

2. Cut the tofu into pieces about ³/₄-inch thick and 2½ inches square. (Portobello mushrooms can be left whole. Domestic mushrooms should have the stems removed.)

3. Place the tofu and/or mushrooms in the marinade, cover, and refrigerate 12 to 14 hours. For the first few hours, turn the tofu and/or mushrooms every 30 minutes or so to maximize exposure to the marinade.

4. GRILLING THE TOFU: Cook over red-hot coals for about 5 to 8 minutes on each side, depending on the thickness of the tofu and the intensity of the heat. Ideally, the tofu should end up dark and crisp, and decorated with black stripes.

GRILLING THE MUSHROOMS: This is a little more subjective than the tofu. Cook the portobellos until they are heated all the way through and *seem* done to *you*. The same holds for their smaller domestic cousins—just be sure you don't cook these too long, or they'll shrink and possibly disappear.

EGGPLANT AND ZUCCHINI OR YELLOW SUMMER SQUASH

Use smaller whole ones, or cut larger ones into slices (at least ½ inch thick) or chunks large enough to not fall into the coals. Brush liberally with Garlic Oil or Garlic-Basil Oil, and grill.

To grill, place the slices high over hot coals, away from extreme direct heat and avoiding any flare-up areas. Move the slices around on the grill if necessary to avoid scorching. Depending on the thickness of the slices, the eggplant should need about 5 minutes on each side and the squash slightly less.

PEPPERS

Stem and seed the peppers and cut them into quarters lengthwise. Brush all surfaces liberally with the seasoned oil. Grill over the hottest part of the fire (a flame is okay, and charring is not only okay but preferable) until the skin is all puckered. If you choose to peel the peppers, the skins will come off easily. (They can also be left on.)

NOTE: Grilled peppers are so delicious and so easy to peel, you might want to throw on some extra if you have room. Peel them and marinate for salads (such as Roasted Red Peppers with Garlic and Lime, page 35), soups (Cream of Red Pepper, page 12), pasta sauces (page 206), etc.

POTATOES AND/OR SWEET POTATOES

Smaller ones (2-inch diameter or less) can be wrapped in foil and cooked in the coals. Poke with a fork to determine when they're done. Larger ones should be parboiled first until just tender, then wrapped in foil and finished in the coals. Sweet potatoes cooked this way taste divine with a little bit of fresh lime juice squeezed on top.

ONIONS

Peel red or yellow onions and slice them lengthwise into quarters or sixths. Grill them over a hot spot—flame is okay. The outside layer will char. Remove it before eating. The inside will be perfect.

MEXICAN-STYLE CORN

1 ear of corn per person

squeezable-sized wedges of lime

Chile Mayonnaise (page 176) (optional)

1. Peel back the husks and remove all the cornsilk. Close the husks back up and wrap the ears of corn tightly in foil.

2. Cook over or in very hot coals until done to your liking. Depending on the intensity of the heat and the distance between the heat and the corn, this can take anywhere from 10 to 20 minutes.

3. Remove the foil and husks, and squeeze fresh lime juice all over the corn. Spread lavishly with Chile Mayonnaise if desired, and it is ready to eat.

SOME OTHER FOODS TO CONSIDER GRILLING

BREAD: Prepare one thick slice of Italian bread or baguette per person. Brush the open surfaces with Garlic Oil or Garlic-Basil Oil, and grill over medium-hot coals until toasted, watching carefully to make sure it doesn't burn.

ARTICHOKES: Precook them until tender (see page 67 if you need instructions). Then cut them lengthwise into halves, and brush all open surfaces with Garlic Oil. Grill over moderate heat. A real treat!

FRUIT

These all taste wonderful served with fresh lemon or lime juice sprinkled on top.

PEARS: Choose firm ripe pears. Bosc work very well for grilling—they stay the firmest during cooking. Core the pears and cut into quarters (peeling is not necessary unless the peel is unappealing to begin with), and grill over moderate heat for about 10 minutes.

BANANAS: Choose firm, ripe ones. Peel and cut them in half or leave them whole. If they are soft to begin with, they will get doubly soft during cooking, and they might turn to mush, or worse yet, slide off the grill and into the coals, never to be heard from again. Cook the bananas over moderate heat, turning frequently, for 5 to 10 minutes.

PINEAPPLE: Peel and cut into round slices $1/2$ inch thick, or into wedges. Grill over fairly hot coals for 5 to 10 minutes on each side.

PEACHES: Peel and cut in half. As with bananas, be sure the peaches are not too ripe (but they should be ripe enough to taste good!), and be sure, also, that they are not too small or they will fall into the coals. Grill over moderate heat 5 to 8 minutes on each side.

VEGETARIAN THANKSGIVING

PESTO AND PEPPERCORN TORTA

RAW VEGETABLES AND CRACKERS

CRANBERRY RELISH-SALAD
(WITH ORANGES, APPLES, AND SUNCHOKES)

CORN BREAD-STUFFED CABBAGE
WITH MUSHROOM-BRANDY SAUCE

SWEET POTATO SURPRISE

WILTED SPINACH SALAD
WITH GARLIC AND HAZELNUTS

CHOCOLATE PECAN PIE

Here is a complete menu for a Vegetarian Thanksgiving with no gaping hole where the turkey would have been. I know that many people love turkey (it's often the hardest meat for new vegetarians to give up), but try this and see what happens.

NOTE: The Pesto and Peppercorn Torta contains pesto, made with fresh basil leaves. If fresh basil is unavailable to you in the autumn, try to plan far enough ahead to make some pesto and freeze it when basil is in season. It will last for several months in the freezer if stored in an airtight jar.

4 DAYS AHEAD: make pesto for torta / for pie: make crust and refrigerate; chop pecans / make corn bread

3 DAYS AHEAD: assemble torta

2 DAYS AHEAD: cook cabbage leaves; assemble stuffing / cook sweet potatoes / chop garlic and hazelnuts for salad / clean and cut mushrooms for sauce / prepare garnishes for torta

I DAY AHEAD: make Cranberry Relish-Salad (minus apples) / assemble and bake pie / assemble stuffed cabbage; refrigerate / assemble Sweet Potato Surprise; refrigerate / clean spinach for salad

SAME DAY: add apples to relish-salad / bake cabbage and Sweet Potato Surprise together / make Mushroom-Brandy Sauce / assemble spinach salad

PESTO AND PEPPERCORN TORTA

PREPARATION TIME: STEPS 1 THROUGH 3 TAKE 15 TO 20 MINUTES, FOLLOWED BY SEVERAL HOURS OF CHILLING; 20 MINUTES TO COMPLETE, FOLLOWED BY 12 TO 24 HOURS OF CHILLING.

YIELD: APPETIZER FOR 6 OR MORE, DEPENDING ON WHAT ELSE IS SERVED. LIGHT LUNCH FOR 4 TO 6.

8 ounces Neufchâtel cheese (lowfat cream cheese)

1 cup ricotta cheese

PESTO:

2 cups (packed) fresh basil leaves

1/4 cup olive oil

2 to 3 medium-sized cloves garlic

2 tablespoons grated parmesan

salt (optional)

a little extra olive oil

about 30 to 40 peppercorns, coarsely crushed with a small, heavy bowl

GARNISHES:

arugula leaves (also known as rocket)

olives (preferably oil-cured or Niçoise)

sprigs of fresh oregano and/or thyme

slices of fresh or sun-dried tomato

strips of ripe red bell pepper

A torta is a combination of soft mild cheeses layered with seasonings, usually served as an appetizer or as a light meal. In classic Italian cooking, the torta is made from a combination of cream cheese and butter. I just couldn't bring myself to make it that way, especially knowing that so many people are trying to eat more healthfully these days. So I used a lower-fat, higher-protein combination of Neufchâtel (which is lower in fat than cream cheese) and ricotta (skim or part-skim).

The torta will keep for up to a week (depending on how fresh the ricotta was to begin with). The pesto will seep more deeply into the cheese the longer it sits.

The pesto can be made as much as two weeks ahead.

You will need cheesecloth for this preparation. Look for it in the housewares section of any supermarket.

1. Combine cream cheese (or Neufchâtel) and ricotta in a small mixing bowl. Beat until thoroughly combined. (An electric mixer at medium-high speed works very well.)

2. Prepare a three-layer rectangle of cheesecloth, about 6 x 20 inches. For easier handling, place the cheesecloth on a tray or cookie sheet.

3. Spread the cheese mixture onto the cheesecloth, making a rectangle about 4 x 16 inches. (It is possible to make a neat rectangle on the cheesecloth by cutting the edges of the cheese with a plain dinner knife.) Refrigerate, uncovered, for several hours before filling.

4. To make the pesto, combine basil, 1/4 cup olive oil, garlic, and parmesan in a food processor or blender. Purée to a paste. Salt to taste (optional).

5. Spread a light layer of olive oil on the cheese rectangle. Then add the pesto, and spread it to within 1/2 inch of the edges.

6. Sprinkle on the coarsely crushed peppercorns.

7. Lifting the cheesecloth from one end, roll up the torta along the long edge as you would a jelly roll. You will end up with a cylinder shape. Wrap it in cheesecloth (use a fresh piece, double thickness) and place it on its side on a plate. Cover

tightly with plastic wrap and refrigerate 12 to 24 hours before serving.

8. To serve, unwrap the torta and place it on a plate. Frame it lavishly with garnishes and serve with dark bread or the finest crackers, and raw vegetables.

CRANBERRY RELISH-SALAD
(WITH ORANGES, APPLES, AND SUNCHOKES)

PREPARATION TIME: 15 MINUTES.

YIELD: ENOUGH FOR 6, WHEN SERVED AS A CONDIMENT.

2 cups cranberries

1/2 cup sugar

1/2 navel orange, cut into 1-inch pieces (rind and all)

1 medium-sized sunchoke (Jerusalem artichoke) the size of a small person's fist

1 medium-sized tart green apple

Crunchy, juicy, sweet, and tart, this condiment is good enough to eat by itself. It is also very easy to make and wonderful to look at. If your guests are late and the cooking is finished, you could have a good time just sitting and staring at the relish.

This keeps well. It can be made a day or two ahead, although I recommend holding off on adding the apple until, at most, a few hours before serving.

1. Use a food processor fitted with the steel blade or a blender. Add cranberries, sugar, and orange pieces. Blend until cranberries and orange pieces are pulverized—but not liquefied. Transfer to a medium-sized bowl.

2. Trim any unsightly blemishes from the sunchoke. (You don't need to peel it, but you could shave off some of the outer skin with a sharp paring knife. This is purely optional.) Cut the sunchoke into very thin pieces and mince it fine. Stir into the cranberry mixture.

3. Core and mince the apple. (I don't recommend peeling, as the juxtaposition of green apple skin with cranberry and orange pieces is strikingly beautiful.) Combine with everything else. Cover tightly and chill.

CORN BREAD-STUFFED CABBAGE WITH MUSHROOM-BRANDY SAUCE

PREPARATION TIME: (AFTER CORN BREAD IS BAKED) 50 TO 60 MINUTES, PLUS ANOTHER 40 MINUTES TO BAKE.

YIELD: ABOUT 16 CABBAGE ROLLS—PLENTY TO FEED 6, OR EVEN 8, DEPENDING ON WHAT ELSE IS SERVED.

The corn bread stuffing is abundantly seasoned with many different herbs and spices, most savory, but with a few touches of sweet. Then it gets wrapped in tender cabbage leaves, bathed in Mushroom-Brandy Sauce, and baked.

The corn bread can be made as much as four or five days ahead. The stuffing can be assembled and the cabbage leaves cooked a day or two ahead. Leftovers reheat well, although the cabbage does get softer. If you are serving it as a leftover, consider making a small batch of fresh sauce to liven it up.

CORN BREAD-STUFFED CABBAGE

1 batch Simple Corn Bread (page 150)

1 large head green cabbage (9 to 10 inches in diameter)

2 medium-sized onions, minced

3 medium-sized cloves garlic, minced

2 tablespoons butter

2 stalks celery, minced

1/2 teaspoon salt

1/2 teaspoon celery seed

1 teaspoon ground ginger

1/2 teaspoon dried sage

1/2 teaspoon dried thyme

1/2 teaspoon dried tarragon

2 teaspoons dried basil

2 teaspoons dried dill

1/4 teaspoon allspice

1 teaspoon paprika

a generous amount of freshly ground black pepper

1 tablespoon fresh lemon juice

1 batch Mushroom-Brandy Sauce (recipe follows)

1. Make the corn bread.

2. Core the cabbage, and place it in a soup pot full of simmering water, core-end down. Cover and cook until the cabbage leaves pull off easily and are supple enough to roll without breaking. (You might have to experiment with one or two to determine when it is ready.) Then remove the head of cabbage, drain well in a colander, and set aside.

3. In a heavy skillet, cook onions and garlic in butter over medium heat for several minutes until the onions become translucent.

4. Add celery, salt, and all seasonings except lemon juice. Cover and cook over medium-low heat, stirring intermittently for 10 to 15 minutes, or until the celery is very tender and everything is definitely well mingled.

5. Meanwhile, transfer the corn bread to a large bowl. Use your hands to crumble it completely. (This is always my favorite part.)

6. Add the sauté to the corn bread, scraping in every last bit.

7. Add the lemon juice, and mix thoroughly.

8. To assemble, break off the cabbage leaves one at a time. Place about 3 tablespoons of stuffing at the core end and roll toward the tip, tucking in the sides. Arrange the cabbage

rolls in a 9 x 13-inch baking pan in rows, touching. This recipe will make about 16 rolls—enough to fit very snugly into the pan. Preheat oven to 350°. Meanwhile, make the sauce.

9. Ladle half the sauce over the rolls. Cover the pan with foil and bake for about 40 minutes, or until the rolls are heated through and the sauce is bubbly.

10. Ladle extra sauce onto each serving. Serve hot.

MUSHROOM-BRANDY SAUCE

1. Heat the milk just to the boiling point. Remove from heat and set aside.

2. In a large heavy skillet, sauté mushrooms in butter over medium heat for about 5 minutes, stirring occasionally.

3. Add brandy or sherry and continue to cook for about 5 more minutes.

4. Gradually sprinkle in the flour and mix it into the mushrooms with a wire whisk. Keep whisking and cooking another 5 minutes. Be sure the heat is not too high.

5. Stir in the hot milk. Cook over low heat, stirring intermittently until smooth and thickened, about 8 minutes. Season with salt and pepper, and remove from heat.

PREPARATION TIME: ABOUT 30 MINUTES.

YIELD: ENOUGH FOR I RECIPE OF STUFFED CABBAGE.

1½ cups milk (lowfat or soy okay)

1 pound fresh mushrooms, cleaned and thinly sliced (12 ounces is okay, if that's how your supermarket packages them)

3 tablespoons butter

3 tablespoons brandy or dry sherry

3 tablespoons unbleached white flour

¼ teaspoon salt

black pepper

SWEET POTATO SURPRISE

PREPARATION TIME: I HOUR.

YIELD: 8 TO IO SERVINGS.

4 pounds sweet potatoes or
  yams

4 bananas, peeled and
  chopped

2 large green apples or ripe
  pears (any kind but Bosc)

2 tablespoons butter or
  canola oil

2 tablespoons minced fresh
  ginger

1/2 teaspoon cinnamon

1/2 teaspoon allspice

I teaspoon salt

1 1/2 cups apple juice

1/2 cup fresh lemon or
  lime juice

1/2 cup chopped dried apricots

2 cups chopped nuts
  (optional)

Puréed sweet potatoes are combined with fresh ginger and sweet spices, plus several surprises. The effect is delicious but subtle, and your guests will have trouble identifying all the ingredients.

This can be assembled a day ahead and stored unbaked and tightly covered in the refrigerator.

1. Peel the sweet potatoes or yams, and boil until soft. Drain.

2. Meanwhile, sauté apples and bananas in butter or oil with ginger, cinnamon, allspice, and salt. Cook slowly, covered, but stirring intermittently for 10 to 15 minutes.

3. Preheat oven to 350°. Butter a 9 x 13-inch baking dish or deep casserole.

4. Purée the potatoes or yams with the fruit juices. A food processor with the steel blade attachment works ideally for this.

5. Stir the sautéed fruit into the purée. (For a smoother texture you can purée the fruit first before adding it to the sweet potatoes or yams.) Add the apricots. Heap into the prepared baking pan and, if desired, top with chopped nuts. (If it looks like the pan is getting too full, butter a pie pan and bake the extra in there.)

6. Bake uncovered for 45 minutes.

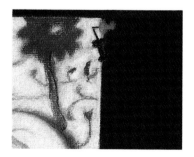

WILTED SPINACH SALAD WITH GARLIC AND HAZELNUTS

PREPARATION TIME: 15 TO
20 MINUTES.

YIELD: 6 SERVINGS.

1½ pounds fresh spinach

¼ to ⅓ cup olive oil

3 medium-sized cloves garlic,
minced

I cup coarsely chopped hazelnuts

3 to 4 tablespoons wine,
champagne, or balsamic
vinegar

salt

freshly ground black pepper

Pouring hot oil over fresh spinach leaves causes them to cook just slightly upon contact. They wilt a little, and tenderize perfectly. After experiencing this soft yet fresh salad, the idea of eating a *raw* spinach salad seems cumbersome by comparison.

You can clean the spinach ahead of time and store it in a bed of clean paper towels within a sealed plastic bag in the refrigerator. If you also peel the garlic and chop the nuts in advance, the final preparation will be very simple. Once assembled, this salad doesn't keep very well, so try to put it together right before serving.

1. Remove the spinach stems and place the leaves in a clean sink or a large bowl. Soak in cold water, then drain. Repeat with another cold water bath. Continue several times until the spinach is very clean. Drain again and spin until absolutely dry. Transfer to a good-sized salad bowl, and break any large leaves into bite-sized pieces.

2. Heat the olive oil in a small skillet and add the garlic and hazelnuts. Cook over low heat for 5 to 8 minutes, stirring intermittently.

3. Add the hot mixture directly to the spinach, scraping in as much of the oil as you can. Toss until all the spinach is coated and the nuts and garlic are distributed.

4. Sprinkle in wine, champagne, or vinegar and salt; grind in some pepper. Toss again and serve immediately.

CHOCOLATE PECAN PIE

PREPARATION TIME: 30 MINUTES
TO PREPARE, 30 MINUTES TO
BAKE.

YIELD: 1 9-INCH PIE.

CRUST:

1/4 cup (1/2 stick) cold butter

1 cup unbleached white flour

approximately 2 to 3 tablespoons cold milk or
buttermilk

FILLING:

1 tablespoon butter

2 ounces (2 squares) unsweetened chocolate

4 eggs

3/4 cup dark corn syrup

1/2 to 3/4 cup (packed) brown
sugar (depending on your
taste for sweetness)

1/2 teaspoon salt

1 tablespoon rum (optional)

1 teaspoon vanilla extract

2 cups coarsely chopped
pecans

a handful of pecan halves

OPTIONAL TOPPING:

1/2 pint heavy cream

3 tablespoons sugar

1/4 teaspoon vanilla extract

1 to 2 tablespoons rum

The two things that used to go through my mind most often while eating pecan pie: (1) this would be delicious if it weren't quite so gooey and sweet, and (2) a good hit of chocolate certainly wouldn't do any harm. A touch of rum wouldn't either, for that matter.

After surveying a lot of people and finding that most agreed with me, I was inspired to create the following recipe. It is now my standard pecan pie.

CRUST:

1. Using a food processor with the steel blade or a manual pastry cutter or two forks, combine the butter and flour until they form a uniform mixture resembling coarse cornmeal.

2. Add just enough milk (1 tablespoon at a time) to hold the dough together.

3. Roll out the dough to fit a 9-inch pie pan, using extra flour to prevent sticking as you roll. Form a crust with artfully fluted edges. Set aside.

FILLING:

1. Preheat oven to 375°.

2. Melt butter and chocolate together. Remove from heat.

3. Beat eggs at high speed with an electric mixer. Slowly drizzle in the chocolate mixture, as you keep beating the eggs. Beat in all other ingredients except the pecans.

4. Spread the chopped pecans into the unbaked pie shell. Pour in the batter, and scatter a few pecan halves on top.

5. Bake 30 minutes, or until solid in the middle. If you want the topping, whip the cream with the sugar, vanilla extract, and rum. Serve warm, at room temperature, or cold with optional whipped cream, if desired.

VEGETARIAN SEDER

NOT-CHICKEN SOUP WITH
   MALKALEH'S MATZOH BALLS

CHAROSET

MATZOH KUGEL

STEAMED FRESH ASPARAGUS
   AND HARD-BOILED EGGS WITH
   HORSERADISH SAUCE

PEAR AND PRUNE TSIMMES

BETTY KATZEN'S MILE-HIGH
   SPONGE CAKE

HAND-DIPPED CHOCOLATES

The Passover seder is a 2,000-plus-year-old ritual annually observed by Jewish people around the world to commemorate the exodus of our ancestors from Pharaoh's Egypt after generations of enslavement. This is a liberation festival celebrating spring and rebirth in a spirit of optimism, gratitude, and compassion.

The seder meal is a testimony of collective memory, and contains foods that symbolize both the bitter and the sweet. This menu reflects such contrasts through the traditional Charoset (sweet tasting, yet a metaphor for bitter experience) and Horseradish Sauce, containing sharp and bitter tastes. Matzoh Balls and Matzoh Kugel utilize various forms of the unleavened bread that the Israelites ate while wandering through the desert.

The seder ends on a hopeful note. Translated into food, what can symbolize that better than chocolate—in this case, lovingly prepared hand-dipped chocolates?

3 DAYS AHEAD: make chicken soup / make matzoh ball dough

2 DAYS AHEAD: cut and sauté vegetables for kugel / make Horseradish Sauce / cook asparagus / separate eggs for sponge cake

I DAY AHEAD: assemble and bake sponge cake / assemble kugel; refrigerate unbaked / assemble tsimmes; refrigerate unbaked

SAME DAY: make chocolates (do this in the morning, if possible) / make Charoset / make and poach matzoh balls / boil eggs; assemble with asparagus and Horseradish Sauce / bake kugel and tsimmes at the same time / reheat soup

NOT-CHICKEN SOUP WITH MALKALEH'S MATZOH BALLS

PREPARATION TIME: 5 TO 10 MINUTES TO ASSEMBLE, 1¼ HOURS TO COOK.

YIELD: AT LEAST 8 SERVINGS. GOES FARTHER WHEN SERVED WITH MATZOH BALLS.

8 cups water

2 teaspoons salt

1 8-inch parsnip, cut in chunks (optional)

2 large carrots, peeled or scrubbed and cut in chunks

2 medium-sized onions, cut in chunks

8 to 10 medium-sized cloves garlic, halved

2 stalks celery, coarsely chopped

2 scallions (optional)

a handful of mushrooms, cleaned and stems trimmed

½ teaspoon turmeric

black pepper

This broth is about as close as you'll get to chicken soup without using chicken. The garlic is essential. It seems like a lot, but it will tone itself down considerably as it simmers.

The parsnip, however, is *not* essential, and may be omitted. (It gives the soup a sweeter taste, which you may or may not prefer.)

You can make the broth up to several days in advance and store it in a tightly closed container in the refrigerator.

1. Combine everything in a large soup pot.

2. Bring to a boil, lower to a simmer, and partially cover.

3. Cook slowly for about 1¼ hours. Turn off heat and let it cool to room temperature.

4. Strain out and discard all the vegetables.

5. Heat the broth gently just before serving.

MALKALEH'S MATZOH BALLS

PREPARATION TIME: ONLY A
FEW MINUTES TO PREPARE, AT
LEAST 30 MINUTES TO
REFRIGERATE, AT LEAST 40
TO COOK.

YIELD: 10 OR 12 MATZOH BALLS.
EASILY MULTIPLIED.

2 eggs
$\frac{1}{2}$ cup matzoh meal
1 teaspoon salt*
a few sprigs parsley
extra matzoh meal for dusting
purposes

Traditionally, matzoh balls are served in soup. Additionally (and nontraditionally), a great way to eat them is hot, cut in half, and buttered, when no one is looking.

The batter can be made several days ahead and stored very tightly covered in the refrigerator.

1. Break eggs into a small bowl and beat lightly.

2. Add $\frac{1}{2}$ cup matzoh meal and salt. Use scissors to snip in the parsley in very small, feathery bits.

3. Mix well, cover, and refrigerate for at least 30 minutes (or as long as several days).

4. About 1 hour before serving, heat a large soup pot of lightly salted water to a rolling boil. At the same time, gently reheat the soup.

5. Dust your hands and lightly coat a dinner plate with matzoh meal. Form 1-inch balls and put them on the dusted plate.

6. Gently drop the matzoh balls into the boiling water, one by one. Partially cover, and keep the water boiling. Cook for 40 minutes.

7. Remove matzoh balls with a slotted spoon and transfer to serving bowls. Ladle hot soup on top and serve.

*This seems like a lot of salt, but it dissipates during the 40 minutes of boiling.

CHAROSET

PREPARATION TIME: METHOD I,
10 MINUTES; METHOD II,
30 MINUTES OR MORE.

YIELD: PROBABLY 6 SERVINGS
(SEE INTRODUCTORY NOTES
ABOVE THE RECIPE).

2 cups shelled walnuts

5 medium-sized tart apples

2 to 3 teaspoons cinnamon

2 tablespoons honey
(optional)

at least ¹/₂ cup grape juice or
sweet red wine (I use
¹/₂ cup plus a few table-
spoons)

Charoset (pronounced ha-*ro*-set, heavy on the "h") is a dense pastelike substance designed to resemble the mortar that slaves in Egypt used for their brickwork. It is ironic that such a sweet and juicy mash of apples, nuts, wine, and cinnamon, with an optional touch of honey, has such a somber symbolic assignment.

This is one of those dishes where there is no standard recipe and no two cooks make it exactly alike (a common occurrence in Jewish cuisine). In fact, no one cook seems to make it the same way twice. Some traditional versions include chopped dates, raisins, and mashed bananas, so there is quite a bit of leeway.

It's hard to give an exact yield for this recipe. Some people take a dab, and some take a whole plateful. I think you could safely expect this amount to serve 6 people.

FOOD PROCESSOR METHOD:

1. Place the walnuts in a food processor fitted with the steel blade attachment. Grind them to a coarse meal by turning the processor on and off in 5-second pulses. Then remove the ground nuts to a medium-sized mixing bowl. (You don't need to clean the food processor before doing the apples.)

2. Core the apples but don't peel them. Cut them into quarters, then eighths. Process in about three batches—until they are ground into very tiny pieces but *not* puréed. (If you do them in less than three batches, you will have a combination of mush and very large pieces—neither of which is desirable. Small batches yield the best results.) Add the shredded apple to the ground nuts.

3. Add cinnamon, honey (if desired), and grape juice or wine. Mix well and taste to see if anything needs adjusting. If all is wonderful, cover tightly and refrigerate until serving.

OLD-FASHIONED METHOD:

1. Use a large wooden bowl and a chopping blade. Add apples and walnuts and chop.

2. Chop a lot.

3. When the mixture acquires the consistency of cement, add cinnamon, optional honey, and juice or wine. Adjust amounts of these to taste. Cover, refrigerate, and take a little rest.

MATZOH KUGEL

PREPARATION TIME: 40 MINUTES
TO COOK AND ASSEMBLE, 50
TO 55 MINUTES TO BAKE.

YIELD: A BIG, HEAVY PANFUL,
ENOUGH FOR AT LEAST 8 OR
10 SERVINGS.

1 10-ounce box plain unsalted
matzohs

4 heaping cups chopped onion
(approximately 3 medium-
sized onions)

2 stalks celery, minced

1 pound mushrooms, finely
chopped (12 ounces is okay,
if that's how your super-
market packages them)

2 tablespoons butter or
canola oil

1 1/2 teaspoons salt

black pepper

6 medium-sized cloves garlic,
minced

5 eggs

1 cup sunflower seeds
(optional)

paprika for the top

This is a savory kugel made with very simple ingredients. The matzohs may be soaked and drained a day or two ahead. The vegetables can be sautéed several days in advance as well, and stored in a tightly covered container in the refrigerator. Leftover kugel stores and reheats beautifully, either in a microwave or wrapped in foil in a regular oven.

1. Preheat oven to 350°. Grease a 9 x 13-inch baking pan.

2. Break the matzohs into pieces (any size) and soak in a large bowl of warm water for about 10 minutes. Drain well and return to the bowl.

3. In a large heavy skillet, sauté onions, celery, and mushrooms in butter or oil with salt and pepper, over medium heat. Stir every now and then, and cover between stirrings. Continue to cook until everything is very tender (12 to 15 minutes). Stir in the garlic during the last 5 minutes of cooking.

4. Add the sauté to the matzohs. Mix well.

5. Beat the eggs in a separate bowl. Add them to the matzoh batter and combine thoroughly. Taste to adjust salt and pepper.

6. Spread into the prepared pan. Sprinkle the top generously with optional sunflower seeds and paprika, and cover the pan tightly with foil. Bake, covered, for 30 minutes. Then uncover and bake another 20 to 25 minutes, or until the kugel is firm and the top is nicely browned.

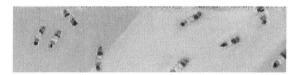

STEAMED FRESH ASPARAGUS AND HARD-BOILED EGGS WITH HORSERADISH SAUCE

PREPARATION TIME: ABOUT
15 MINUTES.

YIELD: 4 TO 6 SERVINGS,
DEPENDING ON WHAT ELSE IS
SERVED. EASILY MULTIPLIED.

3 eggs, room temperature

1 cup sour cream, room temperature

1 cup yogurt, room temperature

1 to 2 tablespoons prepared horseradish (preferably white)

a dash of salt

1 pound fresh asparagus— as slender as possible

a few tablespoons minced fresh parsley

The eggs in this dish should be cooked just to the point at which the whites are firm but the yolks are still slightly wet and soft. If you follow the instructions below, the eggs should come out just right.

All components of this recipe can be made up to several days in advance, although the eggs taste best if served within a few hours of cooking. Store sauce and asparagus separately in the refrigerator, and remember to give them plenty of time to come to room temperature the day you plan to serve them.

1. Fill a medium-sized saucepan with water and bring to a boil. Lower to a simmer, and gently add the eggs. Simmer for exactly 8 minutes, then remove the eggs and rinse them under cold water for about 30 seconds. Peel, and cut into quarters. (If you are not going to serve this right away, don't peel or cut them until, at most, 30 minutes before serving.)

2. Whisk together the sour cream and yogurt in a bowl. Stir in horseradish and salt. You can adjust the amounts to taste. Set aside.

3. Remove and discard tough asparagus bottoms. Steam the asparagus until *just* tender. You can use a steamer over water, or tie the asparagus stalks together and stand them upright in a pan of boiling water (the water level should reach about two-thirds of the way up the stalks). If you are not going to serve this right away, rinse the cooked asparagus in cold running water for several minutes and drain well.

4. To serve, arrange asparagus spears and egg wedges on a serving plate. Spoon the sauce over the top, and garnish with flecks of parsley. Serve warm or at room temperature. (It's also okay cold, although not quite as good.)

PEAR AND PRUNE TSIMMES

PREPARATION TIME: 10 TO
15 MINUTES TO PREPARE,
50 MINUTES TO BAKE.

YIELD: 6 TO 8 SERVINGS.

*10 ripe d'Anjou pears
(or some comparable
juicy variety)*

1 pound pitted prunes

*4 tablespoons fresh lemon
juice*

2 tablespoons honey

cinnamon

Traditionally a tsimmes is made with vegetables, fruit, and meat, and is baked for hours and hours until all its components acquire a mysteriously intermingled quality. Family formulas were conveyed from one generation to the next through nostalgic descriptions. Nothing was ever written down, so there are really no precise recipes, only memories.

This one is simple, with fruit only. Yet when it bakes down, its character deepens to the point where you could swear you were eating more than the sum of its few ingredients.

The tsimmes can be assembled up to a day before it is baked and served. Cover tightly with foil and refrigerate.

1. Preheat oven to 350°. Grease a 9 x 13-inch baking pan.

2. Peel and slice the pears.

3. Halve the prunes.

4. Spread the pear slices in the prepared pan, and place the prunes on top. Drizzle with lemon juice and honey, and sprinkle liberally with cinnamon.

5. Bake covered for 30 minutes and uncovered for another 20.

6. Serve hot or warm, as a side dish.

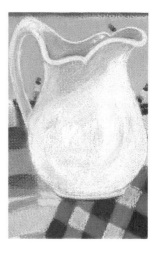

BETTY KATZEN'S MILE-HIGH SPONGE CAKE

PREPARATION TIME: 30 MINUTES TO ASSEMBLE, 1¹/4 HOURS TO BAKE.

YIELD: 1 HIGH SPONGE CAKE.

9 eggs

¹/2 teaspoon salt

juice and grated rind of 2 lemons

water

³/4 cup matzoh cake meal

¹/4 cup potato starch

1 cup sugar

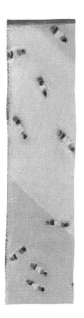

This is one of my mother's timeless specialties. The stereotype of sponge cake as being tasteless and dry can finally be debunked once and for all. This one is so lemony, moist, and rich tasting it's hard to believe there's no oil or butter in there.

Matzoh cake meal and potato starch are generally available in grocery stores during the six weeks or so before Passover. I buy a box of each about once every three years, and keep them in the freezer in sealed plastic bags.

1. Preheat oven to 325°. Have ready an ungreased standard-sized tube pan.

2. Separate the eggs into two large bowls.

3. Beat the egg whites with an electric mixer at high speed, gradually adding the salt, until the beaten whites form stiff peaks. Set aside.

4. Measure the lemon juice, and add enough water to make ³/4 cup liquid. Set aside.

5. Combine the cake meal and potato starch in a small bowl, and stir in the lemon rind. Set aside.

6. Without cleaning the beaters, beat the yolks with the sugar until lightened in color and thick (5 to 8 minutes at high speed). Add everything else except the egg whites, and beat at medium speed another few minutes, or until well combined.

7. Add the whites, and fold in gently. Turn into the ungreased tube pan.

8. Bake for 1¹/4 hours, or until the top springs back when touched lightly. Turn the pan upside down, and cool thoroughly in this position. Remove from the pan and transfer to a serving plate within a few hours of serving time.

HAND-DIPPED CHOCOLATES

PREPARATION TIME: 30 TO 40 MINUTES.

YIELD: PLENTY FOR AT LEAST 6 PEOPLE.

5 tablespoons butter (a little over ½ stick)

1 12-ounce package semisweet chocolate chips

SUGGESTED DIPPEES:

(Have these—or a similar assortment—ready before melting the chocolate)

1 pint whole unhulled strawberries

1 ripe but firm pear, sliced

1 cup dried apricots (whole and plump)

½ cup (half an 8-ounce package) cream cheese, cut into about 20 small cubes

a handful each of almonds, walnuts, and raisins

Hand dipping chocolates sounds like a complicated endeavor, but it's a surprisingly straightforward operation that is only a *little* bit messy. Just be sure you do this on a day that is not too hot or humid.

The idea is very simple. Melt semisweet chocolate and butter, then select an assortment of delicious little morsels to dip into it. After they have been dipped, place the morsels on a foil-covered plate and refrigerate until the chocolate hardens. The only equipment required is a saucepan, knife, spoon, plate, and foil.

My own favorite collection of dipping items includes whole unhulled strawberries, slices of fresh pear, dried apricots, cubes of cream cheese, almonds, walnuts, and raisins. I'm sure there are many other possibilities I haven't thought of. With the fresh fruit, of course, a lot depends on what is in season.

Hand dipping is a wide-open field, open to broad interpretation. So you can have a good time getting creative with this. And as an additional bonus, your guests will be thrilled and feel loved when served such an elegant hand-crafted treat.

1. Place 5 tablespoons butter and the chocolate chips in a small saucepan or in a double boiler over hot water. Heat gently until thoroughly melted. Meanwhile, tightly wrap two or three dinner plates with aluminum foil.

2. Moving quickly, begin dipping the fruits, cheese, and nuts in the chocolate. Hold strawberries, fruit slices, and apricots with your hand, and dip just the tips, about halfway up. For the cream cheese cubes, use small tongs if you want to dip only half (visually quite pretty). If you want to coat the whole thing, drop 1 or 2 cubes at a time into the chocolate, and fish them out quickly with a spoon. The nuts and raisins can also be done in the latter manner, and you can make them into clusters or leave them separate.

3. As you bring each morsel out of the chocolate, place it immediately on the foil-lined plate. Refrigerate until the chocolate is hard. Ideally, hand-dipped chocolates should be served within 24 hours, especially the ones made with fresh fruit.

PASTA DINNERS

PASTA WITH PESTO TAPENADE

SPAGHETTI ELLIANA

LINGUINE WITH QUICK TUSCAN
TOMATO SAUCE

PASTA WITH MARINATED VEGETABLES
(ROASTED PEPPERS, ARTICHOKE HEARTS,
TOMATOES, MUSHROOMS, AND OLIVES)

PASTA WITH GREENS AND FETA

PASTA WITH SPICY EGGPLANT PURÉE

COLD STEAMED VEGETABLES VINAIGRETTE

QUICK SAUTEED CAULIFLOWER AND
RED PEPPERS

RASPBERRIED VEGETABLES

Pasta dinners belong in the weekly repertoire of any busy person's menu plans. Depending on the sauce ingredients, a pasta meal can be quick and inexpensive, as well as elegant, healthful, interesting, and profoundly satisfying. (An added benefit: If you are cooking for children, there is a greater chance of their being happy with pasta—also known as noodles—than with other types of grown-up food.)

The following recipes include a variety of pasta ideas, some with very simple uncooked sauces, and others, slightly more complex, with cooking involved. All of these sauces can be made in advance, so the final mealtime preparations can be greatly streamlined. You can come home from work, put up the pasta water, throw together a simple salad, gently heat the sauce, and sit down to a comforting and sophisticated dinner in less than 30 minutes.

Preassembled, refrigerated sauces need to be brought at least to room temperature, and ideally should be warmed before being combined with hot pasta. A microwave oven can be very useful for this. Put the sauce in the microwave in its serving bowl and the bowl will get nice and warm along with the sauce. If you don't have a microwave, put the bowlful of sauce in a warm oven (250° to 300°) before putting up the pasta water, or heat the sauce very gently in a saucepan on the stove top.

The pasta recipes in this section are accompanied by three ideas for side dishes, any of which can be served with any pasta. All pastas can also be served with a simple green salad. If you clean and dry the greens a day ahead of time, wrap them well in paper towels, and seal them in a plastic bag, the final salad preparation can be done in minutes while the pasta is cooking.

These recipes were written for dried pasta, which is usually much more accessible to busy working people than fresh pasta. Dried pasta can be bought way ahead of time and stored in the cupboard, so you always know it's there. If you prefer to use fresh pasta, however, you can adapt these recipes by increasing the amount of uncooked pasta by 50 percent (i.e., if the recipe calls for 1 pound pasta, use 1$^1\!/_2$ pounds fresh).

Different people prefer different proportions of pasta to sauce. Italian tradition emphasizes the pasta, and the sauce is a secondary subtle presence, laced over the top. American cuisine often has the pasta virtually swimming in a pool of sauce. My own preference is somewhere in the middle, with a fairly equal balance between pasta and other ingredients. The proportions in the following recipes reflect this inclination, so keep in mind that it is just one cook's taste, and adjust the amounts to suit your own.

↝ Make sure there is plenty of water and that it is boiling rapidly. Add a little oil to the water just before adding the pasta, and keep the water hot and moving during the entire cooking process. Dried pasta, depending on its shape, can take 8 to 10 minutes to cook. Check frequently after the 5-minute mark, so it won't be over- or underdone. (Fresh pasta, on the other hand, cooks so quickly that it is just about ready to come out as soon as it goes in.)

↝ While we are talking about being over- or underdone, the second most common error in pasta preparation is to *under*cook it. (The first common error is to overcook it, but lately cookbooks have so emphatically warned about the folly of overcooked pasta, everyone is nervously draining their spaghetti a little too soon.) Overcooked pasta is bad, but undercooked is no better, especially if it is a thickly cut pasta, like penne or shells. Biting into a piece of perfectly done pasta should be a simple and mindless pleasure; there should be only the slightest hint of resistance to the tooth (which is what al dente literally means).

↝ Another common error is to overdrain the pasta. It is fine, and in fact preferable, if a few drops of cooking water adhere to the pasta. You don't want it to be too dry.

↝ Add the parmesan sooner rather than later. It is part of the ritual of pasta eating to pass a small bowl of parmesan so that each guest can individually sprinkle the top of his or her own plateful. But it is best to mix some cheese into the pasta while you are first tossing it with the sauce. More surface area can be coated this way, and more heat is available to melt and incorporate the cheese. (You can still pass the little bowl around for extra.)

↝ Also, if you think of it, warm the plates in a 200° oven while you prepare the food. This will enhance the pleasure, as well as lift the spirits, of those partaking.

PASTA WITH PESTO TAPENADE

PREPARATION TIME: 20 TO 25 MINUTES.

YIELD: 6 OR MORE GENEROUS SERVINGS.

1 cup (packed) fresh basil leaves

1 cup (packed) fresh parsley

1 1/2 cups pitted Kalamata olives

2 large cloves garlic, minced (or more, to taste)

1 tablespoon fresh lemon juice

1 to 1 1/4 pounds spaghetti, linguine, or fettuccine

3 to 4 tablespoons olive oil for the pasta

4 to 6 tablespoons grated parmesan (or to taste)

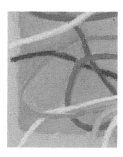

Pesto Tapenade is a rich, aromatic paste featuring basil, garlic, and puréed Kalamata (Greek) olives. It interacts beautifully with hot pasta, coating each strand with potent flavor. Tapenade keeps at least a week in the refrigerator and longer in the freezer. So make the whole batch, even if you intend to serve fewer than the six portions it accommodates. You can just spoon out however much you need onto freshly cooked pasta and put the rest away for later. Cold tapenade can be gently heated—on the stove top or in a microwave—so it won't cool down the hot pasta.

Tapenade has many other uses. It can be a dip for vegetables or crackers, a sandwich filling (wonderful in combination with cream cheese), or a pizza topping. Try spreading it on a split piece of Italian bread, sprinkling some cheese on top, and broiling it, for an elegant lunch or a light supper.

NOTE: You can streamline the preparation time by putting the pasta water up to boil first, and preparing the tapenade while the water heats.

1. Clean and dry the basil leaves and parsley, and run them through a food processor (with steel blade attachment) or a blender until very, very finely minced. Remove to a large bowl.

2. Place the olives and garlic in the food processor. Purée until smooth, and add to the minced herbs in the bowl. Stir in lemon juice.

3. Cook the pasta in plenty of rapidly boiling water until al dente. Drain, and add to the bowl of tapenade. Immediately drizzle with olive oil and sprinkle with a generous amount of parmesan. Then, using tongs or two forks, combine the pasta with the sauce with a gentle lifting motion, bringing the tapenade up from the bottom of the bowl. Serve immediately, preferably on heated plates.

SPAGHETTI ELLIANA

PREPARATION TIME: 35 TO 40 MINUTES.

YIELD: 4 SERVINGS.

3 to 6 tablespoons olive oil

³/₄ cup almonds, coarsely chopped

³/₄ cup walnuts coarsely chopped

4 medium cloves garlic, minced

¹/₂ teaspoon salt (omit if using anchovies)

1 cup raisins

2 to 3 tablespoons minced anchovies (optional)

³/₄ pound spaghetti or linguine

4 to 6 tablespoons freshly grated parmesan cheese (or to taste)

freshly ground black pepper

finely minced fresh parsley

This looks like an odd assortment of ingredients, especially for a pasta sauce. It *is* odd, but it's also delicious and fun to eat. If you are a strict vegetarian or an anchovy-hater, I hope you won't be offended by the presence of those little fish in here. They taste so amazingly good, I decided to include them, letting you make your own decision. (If you leave them out, it will taste fine.)

The sauce can be made up to several days ahead.

1. Heat the olive oil in a deep skillet or Dutch oven. Add chopped nuts, garlic, and salt (if not using anchovies), and cook over moderate heat for 10 to 12 minutes, or until the nuts are coated, golden, and fragrant. Stir occasionally during the cooking. (At some point along the way, put up the pasta water to boil.)

2. Add raisins and cook over low heat, stirring intermittently, another 5 minutes.

3. Turn off heat and stir in optional anchovies.

4. Cook the pasta in plenty of boiling, salted water until al dente. Drain and add to the nut mixture. (You can save a few steps—literally—by lifting the cooked pasta out of its cooking water with a strainer or skimmer, draining it momentarily over the cooking water, and dumping it directly into the nut mixture.)

5. Turn the heat on low under the skillet or Dutch oven, and cook the pasta in the sauce another few minutes. During this process, sprinkle in parmesan, to taste.

6. Transfer to a serving dish or to individual plates, and top with freshly ground black pepper and finely minced parsley. Serve immediately.

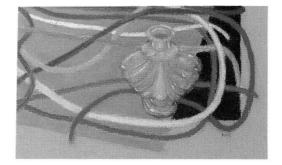

LINGUINE WITH QUICK
TUSCAN TOMATO SAUCE

PREPARATION TIME: 15 TO
20 MINUTES.

YIELD: 4 TO 6 SERVINGS.

4 to 5 medium-sized ripe
   tomatoes

2 tablespoons olive oil

1 cup finely minced red onion

$1/4$ to $1/2$ teaspoon salt

$1/2$ cup (packed) finely minced
   fresh parsley

1 cup (packed) finely minced
   fresh basil leaves

freshly ground black pepper

$3/4$ to 1 pound linguine or
   spaghetti

extra olive oil for the pasta

grated parmesan, to taste

This is a very simple uncooked tomato sauce, best made with fresh ripe tomatoes at the peak of their season. If you have a craving for this dish at other times of the year, consider using high-quality imported canned Italian tomatoes instead. Unripe or hot-house tomatoes will not work in this recipe.

The suggested amount of pasta is flexible, as different people prefer different proportions of pasta to sauce. Experiment to find out how you and your friends and family like it.

The sauce can be made a day or two in advance; just leave out the basil and parsley until shortly before serving. Refrigerated sauce should be permitted to come at least to room temperature before it is combined with hot pasta. If you warm the sauce just slightly (without cooking it!), it will help the pasta hold its heat longer.

If you are making the sauce just before serving, put up the pasta water to boil before you begin the sauce.

1. Half fill a large saucepan with water and heat to boiling. Core the tomatoes, then drop them in the boiling water for about 10 seconds each. Remove from the saucepan, and peel the tomatoes under cold running water. Quarter the tomatoes and squeeze out the seeds. Then finely chop the remaining tomato pulp, place it in a medium-sized bowl, and set aside.

2. Heat 1 tablespoon of the olive oil in a small skillet. Add the minced onion and sauté over medium heat, stirring, for about 2 minutes. Add this to the chopped tomato, scraping in every last drop of oil from the skillet.

3. Stir in the remaining tablespoon of olive oil, plus salt, parsley, and basil. Grind in a generous amount of fresh black pepper. Taste to adjust seasonings, cover, and set aside.

4. Cook the pasta in plenty of boiling water until al dente. Drain and transfer to a large bowl. Drizzle with a little extra olive oil, then add sauce (either room temperature or heated slightly) and parmesan. Toss gently, and serve immediately, preferably on heated plates. Pass extra parmesan and the pepper mill.

PASTA WITH MARINATED VEGETABLES
(ROASTED PEPPERS, ARTICHOKE HEARTS, TOMATOES, MUSHROOMS, AND OLIVES)

PREPARATION TIME: 35 TO 40 MINUTES TO PREPARE THE VEGETABLES, PLUS AT LEAST A FEW HOURS FOR THEM TO MARINATE. THEN 15 TO 20 MINUTES TO COOK PASTA AND ASSEMBLE.

YIELD: 4 TO 6 SERVINGS.

3 red or yellow bell peppers

12 medium-sized fresh mushrooms, cleaned, stemmed, and sliced

2 6-ounce jars marinated artichoke hearts (including all their liquid)

15 to 20 cherry tomatoes, halved

12 to 15 large fresh basil leaves, minced (easiest to use scissors)

3 to 4 medium-sized cloves garlic, minced

3/4 teaspoon salt

4 to 6 tablespoons olive oil

2 tablespoons red wine vinegar

12 to 15 oil-cured olives, pitted and minced

1 pound fettuccine or a tubular-shaped pasta like penne

1/2 cup grated parmesan, romano, or asiago cheese

Be sure to give the vegetables time to marinate. Twenty-four hours of marinating time is optimal. You can get all the other vegetables ready while the peppers are roasting, and thus streamline the whole operation.

The hot pasta can be combined with room-temperature vegetables, but the dish tastes even better if all components are heated first. Warm the vegetables in a microwave or heat them gently in a large skillet over low heat. The drained pasta can be added directly to the skillet, along with the cheese. (Use a strainer or skimmer to transfer the pasta directly from its cooking water to the vegetables, saving yourself the trouble of traveling to the sink with a heavy hot pot.)

1. Preheat oven to 350°. Place the peppers on a baking sheet and roast for 20 to 30 minutes, turning every 5 to 8 minutes or so, until the skin is fairly evenly blistered all over. Remove from the oven, and immediately place in a paper bag for about 5 minutes. Remove from the bag. When they are cool enough to handle, peel off the skin with a sharp paring knife (it should come off easily), and remove stems and seeds. Slice the peppers into strips, and place them in a large bowl.

2. Add all remaining ingredients except pasta and cheese, and mix well. Cover and let marinate a minimum of several hours. Warm the vegetables, if desired, while cooking the pasta.

3. Cook the pasta in plenty of boiling water until al dente. Drain, and combine with the marinated vegetables, adding the cheese as you mix it. Serve immediately.

PASTA WITH GREENS AND FETA

PREPARATION TIME: 35 MINUTES.

YIELD: 4 TO 6 SERVINGS.

3 to 6 tablespoons olive oil

4 cups chopped onion

7 to 8 cups (packed) mixed
   bitter greens, washed, dried,
   and coarsely chopped
   (I used 1 medium-sized
   bunch each spinach and
   escarole)

salt to taste

3/4 to 1 pound penne, fusilli,
   shells, or some comparable
   short, substantial pasta

1/2 to 3/4 pound feta cheese,
   crumbled

freshly grated parmesan
   cheese, to taste (optional)

freshly ground black pepper

Here is a painless way to slip some of those ultranutritious bitter greens into your diet. You can use any combination of kale, mustard, collard, dandelion, escarole, chard, or spinach. I especially like escarole and spinach together.

The instructions call for "short, substantial pasta," and I have suggested a few forms. This kind of sauce, with tender pieces of onion and bite-sized flecks of greens, studded with soft crumbs of feta cheese, adheres best to small shapely units of pasta. Each mouthful of this dish packs in a beautiful integration of textures.

The sauce can be made a day or two ahead of time. Reheat it gently on the stove when you put up the pasta water to boil.

1. Heat the olive oil in a deep skillet or Dutch oven. Add the onions and cook for about 10 minutes over medium heat, stirring occasionally. Meanwhile, put the pasta water up to boil.

2. Add chopped greens to the skillet, salt lightly, and stir until the greens begin to wilt. Cover and cook 10 to 15 minutes over medium-low heat.

3. Cook the pasta until al dente. Just as it becomes ready, add the crumbled feta cheese to the sauce. (Keep the heat on low as you add the cheese.)

4. When the pasta is done, scoop it out with a strainer (in however many batches it takes), hold it over its cooking water momentarily to drain, then add it directly to the potful of sauce. Mix thoroughly.

5. Cook the completed dish just slightly over low heat for a few minutes. Add a small amount of parmesan, if desired, and a generous amount of freshly ground black pepper. Then serve immediately, preferably on warmed plates.

PASTA WITH
SPICY EGGPLANT PURÉE

PREPARATION TIME: EGGPLANT
TAKES 30 MINUTES TO BAKE,
FOLLOWED BY TIME TO COOL;
20 MINUTES OF PREPARATION
THEREAFTER.

YIELD: 6 OR MORE SERVINGS.

1 medium-sized eggplant

a little oil, for baking

2 medium-sized cloves garlic
(or more, to taste)

1/4 cup fresh lemon juice

1/4 cup sesame tahini (toasted
or raw)

1/2 teaspoon salt

freshly ground black pepper

crushed red pepper, to taste

1 to 1 1/4 pounds spaghetti,
linguine, or fettuccine

3 to 4 tablespoons olive oil

grated parmesan (optional)

Spicy Eggplant Purée in this case is none other than the old standard, baba ganouj (an eggplant and tahini dip). You might wonder how this classic Middle Eastern dip happened to wander off into the pasta section. I'd been thinking about just how successfully pasta combines with garlicky, aromatic pastes like pesto and tapenade when I remembered that sitting in my refrigerator was a spicy batch of baba ganouj I had made several days before. The spiciness seemed to increase exponentially with every hour the ganouj sat around, and I knew it needed to be combined with something warm and bland to balance itself out. So I cooked a little linguine and mixed them together. It was fantastic!

The eggplant purée can be prepared several days in advance. You can heat it *very* gently on the stove top or in a microwave just before combining it with the pasta.

1. Preheat oven to 350°. Lightly oil a baking sheet.

2. Slice the eggplant in half lengthwise, and place the halves open side down on the baking sheet. Bake for 30 minutes, or until very tender. Cool to the point at which the eggplant can be handled comfortably. Meanwhile, put up the pasta water to boil.

3. Scoop all the eggplant pulp from the skins. Place in a blender or a food processor fitted with the steel blade, along with garlic, lemon juice, tahini, and salt. Purée until smooth. Transfer to a large bowl, and season to taste with black and red peppers.

4. Cook the pasta in plenty of boiling water until al dente. Drain, and add to the bowlful of eggplant purée. Immediately drizzle with olive oil, and, if desired, add a small amount of parmesan. Use tongs or two forks to mix with a lifting motion, bringing up the purée from the bottom of the bowl until everything is nicely combined.

COLD STEAMED VEGETABLES VINAIGRETTE

PREPARATION TIME: 20 MINUTES TO PREPARE, PLUS TIME TO CHILL.

YIELD: 4 TO 6 SERVINGS.

1 *recipe* Creamy Vinaigrette (*page 125*)

1 *small head cauliflower, cut in small florets*

1 *medium-sized carrot, thinly sliced*

2 *stalks broccoli, cut in 2-inch spears*

Use leftover steamed vegetables or steam fresh ones; serve them cold with a drizzle of salad dressing for a quick side dish. Any vegetables can be used, and any dressing. The following recipe is a suggestion; you can take it from there.

1. Prepare the Creamy Vinaigrette.

2. Steam the vegetables until tender. Remove them from the heat immediately and refresh under cold running water. Drain thoroughly, then chill.

3. Drizzle the vinaigrette over the cold vegetables just before serving. Use just a small amount of the dressing, and pass the extra in a small pitcher for those who want more.

QUICK SAUTÉED CAULIFLOWER AND RED PEPPERS

PREPARATION TIME: 15 MINUTES.

YIELD: 4 TO 6 SIDE-DISH-SIZED SERVINGS.

1 to 2 tablespoons olive oil

1 medium-sized head cauliflower, cut in small florets

2 medium-sized red bell peppers, cut into thin strips

1/4 to 1/2 teaspoon salt

2 medium-sized cloves garlic, minced

1 tablespoon cider vinegar (or more, to taste)

freshly ground black pepper

Here is a wonderful quick way to prepare fresh vegetables. The fast cooking process over high heat seals in the natural juices and flavors, augments the colors, and preserves the texture of the vegetables. I love the combination of cauliflower and red peppers because of their contrasting textures and the bright white and red color scheme. You can also use this technique with many other vegetables. Try small strips of zucchini and carrot, or a wokful of broccoli stems (shaved and cut into julienne strips—surprisingly tender!). Experiment with whatever is in season.

The vegetables can be cut up to a day in advance and stored in sealed plastic bags in the refrigerator; this way, the final preparation will be a breeze.

1. Heat the olive oil in a skillet or a wok.

2. Add cauliflower, and sauté over medium-high heat for 5 minutes, stirring frequently.

3. Add pepper strips, salt, and garlic. Keep the heat fairly high, and sauté, stirring, for another 5 to 8 minutes, or until everything is just tender.

4. Remove from heat, sprinkle with vinegar, and grind in a generous amount of black pepper. Allow to cool to room temperature, then taste to adjust seasonings.

5. Serve warm, at room temperature, or cold.

RASPBERRIED VEGETABLES

Tart raspberry marinade with hot steamed vegetables makes a wonderful, colorful side dish for dinner, especially served with or after a spicy or creamy entrée. The recipe on the next page pairs off beautifully with a simple pasta course.

The variation that follows (Raspberry-Marinated Vegetable Salad) makes cheerful and elegant picnic fare, and is also a great dish to bring to potluck brunches.

Fresh or frozen raspberries can be used with equal success in this recipe. If you use frozen, try to get the kind without sugar. If you are lucky enough to be in the midst of raspberry season, you can easily freeze your own for later use. Just spread the raspberries out on a tray and leave them in the freezer about 20 to 30 minutes until they are individually frozen. Then transfer them to the plastic bag, close it up tight with a bag tie, and put it back in the freezer. You will be thrilled to find it there several months from now.

The vegetables in both of the following variations are somewhat flexible. Experiment to find out which ones work best for you.

The Raspberry Sauce keeps very well, and can be made several days ahead if stored airtight in the refrigerator.

RASPBERRY SAUCE

PREPARATION TIME:
30 MINUTES.

YIELD: 4 TO 6 SERVINGS.

2 cups fresh raspberries (or 2 cups frozen unsweetened)

1/2 cup orange juice

3 tablespoons cider vinegar

3 to 4 tablespoons honey

3 tablespoons extra virgin olive oil

1/4 to 1/2 teaspoon salt, to taste

1 medium-sized clove garlic, finely minced

SUGGESTED VEGETABLES:

1 large head cauliflower, cut into bite-sized florets,

   or

1 large bunch broccoli, cut into 2-inch spears,

   or

1 pound Brussels sprouts, whole or halved,

   or

a combination of the above (enough for 4 to 6 servings)

1. Place the raspberries, orange juice, vinegar, and honey in a saucepan. Heat to boiling, turn heat down to medium, and cook uncovered for 5 minutes. Remove from heat and cool to room temperature.

2. Stir in olive oil, salt, and garlic. Taste to adjust seasonings. Place in a serving bowl and set aside.

3. Steam the vegetables until just tender.

4. Serve the hot or warm vegetables with a little raspberry sauce drizzled over the top. Pass the bowl of sauce, so people can help themselves to extra.

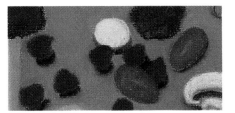

VARIATION: RASPBERRY-MARINATED VEGETABLE SALAD

PREPARATION TIME: I HOUR TO PREPARE, PLUS TIME TO CHILL.

YIELD: APPROXIMATELY 8 SERVINGS.

Follow the preceding directions for the sauce, with these changes:

1. Increase vinegar to ¹/₂ cup.

2. Replace olive oil with ¹/₂ to 1 cup mayonnaise (commercial or homemade, see page 68).

3. Increase garlic to 2 or 3 cloves.

4. Add 1 teaspoon dried tarragon. Chill the sauce until shortly before serving time.

Use a larger assortment of vegetables. I recommend:

2 small carrots, thinly sliced

1 small head cauliflower, cut in florets

1 medium-sized bunch broccoli, cut in small pieces

1 handful each green and yellow string beans, cut diagonally in 1-inch pieces

2 small zucchini or yellow summer squash, sliced

1 medium-sized red, green, or yellow bell pepper, thinly sliced

10 to 12 large mushrooms, sliced

sprigs of fresh tarragon for garnish (optional)

1. Steam carrots, cauliflorets, broccoli pieces, and string beans together until just tender. Refresh under cold running water and drain well. Transfer to a large bowl.

2. Steam zucchini or squash, bell pepper, and mushrooms for just a minute or two. Add to other vegetables in bowl. Cover the bowl tightly and chill.

3. Combine the raspberry dressing and the cold steamed vegetables within 1 hour of serving. Garnish with small sprigs of fresh tarragon, if available.

**STIR-FRY
DINNERS**

ASPARAGUS-TOFU-NOODLE

BROCCOLI AND BLACK MUSHROOMS
IN GARLIC SAUCE

SZECHWAN GREEN BEANS

SPINACH WITH GARLIC

CABBAGE, CARROTS, AND ONIONS
WITH SESAME

SWEET AND SOUR STIR-FRY
WITH COATED WALNUTS

KUNG PAO TOFU

SAUTÉED TWELVE ASSORTMENTS

Here is a series of ideas for stir-fry dinners, ranging from exotic and somewhat complex (Sweet and Sour Stir-Fry with Coated Walnuts) to very simple (Spinach with Garlic, which contains only four ingredients). It's handy to have access to an assortment of recipes that can be cooked in short order on the stove top and that, when served over rice (or, in the case of Asparagus-Tofu-Noodle Stir-Fry, all by itself) make a complete meal.

If your life is busy, and you are struggling to plan healthful and creative, yet straightforward meals, I recommend that you include at least one stir-fry meal per week in your menu plans. Vegetables can be cut the night before and stored in sealed plastic bags in the refrigerator. Rice can be precooked and reheated (microwave ovens do this especially well) or partially cooked before you leave for work in the morning. (For every 4 servings combine 2 cups brown rice and 3 cups water in a saucepan. Bring to a boil, cover, and simmer 10 minutes. Without removing the cover, even for an instant, turn off the heat and leave it all day. When you come home, the rice will only need about 5 more minutes of cooking.)

After trying some of the following recipes, experiment with your own ideas. Use fresh vegetables in season—one or two or several in combination. Add firmer vegetables (carrots, broccoli, cauliflower, etc.) to the wok earlier, and softer, quicker-cooking vegetables (pepper, summer squash, snow peas, leafy greens, etc.) during the last few minutes of cooking. If you cook over consistently high heat and keep the vegetables moving, you can get away with using very little oil. Salting the vegetables lightly during cooking helps release their natural juices, steaming them slightly and further reducing the need for oil.

ASPARAGUS-TOFU-NOODLE

PREPARATION TIME: 25 MINUTES
TO GET EVERYTHING READY,
ABOUT 15 MINUTES TO
STIR-FRY.

YIELD: 4 SERVINGS.

8 scallions, minced

2 medium-sized cloves garlic, minced

1 tablespoon minced fresh ginger

2 tablespoons soy sauce

1/2 teaspoon crushed red pepper

1/4 cup fresh lemon juice

3 tablespoons Chinese sesame oil

3 tablespoons water

3 teaspoons sugar or honey

1/2 teaspoon salt

1/2 pound soft tofu, cut in small dice

5 to 6 ounces uncooked vermicelli or linguine

1 1/2 tablespoons cornstarch

2 tablespoons peanut or canola oil

1 pound slim asparagus, tough bottoms removed, and tops cut diagonally at 1-inch intervals

12 to 15 fresh mushrooms, sliced or quartered

3 tablespoons toasted sesame seeds, for the topping (use a toaster oven, or a heavy cast-iron skillet on the stove top)

Crisp asparagus is minimally cooked with tofu, mushrooms, and noodles in a marinade of lemon, sesame oil, garlic, and ginger.

You prepare the marinade, cook the noodles, and cut the vegetables up to a day in advance. (Store the cooked noodles in a container of water in the refrigerator.) Get everything ready, and then the actual stir-fry takes only about 15 minutes or less.

1. In a small bowl combine scallions, garlic, ginger, soy sauce, red pepper, lemon juice, sesame oil, water, sugar or honey, and salt. Stir in the tofu. Cover and set aside. Let stand for at least 15 minutes. (You can prepare the other ingredients during this time.) Remove tofu with a slotted spoon and set aside.

2. Cook the noodles in plenty of boiling water until al dente. Drain, and immediately rinse under cold water. Drain again.

3. Place the cornstarch in a small bowl. Add about 1 cup of the liquid from the marinade, and whisk until smooth. Return this mixture to the marinade, leaving the whisk in the bowl (you'll need it again).

4. Place a wok over medium heat and wait a minute or two. Add 2 tablespoons oil, and wait 1 more minute. Then turn up the heat and add the asparagus, mushrooms, and tofu. Stir-fry for several minutes until the asparagus is just tender.

5. Add the drained noodles and stir-fry for about 3 more minutes, keeping the heat high.

6. Whisk the marinade from the bottom of the bowl, and pour the entire mixture into the wok. Continue to stir-fry for 5 to 8 minutes more, or until everything is well coated and the sauce thickens.

7. Serve immediately, topped with sesame seeds.

BROCCOLI AND BLACK MUSHROOMS IN GARLIC SAUCE

PREPARATION TIME: 40 TO 45 MINUTES. (THE ACTUAL STIR-FRYING, ONCE ALL PRELIMINARIES ARE READY, TAKES ONLY ABOUT 10 MINUTES.)

YIELD: 4 MAIN-DISH-SIZED SERVINGS.

1 ounce Chinese dried black mushrooms

2 cups boiling water

1/2 cup rice vinegar (cider vinegar will also work)

1 1/2 cups water

1/4 cup (packed) brown sugar

1 tablespoon soy sauce

1/2 teaspoon salt, plus a little more for the broccoli

6 medium-sized cloves garlic, coarsely minced

1 teaspoon crushed red pepper (more or less, to taste)

2 tablespoons cornstarch

2 tablespoons peanut or Chinese sesame oil

1 bunch broccoli (1 to 1 1/2 pounds), stems trimmed and shaved, cut in 2-inch spears

1 8-ounce can water chestnuts, drained and sliced

4 to 5 scallions, cut in half lengthwise, then in 1 1/2-inch pieces

With their seemingly infinite number of little individual surface areas, the broccoli florets catch and hold this sweet and hot garlic sauce perfectly. The soft Chinese black mushrooms and the crunchy water chestnuts contribute significantly to the impact of this dish, so try to get to the Asian grocery store if you can. It will be well worth it. (And while you're there, get rice vinegar and pick up extra of everything. You will probably want to make this dish again.)

About 45 minutes before serving, put up 2 cups brown rice in 3 cups water. Bring to a boil, cover, and simmer very slowly. It should be done about 35 minutes after it reaches a boil.

1. Place the dried mushrooms in a bowl. Add boiling water, cover with a plate, and let stand at least 1/2 hour. Drain the mushrooms, squeezing out all excess liquid. (You may wish to reserve the soaking water for soup stock.) Remove and discard mushroom stems, and slice the caps in half.

2. Combine the vinegar, 1 1/2 cups water, brown sugar, soy sauce, salt, garlic, and red pepper in a bowl.

3. Place the cornstarch in a small bowl. Add some of the sauce, whisk until dissolved, then return this mixture to the rest of the sauce. Leave the whisk in there; you'll need it again.

4. Have all ingredients ready and within an arm's reach before starting the stir-fry. Place a medium-large wok over high heat for a minute or two. Then add the oil. After about a minute, add the broccoli. Salt it lightly, and stir-fry for several minutes over consistently high heat, until the broccoli is bright green.

5. Add the black mushrooms and water chestnuts, and stir-fry a few minutes more.

6. Whisk the sauce from the bottom of the bowl to reintegrate the cornstarch. Pour the sauce into the wok, turn the heat down just a little, and keep stir-frying over medium-high heat for another few minutes, or until the sauce thickens and coats everything nicely. Toss in the scallions during the last minute of cooking. Serve immediately, over rice.

SZECHWAN GREEN BEANS

PREPARATION TIME: 15 MINUTES.

YIELD: 4 MAIN-DISH SERVINGS;
   6 SIDE-DISH SERVINGS;
   6 TO 8 SERVINGS FOR HORS
   D'OEUVRE OR SNACK.

2 to 3 tablespoons Chinese
   sesame oil

2 pounds fresh green beans,
   trimmed

8 medium-sized cloves garlic,
   minced

1/2 teaspoon salt

crushed red pepper, to taste
   (optional)

I had trouble testing this recipe, but not in the way you might think. My problem was that the green beans came out *too* delicious. When I offered samples to family and friends who were hanging around the house that day, they took more than tastes. They devoured the entire batch in minutes flat. Then I had to make more in order to be able to taste it myself, and I, too, found it hard to stop eating these beans. It's difficult to accumulate a dinner-sized amount of something when it disappears faster than you can make it. (So what do I suggest? I don't know. This should be the worst problem one ever has. Serve this as an hors d'oeuvre [*great* finger food!], or buy a large quantity of green beans and quadruple the recipe. I'm confident you'll figure something out.)

Meanwhile, follow the cooking method exactly, as it is critical to the success of this dish. Both the wok and oil should be hot, and the beans should cook quickly over high heat. They will attain an indescribable texture, both crunchy and very tender at the same time. Also, try to hang in there with the full quantity of garlic. The intense cooking heat will take the edge off it, leaving behind just the right amount of flavor.

1. Place a medium-large wok or heavy deep skillet over medium-high heat. After a minute, add the oil. Wait a minute or so, and add the green beans. Turn the heat to high and stir-fry for about 5 minutes, or until the beans are well seared.

2. Add garlic and salt (and optional crushed red pepper). Stir-fry for several more minutes, then remove from heat.

3. Serve hot, warm, or at room temperature.

SPINACH WITH GARLIC

PREPARATION TIME: LESS THAN
15 MINUTES.

YIELD: 4 SERVINGS.

2 pounds fresh spinach

2 tablespoons Chinese
   sesame oil

8 to 10 medium-sized cloves
   garlic, minced

soy sauce

This dish elevates cooked spinach to new heights. The seemingly huge quantity of garlic really works in here; the resulting flavor is strong, but smooth and well balanced.

If your wok is too small to hold all the spinach at once, cook it in two shifts. It all happens so quickly, the first batch won't have time to cool down before the second is ready.

1. Trim just the very tips of the spinach stems, leaving the rest intact. Wash the spinach in several changes of cold water, until absolutely all silt and sand is gone and the leaves are very clean. Spin dry, then finish the job with paper towels. Make sure the spinach is dried as completely as possible.

2. Heat a large wok. Add oil and wait a minute or so.

3. Add the spinach and garlic. Stir-fry over the highest possible heat for 1 or 2 minutes, or until the spinach is completely limp and very deep green. Sprinkle in a small amount of soy sauce at the very end.

4. Remove with a slotted spoon, and serve immediately.

CABBAGE, CARROTS, AND ONIONS WITH SESAME

PREPARATION TIME: 30 TO 40 MINUTES.

YIELD: ABOUT 4 MAIN COURSE SERVINGS.

6 tablespoons sesame seeds

³/₄ teaspoon salt

3 tablespoons Chinese sesame oil

2 medium-sized onions

1 large or 2 medium-sized carrots, thinly sliced

1 small head green cabbage, coarsely chopped (6 to 8 cups)

One of my first cooking jobs (1969) was in Ithaca, New York, at a tiny macrobiotic restaurant called the Ithaca Seed Company. We served a lot of grains and legumes, and only a few vegetable dishes, of which this was my favorite. Almost 20 years later, I remain impressed by how such ordinary, humble ingredients can be enhanced and transformed when combined in just the right way.

The gomasio (sesame salt) made in step 1 can be used to season a wide variety of other dishes. Try making extra, and keep it on the table in a large-holed shaker for everyday use.

1. Combine the sesame seeds and salt in a blender jar, or in a spice grinder or a clean electric coffee grinder. Grind until they achieve the consistency of coarse meal. (This is called gomasio or sesame salt.) Set aside.

2. Heat a medium-sized wok or a large deep skillet. Add the sesame oil and the onions. Stir-fry over medium-high heat for several minutes. Add about a tablespoon of the gomasio. Keep stir-frying until the onions are soft and translucent (5 to 8 minutes).

3. Add the carrots and cabbage, and sprinkle in about half the remaining gomasio. Keep stir-frying until everything is tender (another 10 to 15 minutes). Sprinkle in the remaining gomasio, and serve.

SWEET AND SOUR STIR-FRY WITH COATED WALNUTS

PREPARATION TIME: 30 MINUTES TO PREPARE NUTS; 20 MINUTES TO PREPARE SAUCE AND VEGETABLES; 20 MINUTES TO STIR-FRY.

YIELD: 4 TO 6 SERVINGS.

The walnuts are coated with a touch of sweetness and salt, then precooked until golden and crisp. You can fry them or bake them, and either preparation can be done up to several days in advance. After cooking, store the nuts in a tightly lidded jar and hide them, or they will never make it to their sweet and sour destination.

The coating calls for 2 egg whites. (The yolks can be saved for brushing on unbaked bread.)

WALNUTS:

2 egg whites

1/2 teaspoon salt

4 to 5 tablespoons sugar

4 cups walnut halves

1/4 cup peanut oil, if you fry the walnuts

SAUCE AND ASSEMBLY:

1 cup orange juice

2 tablespoons soy sauce

2 tablespoons cider vinegar

3 tablespoons honey

2 tablespoons cornstarch

1/2 teaspoon grated orange rind (or thin strips of peel)

crushed red pepper, to taste (optional)

freshly minced garlic, to taste (optional)

3 tablespoons peanut or canola oil

1 large onion, cut into 1-inch chunks

1/2 teaspoon salt

2 large carrots, cut diagonally in 1-inch pieces

3 medium-sized bell peppers (red and green mixed, if available), cut in 1-inch chunks

2 cups pineapple chunks (fresh or canned in juice)

1 8-ounce can water chestnuts, drained and sliced (optional)

4 small (or 3 medium-sized) red ripe tomatoes, cubed

5 to 6 scallions, chopped (whites and greens)

2 to 3 tablespoons minced fresh ginger

pepper to taste

About 45 minutes before serving time, put 2 cups brown rice in a saucepan with 3 cups water. Bring to a boil, cover, and simmer until tender.

BAKING:

1. Preheat oven to 400°. Grease a standard-sized baking sheet.

2. Place the egg whites in a shallow pan (a pie pan works well). Beat in the salt and sugar. Add walnuts, and stir until thoroughly coated. You will probably have to do them in two to three shifts.

3. Transfer the coated nuts to the greased baking sheet. Bake 15 to 20 minutes, stirring every few minutes.

4. Remove from the sheet while still hot—into a bowl or container until ready for use.

FRYING:

1. Prepare walnuts exactly as in step 2 above.

2. Heat a wok. Add 1/4 cup peanut oil. Add nuts, and stir-fry quickly over high heat for several minutes until golden brown.

3. Transfer to a bowl or container until ready for use.

SAUCE AND ASSEMBLY:

1. Whisk together the orange juice, soy sauce, vinegar, and honey. Place the cornstarch in a medium-sized bowl, and whisk the liquid into it. Stir in orange rind and optional seasonings (or not), and set aside. (Leave the whisk in there. You'll need it again.)

2. Have all ingredients cut and at hand. Heat a large wok. Add the oil, wait a minute or two, then add onion chunks and salt. Stir-fry over high heat. After several minutes add carrots. Stir-fry another 5 to 8 minutes, keeping the heat steadily high.

3. Add all remaining ingredients except walnuts and sauce. Stir-fry another 5 minutes. Never turn the heat down; just keep everything moving.

4. Whisk the sauce from the bottom, and pour it into the wok. Stir-fry another 5 to 8 minutes, until the sauce is thick and everything is nicely coated. Add pepper to taste, and adjust seasonings. Stir in walnuts and serve immediately over rice.

KUNG PAO TOFU

PREPARATION TIME: 30 MINUTES
TO GET EVERYTHING READY,
PLUS 15 MORE MINUTES FOR
THE ACTUAL STIR-FRYING.

YIELD: 4 TO 6 SERVINGS.

5 tablespoons rice vinegar

1 tablespoon brown sugar

3 tablespoons soy sauce

2 tablespoons Chinese
sesame oil

1/2 to 1 teaspoon crushed red
pepper (more or less, to
taste)

3/4 pound very firm tofu, cut
into dice-sized cubes

1/2 cup minced onion

2 large or 3 small stalks celery, cut into small dice

1 medium carrot, cut into
small dice

1/2 cup bamboo shoots, cut
into small dice

1 cup peas (fresh, if at all
possible; if not, use frozen)

4 medium-sized cloves garlic,
minced

6 scallions—whites only—cut in
1/2-inch pieces

2 small or 1 medium zucchini,
cut first into thin strips,
then into small dice

1 1/2 tablespoons cornstarch

2 tablespoons peanut oil or
Chinese sesame oil for
sautéing

1/2 teaspoon salt

1 cup peanuts (preferably
roasted, unsalted)

This is a vegetarian version of the popular Northern Chinese dish that usually features chicken and diced vegetables in a tangy hot sauce, topped generously with peanuts. Everything here is the same, except the chicken has been replaced with marinated tofu.

Rice vinegar is available at Asian grocery stores. If you can't get it, you can substitute cider vinegar.

The tofu can be marinated and the vegetables chopped well in advance. Cover everything tightly and store in the refrigerator.

About 45 minutes before serving, put up 2 cups brown rice to boil in 3 cups water. When it boils, cover, lower heat to the slowest possible simmer, and cook 30 to 35 minutes or until tender.

1. In a medium-sized bowl combine vinegar, sugar, soy sauce, sesame oil, and red pepper, and mix to combine. Add the diced tofu, and tip the bowl in each direction to allow all the tofu to come into contact with the marinade. Cover, and let marinate for at least an hour.

2. Prepare the onion, celery, carrot, and bamboo shoots, and place these together in a bowl. Set aside.

3. In a separate bowl combine peas, garlic, scallions, and zucchini, and set aside.

4. About 15 minutes before serving time, place the cornstarch in a small bowl. Drain the marinade from the tofu into the bowl. Whisk this mixture until the cornstarch dissolves. Set aside, leaving the whisk in the bowl.

5. Heat a medium-sized wok. Add 2 tablespoons peanut or sesame oil, the bowlful of onions, celery, etc. and the salt. Stir-fry over high heat for about 5 minutes.

6. Add the second bowlful of vegetables (peas, garlic, etc.) and stir-fry another 2 to 3 minutes, keeping the heat high.

7. Add the drained tofu. Stir-fry another 3 to 5 minutes—until all the vegetables are *just* tender.

8. Whisk the cornstarch mixture from the bottom and pour it in. Stir-fry several more minutes, then add the peanuts. Serve immediately, over rice.

SAUTÉED TWELVE ASSORTMENTS

¹/₂ cup diced water chestnuts

1 cup lightly toasted cashews

2 cakes diced tofu kan or 5-spice tofu*

This is a deluxe version of Kung Pao Tofu (which precedes). Follow that recipe exactly. When you reach step 7, add ingredients listed. (You will get a slightly higher yield because of these additions.)

*Tofu kan or 5-spice tofu are very firm cakes of tofu that have been baked or sautéed with dark, sweet spices. They are intensely flavorful and aromatic. You can find them (usually vacuum packed) in most natural food or Asian grocery stores.

GOOD FAST FOOD

PIZZA

POLENTA

BURRITOS, QUESADILLAS, AND NACHOS

ENHANCED RAMEN

FRIED OR BROILED BREADS

The next time you feel harried after a hard day of work, and you are on your way out the door to pick up some fast food (or the phone is in your hand and you are dialing for pizza), write yourself a reminder to read this Good Fast Food section as soon as you finish your dinner. You will find that pizzas, polentas, burritos, quesadillas, nachos, enhanced ramens, and sautéed or broiled breads are all very easy dishes that can readily be expanded into full-blown meals. If you cultivate just a few simple habits, you can make any of these on very short notice and tailor them to fit your own quirks and preferences. They are also very convenient for using up leftovers and will save you considerable expense.

The trick is to keep your kitchen stocked. Pizza dough, biscuit dough, and tortillas can all be frozen for long periods of time, and don't take tremendously long to defrost. Grated cheese can be frozen, and if done so properly, needs no time to defrost at all. (The details are in the recipes that follow.) You can make various doughs and grate cheese once every month or two, and keep your freezer full of possibilities. Also, group leftovers into one corner of the refrigerator for easy inventory. Don't be shy about using them in seemingly strange ways. You'd be surprised at how good drained, leftover bean salad tastes baked onto a pizza!

In addition, make sure you always have salad greens and fresh vegetables on hand. Clean the greens as soon as you get home from the market, dry them thoroughly, and wrap them first in a blanket of paper towels, then in a sealed plastic bag for maximum longevity. Try to keep salad dressing on hand at all times. These advance preparations will make short work of assembling a complete salad.

Also, when you know you're going to be having an especially busy week, cut up some fresh vegetables for steaming and put them in sealed plastic bags in the refrigerator. They will keep this way for several days. You can then pull them out at a moment's notice, and steam them or cook them in a microwave very quickly. Fresh salads or cooked fresh vegetables are all you need to add to make the following fare into complete meals.

PIZZA

On nights when you don't feel like cooking—or you haven't much time to put a meal together—do you call out for pizza? When it arrives at your door nearly an hour later, are you surprised by how much it costs and how mediocre it tastes?

In less time than it takes to make the phone call and wait for the delivery, you could have an exquisite homemade pizza emerging from your oven. Moreover, it can be exactly as you like it, with all your favorite toppings, and it will be very inexpensive.

Though it may seem like a cumbersome endeavor (it involves yeasted dough, which has an undeserved reputation for being mysterious and intimidating), homemade pizza is actually a simple and amazingly easy preparation. From start to finish the entire process takes barely an hour. And you can freeze the dough and many of the fixings way in advance, cutting the final preparation time to less than 20 minutes, including baking!

If you set aside time every month or two to put together and freeze several batches of pizza components, you can have high quality, almost instant pizza dinners whenever you're in a pinch.

Here are some tips:

- ✷ Prepare and freeze the dough as much as several weeks in advance. It takes approximately 12 to 15 minutes to prepare the dough. (Just make sure the water or milk you use to dissolve the yeast is no warmer than the temperature of your wrist, and you can't go wrong with the yeast.) Follow the instructions (step 4) for freezing the dough. It will take about 3 hours for solidly frozen dough to defrost at room temperature, 6 to 8 hours to defrost in the refrigerator.

- ✷ Freeze tomato purée in 1-cup units, and defrost as needed, one unit per pizza.

- ✷ Grate a large batch of pizza cheeses and spread the grated cheese on a tray. Freeze until solid (about 30 minutes), then transfer to individual plastic bags, one pizza's worth of cheese per bag. Return to the freezer for practically indefinite storage.

- ✷ Slice or mince fresh garlic. Figure out how much you like on each pizza, and wrap that amount in a little package of plastic wrap. Attach the package to the container of frozen dough with a rubber band, so you'll be able to find it.

PREPARATION TIME: WITH PRE-
ASSEMBLED, DEFROSTED
DOUGH AND PRE-PREPARED
TOPPINGS, ABOUT 20 MIN-
UTES; FROM SCRATCH, ABOUT
I HOUR. (ASSEMBLING THE
DOUGH TAKES ABOUT
15 MINUTES, PLUS 30 TO 45
MINUTES TO RISE. PREPARE
THE TOPPINGS WHILE THE
DOUGH RISES.)

YIELD: I 12-INCH PIZZA OR
4 PORTIONS, DEPENDING ON
WHAT ELSE IS SERVED.

DOUGH:

¹/₂ cup lukewarm water or milk

I teaspoon (¹/₂ package) active dry yeast

¹/₄ teaspoon salt

I tablespoon olive oil (plus extra, for greasing the container and brushing on the dough)

I ¹/₄ cups unbleached white flour (2 tablespoons of the flour may be rye or whole wheat)

Certain leftovers also make great pizza toppings. Keep this in mind when making grilled or broiled vegetables, Oaxaca Bean Salad, Southwest Salad, Roasted Red Peppers with Garlic and Lime, Marinated Eggplant, and many other dishes. Pizza is fertile ground for improvisation.

NOTE: A popular method for baking pizza is to use a pizza stone, which is preheated in the lower part of the oven. You lift the unbaked pizza with a large wooden paddle (called a peel) and place it directly on the hot stone. While this method is fascinating and yields exceptional results, it requires quite a bit of skill, and involves some risk (i.e., the pizza could become mangled in transit or get dropped onto the floor). Since it is the purpose of this cookbook to simplify, not complicate, people's lives, and because pan-baked pizza is perfectly good, I won't burden you with this exacting paddle-and-stone procedure. Go ahead and use the pan without shame. (Of course, if you are already proficient with the stone and the peel, by all means do it that way.)

1. Place the lukewarm water or milk in a medium-sized bowl and sprinkle in the yeast. Let stand 5 minutes until foamy.

2. Add salt, olive oil, and ¹/₂ cup of the flour. Beat for several minutes with a wooden spoon.

3. Add the remaining flour ¹/₄ cup at a time, mixing after each addition. (Graduate to mixing with your hand as it gets thicker.) The dough will be a bit softer than bread dough, but it should not be sticky.

4. Turn the dough out onto a floured surface and knead for 5 minutes. If you intend to prepare and bake the pizza imminently, clean and oil the mixing bowl, and put the dough back in. Put it in a warm place to rise for ¹/₂ to ³/₄ hour, or until doubled in bulk. If you are going to freeze the dough for later use, oil a 1 pound ricotta cheese container (or a container of equivalent size), and place the dough inside. Cover and freeze.

NOTE: It will take approximately 3 hours for the frozen dough to defrost at room temperature. It is not necessary to let the defrosted dough rise. Plan accordingly.

TOPPINGS:

*3 to 4 medium-sized cloves
garlic, thinly sliced*

1 cup tomato purée

grated provolone

grated mozzarella

crushed red pepper

a light sprinkling of oregano

*thin rings of fresh green
pepper*

sliced mushrooms

OR

Pesto *(page 183)*

*marinated artichokes, cut into
small pieces*

grated parmesan

OR

Pesto Tapenade *(page 203)*

a ripe tomato, thickly sliced

thin slices of mozzarella

OR

*leftover broiled, grilled, or
steamed vegetables*

grated parmesan

OR

a few slices of Marinated
Eggplant *(page 45)*

sliced cherry tomatoes

chopped pitted olives

a few slices of provolone

OR

leftover Oaxaca Bean Salad
(page 146), Southwest
Salad *(page 129),* or
Roasted Red Peppers with
Garlic and Lime *(page 35)*

thin slices of mozzarella

5. Before assembling the pizza, get all the toppings ready, and oil a 12-inch pizza pan. Preheat the oven to 500°.

6. Punch down the risen (or defrosted) dough, return to the floured surface, and knead for a few minutes.

7. Roll out the dough to fit the pan, and press it into place. Brush the top surface of the dough with olive oil, and apply the desired toppings.

8. Bake the pizza in the top third of the preheated oven for 10 to 12 minutes, or until the crust is golden and the toppings are bubbling. Serve immediately.

POLENTA

PREPARATION TIME: LESS THAN 15
MINUTES TO MAKE POLENTA
ITSELF, 30 MORE MINUTES AT
MOST TO PREPARE OPTIONAL
ADDITIONS OR TOPPINGS.

YIELD: 4 TO 6 SERVINGS.

3¹/₂ cups water

1¹/₄ cups coarse cornmeal

³/₄ teaspoon salt (increase to
   1 teaspoon if omitting the
   cheese)

1¹/₄ cups (packed) provolone
   or fontina (optional)

SUGGESTED ADDITIONS:

ricotta cheese

sliced fresh tomatoes

sliced fresh garlic

extra provolone or fontina,
   thinly sliced or grated

grated parmesan

dried basil

freshly ground black pepper

SUGGESTED TOPPINGS:

Pesto (page 183)

Pesto Tapenade (page 203)

SUGGESTED ACCOMPANIMENTS:

bean salads

any marinated vegetable
   salads

any green salads

Polenta is a thick corn porridge that is a staple in North Italian cuisine. It can be made on the stove top in less than 15 minutes, and when combined with cheese and accompanied by vegetables or a salad, it is a soothing and very satisfying quick meal.

You can serve polenta immediately after cooking it. You can also make it up to several days in advance and reheat it either by itself or in combination with cheese, herbs, tomatoes, and other additions. Cooled polenta can also be cut into wedges or squares and fried in butter or grilled (see page 177).

1. Place 2¹/₂ cups water in a medium-sized saucepan and bring to a boil. Meanwhile, combine the remaining cup of water with the cornmeal and salt in a small bowl.

2. Add the wet cornmeal to the boiling water, whisking constantly.

3. Cook over medium heat, stirring frequently, for about 5 minutes, or until thick and smooth.

4. Stir in the cheese, if desired, and remove from heat.

At this point you can serve the hot polenta as is. You can also put it in a casserole, combine or top it with any of the suggested additions or toppings, and place it in a 350° oven until heated through. For a final touch, try sprinkling the top with grated cheese and broiling it for a few minutes.

If you are making the polenta in advance, spread it in a buttered or oiled 9 x 13-inch baking pan to cool. To serve, top with SUGGESTED ADDITIONS (I like to use all of them!) and heat in a microwave or a 350° oven. Finish it off under the broiler, if desired.

BURRITOS, QUESADILLAS, AND NACHOS

flour tortillas, frozen or refrigerated

corn tortillas, frozen or refrigerated

cooked beans, canned or frozen (cook extra when making beans for something else)

mild white cheese (Monterey jack or something similar), grated and frozen (to keep frozen cheese from sticking together, spread it on a tray and freeze for about 30 minutes, then transfer to a sealed plastic bag and return it to the freezer)

salsa, either a good commercial brand (which keeps a long time in the refrigerator), or homemade (page 74)

raw vegetables—tomatoes, lettuce or cabbage, onions or scallions, carrots, cucumbers—all of these can be finely chopped and added to or served alongside any tortilla-based dish

leftover cooked vegetables—good in burritos

olives

sour cream

avocados, plain or mashed into guacamole (to make guacamole, add 3 to 4 tablespoons fresh lemon juice to 1 mashed avocado, plus 1 clove crushed garlic, a dash of cumin, and salt and pepper to taste)

↬ A burrito is a soft flour tortilla wrapped around a filling of meat or beans, plus cheese and vegetables.

↬ A quesadilla is a soft corn or flour tortilla with cheese melted on top.

↬ Nachos are crisp strips of corn tortilla topped with cheese and baked or broiled.

Other toppings are often added to quesadillas or nachos. These usually include some combination of beans, salsa, sour cream, and guacamole. In general, these tortilla-based preparations are as substantial as what you choose to put in or on them. They can be snack food or light suppers.

With the following items on hand, burritos, quesadillas, and nachos can become part of your repertoire of quick meals:

BURRITOS

For each serving, place about ¹/₂ to ³/₄ cup cooked beans inside a flour tortilla. (If you are using canned beans, drain and rinse them first, as they tend to be salty.) Add grated cheese, salsa, and raw or cooked vegetables as desired. Roll it up tightly, and heat in a 325° oven or toaster oven, or very gently in an ungreased skillet over medium heat.

QUESADILLAS

For each quesadilla, place 3 to 4 tablespoons of grated mild white cheese on a flour or corn tortilla. Spread the cheese to distribute it evenly. Bake at 350° or broil for just a few minutes, until the cheese is completely melted. (A toaster oven works very well for this.) You could also try heating it in a lightly greased heavy skillet with the cover on. Keep the heat fairly low; just cook it enough to melt the cheese. If desired, you can top the quesadilla with cooked beans, salsa, sour cream, guacamole, and/or olives. Plan on one to two quesadillas per person, depending on how much stuff is piled on top.

NACHOS

Use strips of corn tortilla chips. Spread them on a lightly greased baking sheet, and top generously with grated mild white cheese. Bake or broil for just a few minutes, or until the cheese is bubbly. Top with salsa and sour cream or guacamole. Serve with a big salad for a crowd-pleasing light meal.

ENHANCED RAMEN

This is the dinner I make most often when I'm in a pinch.

Ramen is a little soup kit containing a clump of dry noodles and an envelope of broth mix. It can be put together in minutes flat once the water is boiling. You can find ordinary white flour ramen in most grocery stores, but it has little food value and I don't recommend it. Look instead in a good natural food store for the whole grain, variously flavored ramen packages that are imported by Westbrae Natural from Japan. This brand contains all natural ingredients, and is very well seasoned. It's also quite inexpensive.

You can enhance each batch of ramen, moving it up a notch from soup to main dish. Do this by adding some chopped vegetables and tofu to the boiling water when you add the noodles. (Broccoli and mushrooms work very well. Spinach leaves can be added just a minute or two before serving.) Top each bowlful with a few toasted cashews, if desired, and serve. It's a light meal, but when you get to the bottom of the bowl, you'll know you've had supper.

FRIED OR BROILED BREADS

If you have remnants of good unsliced bread lying around, try salvaging them by adding toppings and frying or broiling them. This is a quick meal that can be quite creative and frugal, especially if you use leftovers to spruce up the bread.

Here are some examples of what can be done:

- Fry thick slices of French bread in olive oil on both sides until golden. Spread with a little Pesto (page 183 or 203), add a substantial slice or two of fresh tomato, spoon on a teaspoon or so of vinaigrette (page 28 or 125), sprinkle with parmesan, and broil for a few minutes.

- Toast thick slices of any whole-grain bread. Add leftover cooked or marinated vegetables (or bean salad), top with grated cheese, and broil until the cheese is bubbly.

- Toast medium-thick slices of whole-grain bread. Spread with a very thin layer of miso (fermented soybean paste, available in Asian grocery stores or natural food stores) and a thicker layer of nut butter and/or tahini. Top with $1/2$-inch slices of firm tofu, and broil for about 5 minutes. Serve with steamed green vegetables.

Experiment with your own ideas (and leftovers). There are no rules about this, so anything goes. You just might come up with something that you'll want to make over and over again.

INDEX OF INGREDIENTS

NUT BUTTER
  on toast, 232
  see also ALMOND BUTTER;
    PEANUT BUTTER

NUTS
  almonds
    chocolate-dipped, 199
    in cookies, 126
    with noodles, 171
    in pâté, 40
    in spaghetti Elliana, 204
    in stuffed dates, 143
    in torte, 70
    see also ALMOND BUTTER
  cashews
    with noodles, 60, 171
    in ramen, 231
    in stir-fry, 223
  in green salad, 50
  hazelnuts
    in spinach salad, 188
    in torte, 70
  peanuts
    in cabbage salad, 165
    in chutney, 162
    with noodles, 155
    sauce, sweet and pungent,
      158
    in spinach roll-ups, 162
    in stir-fry, 222
    see also PEANUT BUTTER
  pecans
    and chocolate pie, 189
    in praline-butterscotch
      bars, 15
    in rice salad, 22
  in pilaf, 140
  pine, 105
  pistachio
    to blanch, 135
    for eclairs, 135
  with sweet potatoes, 187
  walnuts
    in broccoli salad, 55
    in cake, 84
    in charoset, 194
    chocolate-dipped, 199
    coated, for stir-fry, 221
    in cookies, 29, 102
    in pâté, 40
    in piecrust, 37
    in pilaf, 110
    in salad, 87
    in spaghetti Elliana, 204

O

OATS, rolled
  in cookies, 29
  flour from, 41
OIL
  Chinese sesame, 53, 54, 60, 218
  garlic, 176, 178, 180
  garlic-basil, 176, 178, 180
  walnut, 28, 36, 50, 55, 87
OLIVES, 228, 230
  black, 86, 145
  Greek, 98
  green, 77, 86
  Kalamata, 203
  Niçoise, 183
  oil-cured, 98, 183, 206
ONION/S
  broiled, 134
  with cabbage, 101
  caramelized, 159
  in casserole, 128
  in cheese pâté, 40
  in chili, 117
  in chutney, 162
  in creamed vegetables, 166
  with eggplant, 105
  in fries, 145
  green, *See* SCALLIONS
  grilled, 179
  in kugel, 195
  in pilaf, 110, 122, 140
  in relish, 124
  in salad, 34
  in sauce, 91, 207
  in soup, 12, 17, 25, 31, 59, 161,
    192
  steamed, 171
  stir-fried, 222
    with sesame, 220
    with walnuts, 221
  in stuffing, 185
  red
    broiled, 134
    in salad, 129, 146, 156
    in tomato sauce, 205
ORANGE JUICE, 29, 123, 212,
    221
  concentrate, 151
ORANGE/S
  with cabbage, 101
  glaze, for lemon-nut torte, 71
  in lentil salad, 18
  in relish, 124, 184

P

Pad Thai, 155
PANCAKES, *see also* LATKES,
    potato
PARSLEY
  with hard-boiled eggs, 98
  in pesto tapenade, 203
  in pilaf, 110
  in salad, 22, 111, 129, 146
  in salad dressing, 79
  in tomato sauce, 205
PARSNIP, in soup, 49, 192
PASTA
  to cook, 202
  dinners, 200–208
  with eggplant, 208
  with greens and feta, 207
  with marinated vegetables, 206
  with pesto tapenade, 203
  see also individual kinds; NOODLES
PASTRY DOUGH
  choux, 135
  empanada, 74
  see also PIE CRUST
PÂTÉ, cheese-nut, 40
PEACHES
  in crumble, 88
  to freeze, 88
  grilled, 173, 180
PEANUT BUTTER
  in cabbage salad, 165
  and chocolate chip cookies, 120
  with noodles, 155
  in Pad Thai, 155
PEANUTS. *See* NUTS, peanuts
PEAR/S
  chocolate-dipped, 199
  in fruit sauce, 79
  in green salad with walnuts and
    feta, 50
  grilled, 173, 180
  pie, with walnut crust, 37
  soup, with yams, 39
  with sweet potatoes, 187
  tsimmes, with prunes, 197
  types of, about, 37
PEAS
  black-eyed, and greens, 149
  green
    in Chinese soup, 59
    in rice salad, 63
    in stir-fry, 222

ALSO BY
MOLLIE KATZEN

MOLLIE KATZEN'S STILL LIFE SAMPLER

For all those readers who love the art in *Still Life with Menu*, but aren't quite willing to tear up a favorite cookbook to decorate their walls, here's the solution. This quality art book collects twenty framable 12 x 9 inch prints, perfect for kitchen, hallway, or children's rooms. Also included: sixteen recipe cards featuring Mollie's favorite *Still Life* recipes, perforated to be torn out and added to your own recipe file. A great gift!

> ISBN 0-89815-573-8 paper
> 12 x 9 inches, 48 pages

PRETEND SOUP AND OTHER REAL RECIPES

Mollie Katzen and Ann Henderson

Working with early-childhood educator Ann Henderson, Mollie has created this "first cookbook" for preschoolers and up. With whimsical watercolors, easy-to-follow instructions for grown-up kitchen assistants, this is a great resource for playtime, and for teaching kids to cook healthful, fun vegetarian dishes. As seen on *Good Morning America*, with Julia Child.

> ISBN 1-883672-06-6 cloth
> Reinforced binding, full color throughout
> 8 x 10 inches, 96 pages

MOOSEWOOD COOKBOOK (REVISED EDITION)

"Mollie Katzen, beloved mentor of many a counterculture kitchen, is back with a revised and expanded version of her original."
> —*Newsweek*

"The cookbook is an alternative classic. For the leaner '90s Katzen has added some lighter dishes and cut down the amounts of butter, cheese, and eggs."
> —*Entertainment Weekly*

> ISBN 0-89815-490-1 paper
> ISBN 0-89815-503-7 cloth
> 8½ x 11 inches, 256 pages, illustrated

THE ENCHANTED BROCCOLI FOREST (REVISED EDITION)

"Mollie Katzen has done it again! There is a sense of warmth, a spirit of caring about the dishes in this book."
> —*Toronto Star*

> ISBN 0-89815-601-7 paper
> ISBN 0-89815-695-5 cloth
> 8½ x 11 inches, 320 pages, illustrated

Available at your local bookstore, or order direct from the publisher. To order, or for more information, call 800-841-BOOK. Write or call for our free catalog of over 500 books, posters, and tapes.

Ten Speed Press / P.O. Box 7123 / Berkeley, CA 94707 / 800-841-BOOK